Free Market Economics

An Introduction for the General Reader

Steven Kates

*School of Economics, Finance and Marketing,
RMIT University, Melbourne, Australia*

Edward Elgar

Cheltenham, UK • Northampton, MA, USA

Published by
Edward Elgar Publishing Limited
The Lypiatts
15 Lansdown Road
Cheltenham
Glos GL50 2JA
UK

Edward Elgar Publishing, Inc.
William Pratt House
9 Dewey Court
Northampton
Massachusetts 01060
USA

A catalogue record for this book
is available from the British Library

Library of Congress Control Number: 2010939247

ISBN 978 1 84542 322 3 (cased)
ISBN 978 0 85793 244 0 (paperback)

Typeset by Servis Filmsetting Ltd, Stockport, Cheshire
Printed and bound by MPG Books Group, UK

Contents

Introduction   1

1   The axioms and underlying principles of a free market economy   8

2   The economics of the free market   22

3   Value added   46

4   Governments and the market   56

5   Factors of production, finance and the role of the entrepreneur   71

6   Supply and demand   88

7   Supply and demand: beyond equilibrium   107

8   Marginal analysis   127

9   Measuring the economy   153

10   An interlude on the history of economics   181

11   The Keynesian Revolution and Say's Law   204

12   The basic Keynesian macroeconomic model   219

13   Aggregate demand and aggregate supply   243

14   The classical theory of the business cycle   260

15   Cyclical activity and governments   282

16   The financial system   296

17   Controlling inflation   319

Afterword   336

References   338
Index   341

Introduction

This is a book about the market economy.

A market economy is one in which overwhelmingly the largest part of economic activity is organized by private individuals, entrepreneurs, for personal profit. Such entrepreneurs are private citizens, not government employees. They make decisions for themselves on what to produce, who to hire, what inputs to buy, which machinery to install and what prices to charge.

There are, of course, in every nation state legislative barriers put in place by governments which limit every one of these decisions. No market is or ever has been even remotely laissez-faire. Entrepreneurial decisions are circumscribed by the laws, rules and regulations that surround each and every such decision.

And in every economy there are various areas of production undertaken by governments to a greater or lesser degree. There is no economy without government production of various kinds.

But in a market economy, although governments impose their will on the market process and engage in production themselves, it is the individual entrepreneurs who make the ultimate decisions on the largest part of what is produced, how it is produced and the prices that are to be paid.

It is from these activities that entrepreneurs earn their incomes. It is how they earn the money they spend. It is through their value adding activities that their own purchasing power is created, and not only their own but the purchasing power of their employees as well. Indeed, since governments live off tax revenues, a government's own ability to spend on what it buys is largely dependent on that same entrepreneurial success.

SHARING THE WEALTH

There are, of course, other ways of claiming a share of the output of an economy. Theft, charity, welfare, government grants of various kinds all provide an opportunity to receive some part of what has been produced.

But while each of these have economic consequences, they are not forms of market activity. Providing charity is an individual choice that will have as much, if not more, to do with the surrounding culture than it has to do with the nature of the economic system.

The provision of welfare by governments is a political decision that is generally unrelated to the economic system, except to the extent that welfare is more likely to be provided in strong economies than in weaker ones.

Government grants – the receipt of income through political decisions rather than through the market – is a major industry in itself. Governments are prevailed upon at every turn to hand out money; usually, but not always, with some stated social purpose attached.

Many such projects do not even achieve the social purposes that their advocates have promised, but whatever may be the outcome, the decision is made by those with political power for political reasons. Not all decisions to direct money in some particular direction are intended to strengthen the economy, and even where it is the intent, governments are often poor judges of the economic benefits of what they do.

But this at least can be said. The ability of governments to make such grants is ever-dependent on the underlying strength of the economy from which the expenditure must be funded. There is therefore always at least some interest in governments to see the community prosper. It is well that there is.

Because it is here that the market comes into its own. It is only in market activity that those who receive incomes give something back in return and, by the nature of the system, give back at least as much in value, if not more, than what was received. It is only through market activity that those who receive do so because they have also produced.

It is therefore only through the market that wealth and prosperity can be achieved. It is within the market-based exchange economy, one of the greatest social discoveries ever made, that our living standards depend.

THE NATURE OF MARKET ACTIVITY

Market activity is about earning an income of one's own by creating goods and services for others to buy. It is a natural part of human life in the complex societies in which we live.

But to speak of a market economy is to speak of an abstraction. By focusing on production, exchange and the enjoyment of the produce of economic activity, it seems to remove the processes involved in earning a living from the day-to-day lives of people. It seems to suggest that there is economic activity over here and then over there is something else which makes up the rest of life somewhere else.

One of the greatest English economists, Alfred Marshall, defined economics in this way. 'Political economy', he wrote on the very first page of his book first published in 1890, 'is a study of mankind in the ordinary business of life' (Marshall, [1920] 1947:1). There is a great deal of compartmentalization that often goes on when economics is discussed formally. There is a sealing off of economics from the everyday world when it is, in fact, seamlessly connected.

Contrasting economic activity with the study of economics is quite instructive. Economic activity is, as Marshall said, about getting on with life itself. The study of economics is about trying to understand the processes involved.

Economic activity is about people doing things that make them materially better off. The study of economics is about putting together formal analytical structures that neatly wall off such activities from everything else. Economic activity is about doing things. The study of economics is about explaining things.

What is important, therefore, in thinking about economics is that it is understood that outside the text and the theory are just people going about their lives, producing things for others and trying to earn incomes for themselves. In burying oneself in the formal study of economics, strangely enough it is possible to forget that for most people economics is just about getting on with the ordinary business of living.

There is also a notion that exists in some areas that the economics of the market and markets themselves ignore such problems as poverty, disadvantage or economic harm. That the attitude of a 'market' economist is to leave the economy to sort things out and let the chips fall where they may.

An economy is part of a community's political structure. There are innumerable ways that the political process will deal with various economic concerns.

Economic theory does not pretend to provide answers for all of life's problems, not even for all of our economic problems. No matter how you run an economy, there will be differences of income, differences in wealth, differences in power and ultimately differences in outcomes.

But what economics does do is let you understand the trade-offs that are intrinsically involved in making decisions. You cannot have everything, economists point out. You have to choose, sometimes between two goods and sometimes between two bads to work out which is the least worst.

And no matter what you do, from time to time there will be recessions and unemployment. There will be disappointment and failure.

But as history has so amply shown, the one and only road to improving the living standards of a community is through putting in place institutional structures that encourage entrepreneurial activity, continuous innovation and market-driven change.

FREE MARKETS AND POLITICAL FREEDOM

And then there is this. The free market is the only economic system consistent with personal freedom. It thus not only provides the basis for the
greatest improvement in living standards, it also provides the basis for
remaining free of political control over our lives.

The only other way to organize an economy is through central control
and centrally determined collective action. There is a belief held by many
that it is only possible to coordinate the required actions of an economy
through some form of government planning and direction. With no government to coordinate activity, it is said, there is no basis for individuals
working together.

It is, in fact, the opposite which is true. It is the market, and market-
based activity, that is irreplaceable as the means to foster cooperative
action, to encourage people to work together. And it encourages such
cooperative activity because it harnesses the self-directed interests of
individuals.

But it is only where such individuals are free to make decisions on their
own without reference to anything other than the law of the land – where
the law is itself designed to allow individuals the widest scope for making
such decisions on their own – that the most productive economic decisions
are made that raise, over time, the living standards of all.

ECONOMICS IS POLITICAL ECONOMY

Economics is, moreover, a branch of politics. No economic decision is ever
made by economists unless the authority to make that decision has been
given by those who hold political power.

Economics is also a branch of philosophy, but it is political philosophy
of which it is a sub-branch. Economists think about the good life and how
to get it. There has never been an economics tract of any consequence that
did not outline how its author believed the lives of individuals could be
improved by organizing the economy in one way rather than another.

Economics is also by nature a guide to action. It sketches out the contours of the economic system, explains how the various bits and pieces are
related to each other, and brings the lot together in such a way that those
who make economic decisions are able to understand how to achieve the
political ends they seek.

When all is said and done, it is those who hold the political levers of
the state who decide about many, if not most, of what will determine the
ability of a nation's economic system to perform to its potential. And

overlaying all of the economic considerations will be the political demands placed upon an economy by those with political power who, in an ideal system, are responsive to the individuals in whose interests they govern.

The ancient name of economics was political economy. This was in many ways more accurate as a description of the subject matter of this area of study. Politics dominates. There is no economic system anywhere that is now or ever was that has not been profoundly shaped by the political world in which it is found.

It is why books on economics are so frequently designed as manuals for government.

But there are still many reasons for the rest of us to understand how economies work. We each have to make our own way in the world based on our own assessments of what is going on. Having an understanding of economic matters is amongst the most useful areas of knowledge one can have.

By studying the economy we can judge, assess and see the consequences of the many events that will affect our own lives. It helps explain the world we live in and can help in making decisions in the face of the uncertainties we face.

It is also useful to understand what governments are doing even when there is nothing we can do to change it. Government economic blunders of the most expensive kind are common. A knowledge of economics provides the necessary insight for a ringside seat in what is often the most intensely contested area of political debate. As with any sport, only if one knows the rules can one genuinely follow the game.

HOW THIS BOOK IS DIFFERENT

This book describes itself as being about free market economics. How, it might be wondered, does this approach differ from any other? There are a number of ways, but a few stand out.

To begin with, this book is about the entrepreneur. At the very centre of economic activity are those individuals who decide for themselves to earn their incomes by owning and running a business. Other texts seem to take a cosmic approach where things just happen without identifying the role that specific individuals have played. Ignoring the role of individuals ignores everything important about how a market economy works, indeed about how any economy works.

And then there is this. The book embeds uncertainty at every step. Much of economics is taught as if not knowing what the future will bring is just one of those things that have no effect on how economies are managed or on how economics should be taught. In reality, the fact that the future is unknown, that tomorrow may bring the most profound forms of change, means that economics and economic management must be approached in a very particular way. Uncertainty means that an economy can never be managed from the centre, that it must always be managed in as decentralized a way as possible.

To think that governments or public servants or any central body can know and understand anything other than the most minute part of what needs to be known is to be blind to the ultimate reality of economic life.

Thirdly, this book more than just dispenses with an innovation introduced into economic theory in 1936, which is the concept of aggregate demand; it attempts to demonstrate at every turn just how fallacious and misguided this concept is. There is now virtually no text on the economics of output, employment and growth that does not start from the notion that variations in the level of demand are needed to account for variations in the level of activity. It is the argument of this work that this is not just a poor way of thinking about such issues, it is positively wrong and guaranteed to mislead.

But because aggregate demand is now the bedrock foundation of the branch of economic theory dealing with the economy as a whole, the theory of aggregate demand is explained in this book in exactly the same way it might be found in any normal work of economics. It is essential to understand the frame of reference in which decision makers are making their decisions.

The largest revolution in economic theory during the twentieth century was brought about by the English economist John Maynard Keynes, who published his *General Theory of Employment, Interest and Money* in 1936. It was he who introduced aggregate demand into economics by rejecting a principle that had until then been part of the very foundations of economic theory.

That principle, known as Say's Law, denied in absolute terms the validity of the theory of aggregate demand. No discussion of economic theory in general since 1936 has attempted to return Say's Law to the central position it had previously held. This book does.

The full name of Say's Law was Say's Law of Markets. It is the essence of market-based economics. Without the clarity that the Law of Markets brings, economic theory has lost its moorings and the irreplaceable value of leaving things to the market in directing economic activity cannot be understood.

And because this book looks back at economic theories that had flourished before Keynes wrote his *General Theory*, it presents the classical theory of the business cycle which, since 1936, has all but disappeared from economic discourse. The theory of the cycle, however, has the ability to penetrate the darkness left by Keynesian theory in understanding the causes of recession and the steps that are needed to bring recovery about.

Finally, the book looks at the nature of the money market and uses pre-Keynesian forms of analysis to understand the nature of the inflationary process. No one can promise to settle for all time the theory of money and inflation, but what this book at least does is examine and explain theories of inflation that were common before Keynesian economics swept the field. These are market-based theories that still make logical, coherent sense and shed light on what remains one of the most difficult areas of economic thought.

1. The axioms and underlying principles of a free market economy

Before taking a single step into the formalities of economic theory, there are some things that have to be understood about the nature of the world if one is to understand how market economies work. Call these the basic axioms of the market mechanism.

- Nobody knows the future.
- Everything is always in the process of change.
- Commercially useful knowledge is diffused everywhere across an economy.
- Without market prices no one can tell what anything costs.
- In the commercial world, everyone does what is best for themselves.

What we have here are statements about the world that are the bedrock foundations for understanding why a free market economy is the only kind of economy that can deal with the world as it actually is. The opposite of each of these cannot be entertained. No one can genuinely argue any of the following:

- that the future is known and knowable;
- that change either never happens or takes place so slowly it makes no difference;
- that there is someone or some group who knows everything about the economy that needs to be known;
- that it is possible to tell what something costs without prices that reflect relative scarcity or the intensity of demand;
- that individuals within an economic environment can realistically be expected to act in the best interests of total strangers rather than themselves.

Because these axioms are true statements about the nature of the world, we need an economic system able to cope with things as they actually are. Let's look at these axioms one by one.

NOBODY KNOWS THE FUTURE

If the future were known, or even knowable, there would hardly be a need for economics. It is because the future is invisible, except as inferences from what we see in the present and what we have learned from the past, that economic decision making is so difficult. The possibility of error is always present in every decision, and the farther into the future a return is expected, the greater is the risk of loss.

This is the most basic fact about economies: all decisions are made about the future before the future becomes known. There is therefore a need to find institutional arrangements that reward good decisions and punish those decisions which turn out to have been wrong. No one may be at fault, but unless those who run a business understand that it is their own responsibility to make that business succeed, the kinds of incentive to get things as right as possible just will not occur.

And the reason that some decisions are rewarded while others are punished is because only in this way can we guide the economy in the direction of creating more net value than is used up in production. Bad decisions are wasteful. They take an economy in the wrong direction. They cause the production of things for which others do not wish to pay the full costs of production. People end up less wealthy and less prosperous. Their living standards are lower. The aim of setting up our institutions as best we can is to limit as much as humanly possible the damage that such bad decisions can cause.

And because the future is invisible, it is amongst the most difficult tasks to decide, in the present, which forms of investment made today will produce a profitable outcome. For every successful enterprise there are many others which have fallen by the way.

There are, in fact, no guarantees of success.

Because all economic decisions aside from the most trivial are about the future, economic decisions are built around individuals in the present trying to work out what the future will be like. And because the future is always different from how it was imagined, economic decisions often turn out to have been mistaken.

This is the way of the economic world in which, by the nature of circumstance, we will always be forced to live. It is therefore imperative that the economic system provide as much incentive as possible for decision makers to get it right and that we remove from the control of businesses as quickly as possible those decision makers whose judgements are, for whatever reason, habitually wrong.

EVERYTHING IS ALWAYS IN THE PROCESS OF CHANGE

In an economy, as with just about everything else, the processes of change never come to a halt. Some of these changes are visible to all and some are virtually invisible. Indeed, some changes are unknown to anyone at all although they will ultimately affect everyone; think of an impending natural disaster such as an earthquake or an invention that will be made one year from today.

There are major economic and political events that no one can predict. Economies expand and contract. New regulations are regularly introduced. Governments come and go. Wars are declared and peace resumes.

There are new products, new technologies, new ways of doing things, and many of these have commercial possibilities that will completely upset the best laid plans of those who are already in the market.

Amongst the most important features of an economy is that it be designed to cope with change. The phrase 'creative destruction' captures the way a modern economy adjusts. The new does not arrive and then live side by side with the old. The old is instead driven from the field, and unless adjustments are made, what was there before ceases to exist.

There was a time when the only way to cross the oceans was to go by sea, but now virtually no one does. The businesses who built and sailed the world's ocean liners were some of the largest businesses of their times. These businesses have now almost entirely disappeared and have been replaced by aircraft and airlines.

But there are also many changes that are quite trivial except in the particular workplaces they affect. A change in the price of an important input, or in the prices charged by some competitor, can come as a bolt from the blue but with devastating consequences.

The cancellation of orders from a major customer or an illness for one of the key personnel in an enterprise can create major difficulties impossible to accommodate.

This business about change being a constant has all the force of any old cliché, except that like many clichés, it expresses one of the profound truths about the economic world.

No economic system, nor the businesses contained within it, can survive without the means of accommodating change. The better they are at adapting themselves to new circumstances as they arrive, the more successful they will be.

KNOWLEDGE IS DIFFUSED EVERYWHERE ACROSS AN ECONOMY

The knowledge needed to run an economy is dispersed everywhere. No one has anything other than an infinitesimal amount of the knowledge required to keep an economy working.

Useful knowledge is contained within actual people, embedded within the individuals of whom the society is composed. This is not knowledge contained in books, but the active knowledge held by actual people who are personally capable of applying that knowledge in a real world workplace.

No one knows everything commercially useful to know. Virtually everyone has specialist knowledge that is economically useful, some with knowledge more valuable than the knowledge held by others but each with something to contribute towards a final outcome. One of the major purposes in structuring an economy is to put that knowledge to work as efficiently as possible.

Even the most knowledgeable people have only a smattering of the relevant knowledge in any society. Most commercially useful knowledge is of quite a basic character (Where are the paint brushes usually kept? What is the quickest way to get to Major Street?) yet it is essential for making an economy work efficiently.

Getting the knowledge that is at hand into the most commercially useful places is among the great and difficult tasks an economy is forced to perform.

Beyond that, the sum total of all the knowledge in existence is continually growing and changing shape. Things that were known on one day (where the brushes are kept) may be different the day after. A price that was charged on one day may be different a day later. A new innovation or invention may have just been released on the market or an old product removed.

Relevant knowledge is scattered everywhere. How to increase the knowledge base of a society and then coordinate and focus such knowledge towards economically useful and productive ends is the single greatest challenge an economy must face. How well or poorly it is done will determine the prosperity of an entire community.

WITHOUT MARKET PRICES NO ONE CAN TELL WHAT ANYTHING COSTS

Think of costs as representing a proportion of the totality of productive resources available within a community. Therefore, the more any particular product costs, the less of everything else that can be produced. Some mechanism is therefore needed in any complex society to allow consumers and producers to work out how to satisfy their wants at the lowest possible cost.

The centre, the absolute centre, of a properly functioning market economy is therefore based around the price mechanism. It is almost impossible to emphasize enough just how important to an economy the generation of *market* prices is.

Market prices reflect the intensity of demand on the one side and the relative scarcity of the good or service on the other. Prices instruct economic agents (that is buyers and sellers) on how to economize.

In very simple terms, the price mechanism identifies which products, services or resources are the least abundant relative to demand. Prices therefore guide producers to use relatively more abundant resources and smaller amounts of relatively less abundant resources.

Without prices set in the market no business can make economically rational decisions on what to produce, since there is no actual information available to producers about what others want to buy. (They want shirts, you say – then tell me what colour, what size or what style?)

And even if businesses knew in detail which final products to produce for consumers, which they never would, there would be no means whatsoever to determine how to find out which inputs would keep costs to a minimum.

A business would never know, without market prices to tell them, whether it was using scarce inputs which were relatively hard to find and expensive to produce. It would be impossible to determine what proportion of the entire productive potential of an economy was being used up to produce any particular array of goods and services.

Without prices to guide them, businesses could not know what forms of production would earn a profit since they could not know how much each input cost. Without a realistic set of prices to indicate the relative scarcity of inputs, no business would have the foggiest notion about which set of factors of production would keep their costs to a minimum.

Prices also connect the present to the future, at least to the limited extent we can ever know the future. What we know we know today, and part of what we know in the present is what is *believed* about the future. Market prices therefore adjust as assessments about the future shift.

Change in the economy is also automatically reflected in movements in market prices. Irrespective of what happens, if it comes to the attention either of those who sell and set prices or to those who wish to buy, forces are commenced which move prices in the direction to reflect either increased or diminished scarcity or an increased or diminished willingness to buy the product.

The thread that connects all of the parts of the economy is the price mechanism. It allows what could never otherwise be done by bringing together inputs from all over the world to produce goods and services sold all over the world; it allows activities to be coordinated which could not be coordinated in any other way.

The crucial point is this. Without the information provided by market prices, no complex economic decision could ever be made.

IN THE COMMERCIAL WORLD, EVERYONE DOES WHAT IS BEST FOR THEMSELVES

The way this is traditionally stated in economics is to say that individuals act in their own self-interest.

Since everyone has their own perspective on the world, everyone acts in the way they think is best based on their own morality, background and personal circumstance. Everyone does what they believe will be, given their own perspective, the 'best' thing to do.

Moreover, everyone acts as a moral agent in trying to do what they see is the right thing to do, but the only perspective from which anyone can see the world is from their own. To point out that we all do what is best for ourselves does not mean we necessarily act in selfish ways. It means that even when we try to help others, we are acting in this way because we personally believe that is the right thing to do.

A mother looking after her children, someone giving money to a charity, others doing what they can to help the poor, are all examples of acting in ways that each of these people believe will be best.

But moving away from such intense personal circumstances, virtually all economic activity is undertaken between strangers, frequently between people who live in different countries and often on entirely different continents.

Market-based activity is not a personal relationship between people. The different individuals who go into the making of an item of clothing, for example, whether harvesting the cotton, spinning the yarn, weaving the cloth or cutting and sewing the fabric, are undertaken far from the person who will eventually buy the shirt.

Producing goods and services that others wish to buy should there-fore be seen as actions intended to serve consumers by allowing sellers to achieve ends of their own. People undertake the various productive activities for a variety of reasons, but to believe that the reasons are ever independent of their own personal interests will make understanding the nature of the economic world impossible.

There are personal relationships and then there are commercial relationships, and sometimes, but not very often, they are the same. An economy is run on self-interest, in which the central aim for all, whether the owner of the firm, the workers employed or the lenders from whom funds are borrowed, is to earn an income.

The greatest protection for a buyer is that the self-interest of firms which intend to stay in business lies in producing quality products at the lowest possible price. In a commercial competitive environment, self-interest works for customers and not against them.

THE BASIC RULES OF A MARKET ECONOMY

These are the basic axioms, not of a market economy but of any economy. If even only one of these axioms were true, the need for a market would be proven. That all five are true and obviously true makes market-based economies an imperative.

From the above axioms are derived the basic rules of a free market economy. They are also almost entirely invisible. Yet they are the fundamental background principles one needs to know to have an understanding of the economics of the industrialized world.

Anyone trying to understand the operation of such an economy must always bear these principles in mind.

These principles are also important because they are not always followed. And where they are not followed, where any of these principles is not permitted to be the operating principle in the management of an economy, that economy will experience slower growth and lower incomes than it would otherwise have achieved.

1. No One Runs a Free Enterprise Economy: It Runs Itself

The structures of a free enterprise economy are designed so that the personal decisions of producers and consumers shape the economic environment in which they live. Laws and regulations determine the decisions that can legally be made. But within the law, the decisions made are personal and private.

The shape and structure of the economy has been designed by no one. It is just the outcome of millions upon millions of individual decisions.

The driving force on the production side is profit. The driving force on the consumption side is personal satisfaction, often referred to as 'utility' by economists. Businesses make decisions that are expected to bring them the greatest excess of revenue over cost which they can only do by providing buyers with the goods and services they want.

2.   Everyone is Expected to Make Economic Decisions for Themselves

Individuals decide for themselves what they will produce and for whom they will work. Each individual decides what investments to make and which skills to acquire. Each decides what to produce and what to buy.

On the consumption side, the driving force is personal satisfaction. Individuals make decisions, based on the purchasing power at their disposal, to buy those goods and services which are expected to give them the greatest level of economic utility.

All of the various considerations that go into making their various purchases are balanced one against the other with the intention of causing the specific goods and services they buy to create the highest level of personal satisfaction possible.

That both producers and consumers are often wrong about the profitability or utility of the different actions they take is neither here nor there. No one else is seen as even remotely having a better prospect of making the right decisions on their behalf.

3.   Businesses are the Spontaneous Creation of Members of the Community

Virtually all businesses have their origins in decisions made by private citizens. The only alternative is that businesses are started by the government or by those with political authority. In a free market economy, that almost never happens.

The commencement of a business is through the decision made by individual members of the community. They decide that they wish to be in business, which business they wish to be in and then make the arrangements themselves to turn their intent into a physical reality.

In so doing, there are laws to follow and regulations to conform to, both of which are determined by government.

Businesses are almost never started or run by governments. Nor should they be, other than in some very restricted circumstances. That is not what governments are for.

4.   Businesses are Far More Likely to Make Good Economic Decisions than Governments

This is a more concrete way of trying to say that tasks undertaken on one's own behalf for one's own personal benefit are done better, more efficiently and with less cost than tasks done by others with no personal stake or interest in the outcome.

Businesses are run by individuals who want to see those businesses succeed. Governments are run by individuals whose interest is in politics. The self-interest of those who run or manage their own firms lines up very closely with the need to meet their customers' demands.

It is also a crucial determinant of success that there is a major risk of failure. In business, there is constant attention by management to the details of the firm's operation, and the attention is applied by people whose own livelihoods depend on the financial success of the firm. Business firms are responsive to customer demands in a way that government businesses are not.

There is no comparable situation in a government-run enterprise. It would be rare for a government to stand or fall on the success of one of the businesses it owns or runs.

In general, governments are able to run businesses where there is either a natural or legislated monopoly, or where tax money is available to subsidize the loss. But running businesses is not what governments are designed to do, and where they do it they do it badly.

Incentive structures within private sector firms are properly aligned with community demands because profitability is the main guide to action. Businesses do not typically have access to taxpayers' funding to maintain projects which are not desired by the public. They are therefore responsive to external demands. And very importantly, businesses are not typically subject to political pressures which can and often do override commercial considerations.

5. The Most Important Economic Role of Governments is to Structure Laws and Regulations in Ways that Encourage Private Sector Economic Activity

Properly structured laws and regulations allow businesses and individuals to coordinate as productively as possible the economic activities that take place amongst themselves.

The most important economic role that governments have is to create an economic environment in which individuals can go about their lives while being as personally productive as possible.

Part of that is legislative, part is regulatory and there is then a third aspect, which is the provision of various forms of infrastructure. Governments are judged on their ability to foster an expansion in the level of private sector activity, high rates of economic growth, low rates of unemployment, high and rising levels of real wages and a stable level of prices.

Governments are thus held responsible for the outcome of economic activity in general but in a market economy are not expected to contribute to such activity themselves.

The techniques of economic governance have been developing continuously. But all of these techniques are designed to occur at a distance from the operation of the productive parts of the economy.

Governments have neither the knowledge nor expertise to make business decisions. Neither do the public servants who work in public administration. Their knowledge of the commercial realities that face each business are extremely limited. They are seldom, if ever, in a position to productively second guess the decisions made by firms.

6.   The Goods and Services Bought in an Economy are Financed by the Sale of the Goods and Services Sold in an Economy

This may be amongst the most important principles of an exchange economy. Demand is financed by supply. We buy with the revenues earned from selling.

Whether goods or services, it is the income earned from their sale that is turned around and used as the income with which to buy. In an exchange economy, unless one has sold, one cannot buy.

Why does this matter? To begin with, it matters because it is a reminder that value adding production is the source of all demand. Only what has been produced can ever be bought and only what has been bought can be the source of someone's income that they can themselves use to buy from others.

It is also a reminder that production that cannot be sold at prices that cover each and every one of the costs of production is not a source of demand in an economy but is, in fact, a step in the opposite direction. The community is less well off because of such production rather than more prosperous.

Beyond that, it is a reminder that recessions are caused by production failing to find buyers who collectively cover all of the costs of production. If businesses in aggregate produce what buyers do not want to buy, the result is a downturn in economic activity in general.

Finally, it is a reminder that the money governments spend comes from the efforts of the productive parts of the economy. Governments seldom create value themselves. What they spend is therefore nothing other than a transfer from those who have produced value. Whatever it is that governments might do, what they spend is almost invariably financed by the productive activities of others.

7.   Money Has Purchasing Power Only Because of the Value Added Created by Those Who Earned the Money in the First Place

Money in an exchange economy is received as incomes for producing goods and services which are *sold* to others. Money cannot be earned unless what was produced met with the sufficient approval of buyers so that they were willing to pay money to receive what had been put up for sale.

Money, to the extent that it represents exchangeable value, only has that value because there are actually goods and services in existence that can be purchased.

There are other ways money can enter into an economy, most notably from banks creating deposits and governments spending more money than they bring in through taxation.

Banks should, of course, ensure that the bank deposits they create will actually reflect the value being created in an economy. They do this by taking whatever measures they can to ensure that those who borrow will be able to repay.

That is the crucial test that every financial institution must put on every decision it makes to lend funds to others. They must do whatever they can to guarantee for themselves that borrowers either intend to invest and produce, or that they have other sources of productive income that will allow them to repay their debts.

Governments meet this same test when they spend tax money raised from the community. The community earned their own incomes in the first place by producing goods and services, with some of that money being taken by governments.

But the money received as taxes is the counterpart to the products and services produced to earn that money. In a properly functioning economy, the goods and services are there because incomes have been earned which is in turn because value adding goods and services had been produced.

Governments, however, sometimes spend more money than they receive in taxes, just as sometimes banks lend money to borrowers who, for one reason or another, do not pay it back. The result is a misfiring of the economy, with the potential for higher inflation and slower growth.

Maintaining the value of money in terms of goods is one of the most important functions a government has. Keeping an eye on the financial system to make sure it is lending prudently and by keeping its own expenditures within the framework of its own level of spending are critically important if an economy is to maintain a stable price level and a rising level of prosperity.

8.   Production Decisions Should Be Left to Businesses to Make for Themselves

No one decides what a business should produce, nor how it should produce, other than the business itself.

A business determines its own fate by deciding for itself what it is going to produce. Those who own and manage the business make these decisions based on their own assessment of what they are capable of producing and what they believe they can sell while covering all of their costs.

The structure of the economy is thus determined by the personal decisions made by such owners and managers. Over time, the economy changes the array of what is produced because the owners and managers of businesses have made the decisions they have.

No one plans an economy from above. What you see now, and what you will find in the future, are nothing other than the aggregated outcomes of the evolution of the economy which are the consequences of the individual decisions made by one business after another.

9.   Investment Decisions Should Be Left to Businesses to Make for Themselves

No one decides what forms of investment a business should undertake other than the business itself.

Investment is made up of the various forms of plant, machinery and other forms of produced inputs that are used in the production process. These are amongst the most important decisions a business needs to make.

A business must decide not just what to produce but how to produce it. It must decide where to produce and which forms of capital it will need. No one tells a business how it ought to produce. These are decisions that are left to the business itself.

10.   Pricing Decisions Should Be Left to Businesses to Make for Themselves

No one decides what prices a business should charge other than the business itself.

This is a principle of the highest order of importance. From the perspective of the individual firm, choosing the right price requires the weighing up of a vast number of considerations.

The price will have a major effect on the level of sales of the product. It will therefore have a major impact on profitability. There must also be thought given to the short and long term since the price today will be reflected in prices in the future. And the effect of a given price on the prices charged by one's competitors will be significant.

But beyond the importance of pricing for the individual firm, for an economy taken as a whole, prices play a crucial role. The price system is an interlocking process through which businesses can estimate the relative costs of different forms of production.

Prices when they are set by businesses reflect scarcity. They reflect other aspects of the market as well, such as the number of competitors and the strength of demand for the product. But most crucially, prices reflect scarcity.

If businesses are not free to decide their prices for themselves, but are instead an artificial construct of a political process, they then fail to provide information on which inputs are cheapest, where increased production is required and which inputs to use in a production process.

Interfering with the setting of prices will cause an economy to underperform badly.

SOME QUALIFICATIONS

These are the principles of a market economy in which individual entrepreneurs determine the overall direction of economic activity through making choices for themselves on what to do and how to do it.

But no one lives in a laissez-faire economy where the decisions of businesses are the last word. Business decision making is hemmed in at every turn by government regulation and control. It is the government that is the final arbiter of what can and cannot be legally done.

Economics is a branch of politics.

An economy runs itself but will only do so productively if the proper legal and institutional structures have first been put in place. It requires a government to understand what is required and to legislate to ensure proper structures exist. This, in turn, requires governments to understand the tremendous productive powers of private sector activity, and to appreciate what is required to make individual decision making work.

Institutional arrangements must be designed to accommodate the needs of private decision making. Meaning what? Meaning this: that governments must stand almost completely apart from the business decision making going on across the economy.

There is also a role for governments to set limits on permissible actions. Commercial activity is not a system of survival of the fittest. It is a system in which custom and law separate the permissible from what is not allowed. These rules and regulations will almost as often specify what individuals and businesses must do (for example, pay their taxes) as it will decree what is forbidden (pouring waste products into the nearest river).

Government is also responsible for administering the justice system. Courts to adjudicate and a legal system to enforce are necessities.

Governments must also provide a safety net for those whose incomes do not reach some socially determined minimum standard and assist those who might otherwise fall by the wayside.

But when all is said and done, the success of a government will be judged on how well it is able to put in place a set of rules that will permit the private sector to get on with producing without government involvement. The certainty is that rules of one kind or another will be set by governments But if the aim is economic success, the rules should be designed so that governments are almost never directly involved in the decision making processes of firms.

GOVERNMENTS ARE SOCIAL INSTITUTIONS RUN BY INDIVIDUALS

Government involvement is everywhere, often by popular demand. But you wouldn't want to get too carried away with the notion that governments are some kind of noble institution that anyone can depend on for their health, happiness and general welfare.

There is no 'social' in the sense that there is some collective entity that watches over what individual decision makers do. The collective is itself made up of other individuals who have different economic functions but who are human beings all the same, with all of the limits that being human brings.

Social decisions are decisions made by individuals on behalf of the entire community, but simply because they are made on behalf of the entire community does not guarantee they will be good decisions either in intent or consequence. They are still decisions made by individuals who have their own motivations and purposes clearly in mind.

Governments often have a will of their own that produces outcomes that sometimes benefit the community and sometimes harm the community, but in all cases benefit the governments that make those decisions, or at least attempt to.

Governments should never be thought of as doing things with a benevolent purpose in mind. Self-sacrifice is not in the nature of government action.

Only a government over which a population has some control can be expected to act in the interests of the community it represents. Representative government, where the representatives must frequently renew their mandate with the population at large, is the least worst form of government if the interests of the community at large are a prime consideration.

2. The economics of the free market

This is a book for those whose intention is to understand economic issues. It is for those who wish to follow policy discussions with some insight, read a newspaper with some clarity and discuss economic questions within a solid frame of reference. It is designed for those who wish to have familiarity with the underlying concepts and theory without being overwhelmed with the detail. It is for those who would like to know how those in decision making roles think and the kinds of analysis they apply when those decisions are being made.

It is foremost for those who want a good working knowledge of how economies work so that they can understand economic events as they unfold. The aim is to assist them in becoming informed followers of public discourse. It should allow them to understand what policy makers and professional economists are saying to each other and to the public. It should provide them with the tools needed to make sense of the decisions made by governments and various economic agencies. It should allow them to make sense of economic events, to have some personal idea of the complexities of such events and to be able to make their own judgements on how such events might unfold.

The aim of this book is to allow an attentive reader to follow the policy debates that inevitably find their way into the media and which are played out within governments.

They should then be able to make their own judgements on the policy actions being taken since the intent is to provide a framework from which such judgements can be made.

WHAT THE STUDY OF ECONOMICS IS FOR

The first question though, is this: why bother? Why take the trouble to know anything at all about how economies work?

At the most basic, the aim is to understand how communities become prosperous, how the individual members that make up the community can themselves become prosperous and, still within the same framework, to understand how economic theory can provide guidance to decision makers to help them devise appropriate economic institutions to create the sought-after prosperity.

Economics is a policy science to inform decision makers on the different consequences that can be expected to follow from different decisions. In dealing with economic questions, there are seldom choices that do not require some kind of balancing between different sets of outcomes.

Some of the harm may come early but lead to improvements later. On other occasions the good bits come first but are followed by harsher medicine. There is often a necessity to choose between one thing or another in which both would be desirable but where only one is possible at a time.

In economics, having it all is never an option. Having to choose is the only option ever available.

DEFINITION OF ECONOMICS

Economics, as Adam Smith in the first great work in the subject stated in his very title, is *An Inquiry into the Nature and the Causes of the Wealth of Nations*. This is the classical conception written in 1776. It was the way of thinking about the subject matter of economic theory that lay behind economic thinking for a hundred years.

It is the right definition. Economics is about the national economy and how a nation and its citizens can become more prosperous.

Economics is the study of what it takes to provide material well-being, not just to a community but to the individual members of that community as well.

And beyond that, the study of economics explains how that same community and the individuals within it should be able to live with a continuous expectation that, over time, their material well-being will continue to improve.

And finally, economics explains why economic conditions can and often do deteriorate, and provides remedies to halt and reverse such deterioration when it occurs.

Economics is about making people better off. In some ways, it might be thought of as an abstract science, like astronomy, in which the subject matter is looked at without any means or intention of becoming involved in changing how it performs. Knowledge for knowledge sake.

That, however, is not what economics as a science does, nor is it why it is studied. It is an area of study because an understanding of how an economy works is the start of a process towards making our economic arrangements work to our own benefit to a greater extent. That is what it is for and that is what economists do.

The most common definition of economics nowadays is somewhat different. It comes from the economist, Lionel Robbins, who in the 1930s defined economics as:

> The science which studies human behaviour as a relationship between ends and scarce means that have alternative uses. (Robbins, [1935] 1945)

This is a different kind of definition. There is much merit in this definition which is why it is so commonly used. It draws attention to the major problem in all economies, which is to try to satisfy the almost infinite demands of a population with the very finite amount of resources available.

But as a definition of so vast a subject as economics it is not quite right. It is technical. It narrows the focus from outcomes to process.

In this definition there are people who have numerous ends they want to achieve and only limited means with which to achieve whichever amongst those ends they choose to pursue.

This is, of course, the human dilemma of economics. So much to do with so little to do it with. The nature of economics is therefore, according to this way of thinking, an investigation into the ways in which such choices are made with the unstated aim being to improve the decision making process.

But while economics often involves having to choose, that is not the whole story. Economics is about all aspects of how economies work, with the focus on how they bring food to our tables and shelter over our heads. It undoubtedly involves scarcity of means and limitless human ends. But it is more. Any definition that fails to recognize what that more is, does not describe what most people who choose to study economics are there to find out.

SOCIAL CONDITIONS

There are also many aspects of what makes an economy succeed that are not themselves intrinsically economic in nature. The surrounding moral, ethical and institutional environment is crucial. You cannot make a community prosperous where the population does not regularly act in a moral or ethical way.

Rule of Law

Amongst the most important aspects of the social arrangements needed to create prosperity is the rule of law. The rule of law, a phrase hardly found

in the normal economics text, is as important a component in the creation
of a successful economy as one can possibly find.

The most fundamental point is this. Economies will never be productive if the legal system does not protect the incomes and the property of
those who produce a nation's wealth. The people who run businesses are
seldom, if ever, the same as those who are in control of the government.
Only where the civil authority is used to protect the incomes and profits
earned through productive activity will that productive activity occur.

How often do those who understand nothing about the basic requirements for economic growth and prosperity act as if those who run a
nation's businesses are also, and for that reason, in control of its government as well?

The order is absolutely the other way round. Business never controls the
government of any country. But it is only in countries where those who
run the political structures are resolute in protecting from thievery and
plunder those who run their nation's firms and businesses that prosperity
can occur.

Moreover, this thievery and plunder can come just as easily, indeed
more easily, from governments as it can from the community generally.
The self-restraint of government in allowing businesses to succeed and
thrive is the most basic requirement for an economy to succeed.

If governments are determined to take from businesses the profits that
ought to have remained within the business, whether the profit is taken by
governments for their own purposes or, as it is said, 'to share the wealth'
with the whole community, the result is, at best, diminished prosperity,
lower incomes and a slower improvement in the standard of living for the
population as a whole. At its worst, it causes wealth not just to grow more
slowly than it otherwise could but actually to decrease, often leaving large
segments of the population in desperate poverty.

Laws must protect commercial activity, enforce contracts and ensure
fair dealing between those who buy and those who sell.

Beyond this, no society in which some are privileged by the structure
of the legal system while others are kept in a subordinate position can
ever hope to succeed. Within this legal structure, there should be clarity in
terms of the importance of governments, and especially of the importance
of the popular control of governments, in seeking to achieve particular
economic outcomes.

No one is above the law. All should be subject to the law. And the
laws must be designed in ways that provide impartial abstract justice so
that commercial disputes are decided according to the laws of the land,
not by who can bribe the most or who happens to be related to someone
else.

Honesty and Character

The character of a population makes an all-important difference to its economic success. The rule of law and the role of the courts are important but the personal ethics and values of a population are possibly more important still.

An exchange economy only works where those who engage in production and trade are personally honest in their dealings with others. If agreements can only be enforced through courts of law and the involvement of the civil authorities, then an economy will not work.

One cannot push this to any extreme. Dishonesty exists everywhere. With so much wealth at stake, one must accept that the commercial world will inevitably attract towards it a fairly large number of those who will be dishonest in their dealings with others, and who will rob and defraud others if they can.

No economic system can rid itself of such individuals. Theft occurs only where there is something to steal. In the commercial world, corrupt practices are an everyday occurrence and a normal, if regrettable, part of the ongoing activities of those who are involved in trade and finance.

The fact that such activity occurs should not be seen as anything more than a product of human nature. But that such activities can and should be weeded out to the greatest extent possible is an imperative.

An economy works best where the population at large is disgusted by corrupt practices and refuses to accept dishonesty at any level. Those who act in a dishonest way need to be culled from the normal activities of economic life. The various forms of identifying such people – whether through credit agencies, personal references, criminal prosecution and the disgrace that comes from the publicity that can surround unfair dealing – should lead to there being severe penalties for dishonesty.

Where dishonest practices become the norm, especially where dishonest and corrupt government practices are common, no economy can expect to succeed. Corruption regularly drains away the potential profits of a successful business. It bleeds business dry and vastly reduces the incentives for productive economic behaviour while limiting the ability of business to finance innovation and internal growth.

An ethical, honest population is a necessary part of any successful economy. Whether it is in employer–employee relations, in the dealings between one business and another, or where it is governments involved with business, honest and fair dealing is essential. Acceptance of corrupt practice as just one of those things that no one can do anything about may seem realistic but it will condemn a society to economic stagnation.

Property Rights

As important as the rule of law are the rights to property. Who owns what, and what those who own are allowed to do with the rights they have, are major questions. Only where ownership is recognized, and the full weight of the legal system is designed to maintain the security of the owners of property in the possession of what they own, will an economic environment be created in which prosperity can be achieved and maintained.

It is the law that defines what can be owned and the various forms of ownership. Property comes in the widest variety of forms from actual land and structures, to pieces of paper that are promises to pay certain amounts of money on certain dates.

If the owners of property must continuously be on the lookout for thieves and governments – different in theory but potentially equally disastrous in their effects – the basis for wealth creation, a very patient and long-term process, will seldom be achieved. And it is the poor more than anyone else who benefit from the strong protection of property rights.

The wealthy and powerful can usually take care of themselves. It is those possessing little wealth or power who have almost no means to protect even the little they do have and who are vulnerable to the depredations of thievery and lawless governments.

MACRO AND MICROECONOMICS

Economics, as it is now taught, is divided into two halves: microeconomics and macroeconomics. This has become a major division in which issues are approached, but it was not always so and it need not continue to be so.

Macroeconomics refers more or less to the movements in various economic aggregates, such as the level of national output or the price level of all goods and services taken together. Microeconomics looks at the smaller units that make up an economy, such as the demand for particular products and how their prices are determined. As now taught, macro is almost totally isolated from micro since microeconomic shifts are not seen or related to movements in the microeconomic world.

This is not how things should be or previously were. What we now refer to as macroeconomics was once built around the theory of the business cycle. And in the theory of the cycle, the overall direction of the economy, its pace of growth, the movement in prices, the generation of jobs, were seen as a direct counterpart of the actions at the micro level. The division of economics into macroeconomics and microeconomics is part of a confusion that pervades much of economic theory to this day.

Macroeconomics

As economic theory is now constituted, *macroeconomics* looks at the entire economy as one large productive unit. The role of macroeconomic theory is to explain how all the parts fit together and in fitting together how the entire mechanism taken as a whole leads to increased or diminished employment, a higher or lower price level, faster or slower rates of growth and a balanced or unbalanced level of international trade.

It also looks at the financial side of economic activity. It looks at how interest rates come to be what they are and at how the financial system is interconnected with the production parts of the economy.

And it looks at the policy actions that should be taken to achieve what are the traditional aims of economic policy:

- low rates of unemployment;
- high rates of economic growth;
- low rates of inflation;
- stability on the balance of payments.

All of these issues are related to the material well-being of communities and all are related to questions about how to get more output from available resources.

There is a fifth aim of policy that sometimes is and sometimes isn't included, and that is making an 'equitable' distribution of income one of the objectives of a sound economy. Whether it really belongs as an economic rather than a political objective is more of a philosophical question. But there can be no doubt that governments do take actions to equalize incomes through the tax and welfare systems, and such issues are frequently a major political issue in many countries.

Like it or not, questions about the distribution of wealth and income do become part of the economic debate, so that reducing disparities within populations becomes one of the tasks that economists find themselves having to examine and provide policies to achieve in ways which do not affect the achievement of the other economic objectives in the above list.

Microeconomics

Microeconomics is the part of economic theory that looks at the actions taken by individual producers and buyers. It looks at who does what and the motivations behind the economic decisions made by individual people, either as consumers or producers.

An economic decision concerns itself with whatever it is that provides individuals with their material well-being. Food, clothing, shelter at its most basic. The vast array of the most exotic and varied goods and services at their most expansive.

But one way or another, microeconomics is about the decisions that individuals make, as buyers and producers, that cause particular goods and services to be produced and to end up in the hands of the particular people to whom they find their way.

When economies run well, the entire process is invisible. No one sees it happen and thinks for so much as a second about how they were fed, clothed and sheltered.

Although virtually every single item in any inventory of a person's possessions, and virtually every single service received from the market, was the result of an extraordinary web of decisions that had been made, some of which might have been made years before in far-off lands, it is normally taken as no more remarkable than the daily appearance of the sun in the sky.

Microeconomics is about the economic coordination between various producers who buy inputs from each other and the further coordination between producers and those who finally buy the consumer goods and services at the end of the trail.

A shirt bought today will be made from cloth that might have been spun in the last six months from cotton that had been picked in Egypt a year before. The plants from which the cotton had been picked might have been put in the ground five years before that.

All of the machinery used at each stage in the preparation of the cloth might have been designed and built 25 years before the cotton was grown and the different parts of the process might have taken place, not just at different times but in different countries. And then there is the thread that finds its way into the shirt, and the buttons and the colours.

And at every stage there will be individual workers who have specialist skills in the specific tasks that have been required, from the planting to the spinning to the weaving to the sewing to the packaging and then finally to the retailing at the very end. And each of those skills will have had to be taught and each individual will have had to decide to learn how to do just those tasks that have been required to complete everything that needed to be done.

How just the right amount of the ingredients that went into making up that shirt happened to enter the world and were brought together in just the right proportions is the mystery that microeconomics tries to explain.

THE MARKET MECHANISM, PRICE SYSTEM AND SUPPLY AND DEMAND

Here is a distinction you need to keep in mind. There is something called the market mechanism. There is then something else called the price system. And finally there are the forces of supply and demand. Knowing the difference is essential to understanding the market and how it works.

The *market mechanism* refers to a system in which individuals produce goods and services for others. Moreover, in virtually all instances, those from whom purchases are made are people generally unknown to the buyers, and are usually, in fact, total strangers.

We may know the retailer, although even that is becoming less frequent, but we almost certainly do not know the identity of the persons who made the particular products we buy.

The *price system* is the determination of *relative* prices within the market so that the prices of some goods or some inputs become relatively more expensive, while others become relatively cheaper. Prices, of course, almost invariably are shown specified in the local currency. The price system is an institutional arrangement through which prices are placed on products.

And then there are the forces of *supply and demand* which determine the prices for individual goods and services and also explain how those prices change. It is such prices that become elements within the price system which is the essential mechanism through which products are distributed through a market.

MARKET COORDINATION

Although seldom ever asked even though we see the process in front of us every day, the central question that surrounds economic activity is: how are the actions of consumer and producers, and of producers with other producers, coordinated across the untold millions of transactions that take place?

More difficult still is the question of how this coordination ends up working so well that there is virtually no interruption in the flow of the innumerable varieties of every imaginable commodity and service found in the world today.

At the heart of this mystery is the market mechanism. It is this 'market mechanism' that coordinates the commercial, productive and economic actions of total strangers. Whether these are total strangers from across the world or best friends from across the street, the market mechanism coordinates what they do so that a business in Cairo and a buyer in Saigon can make rational decisions about what to produce and which inputs to use.

Because of the nature of the market, in a well-ordered economy everything that commercially exists, with only trifling exceptions, has an owner. The owner may be a government, but in a properly functioning economy, for the most part most of what exists in the commercial world is owned by private individuals or the businesses these individuals own.

This is not just a description of the way things are. This is a statement of how matters must be arranged if a nation's resources are to be properly used in the most productive ways. Private property is an essential part of the foundation of any prosperous economy. Without a legal system dedicated to the protection of individual property rights, no economy can prosper.

In that same properly functioning economy, there must also be clearly understood rules for the way in which the rights associated with any single item of property – from an apple to an orchard – can be transferred from one person to another.

Most things produced are produced for others. Most things owned will one day be owned by someone else. The orderly transfer of goods and services from one person to another, or from one business to another, is an essential part of the operation of an economy.

PRICE SYSTEM

At the core of the market mechanism is what is known as the *price system*. To understand how the market works it is necessary to understand the price system. But understanding the price mechanism and how it works is different from understanding supply and demand.

Supply and demand is a description of how an individual good or service ends up with a particular price. Knowing how prices become attached to particular things is important, but it is not as important as understanding that it is *relative* prices that matter most.

What is a price? It is a number, a number stating how many units of currency have to be paid in exchange for some object or service.

For buyers, that number only has relevance when looked at against all of the other prices in that economy, the incomes being earned and the alternative ways that their incomes might be spent.

For a business buying an input, the number of units an item costs has to be looked at against the prices of other possible inputs and most importantly against the backdrop of how many units of currency the products being produced will themselves attract when put up for sale.

The market mechanism should therefore be seen as a continuous process in which every good and service competes with every other good and service to find buyers, with prices of every item offered to the market under ongoing and relentless pressure to fit into the entire framework of purchase and sale.

Every product must pay its own way. Each purchase must satisfy some need. But since costs are always changing in the same way that the needs, wants and desires of buyers are always changing, prices are in constant flux, shifting relative to each other to reflect the costs of production on the one hand and the willingness of buyers to pay the price on the other.

Getting in the way of the price mechanism to prevent prices from showing the relative costs of putting things onto the market will inevitably lead to economic problems that will not go away until prices are again allowed to reflect relative scarcity. Price controls of various sorts are often seen as the answer to various economic problems. They never are. They only add to problems in the longer run and economically speaking solve nothing.

SUPPLY AND DEMAND

The forces of supply and demand are the basic unit of analysis for the market mechanism. Supply and demand explains how an individual price for an individual product ends up being set.

The process starts from the decisions by sellers to produce something for sale to others.

It then turns to examine the actions of buyers who, once the various goods or services are offered up for sale, will buy more at lower prices and less at higher prices.

And finally, it points out that somewhere there exists a price in which the amount that the sellers wish to sell and the amount that buyers want to buy will be the same. This is known as the point of equilibrium, where how many units in total will be sold and the price at which those sales will take place is simultaneously determined.

It shows how the market, if left to its own devices, will satisfy the demands of all those willing to cover costs through the prices they pay. It shows how prices change and why allowing prices to follow the movements of supply and demand is essential if an economy is to prosper. It points out how the emergence of equilibrium prices ensures that neither shortages nor surpluses occur. It tells governments and other would-be regulators the consequences of trying to set prices against the market.

DECISION MAKING AT THE MARGIN

At the core of economic analysis is the assumption that individuals making their own decisions about their own economic circumstances will lead to the best outcomes for themselves. No one can ever know what anyone else truly desires. Therefore no one else can make decisions that will create as much personal satisfaction as those that are made by individuals acting on their own behalf.

Each person is therefore seen as weighing up all of the alternatives they have before them and making a decision based on their own judgement of what is best. No one else is seen to be better placed to decide than the individual person who is given both the freedom and the responsibility to make their own decisions within their own life.

This same freedom to apply one's own judgement is bestowed upon the production side of the economy as well. Incomes are earned largely by selling what one has to the market, whether it is a manufactured good or a personal service. All producers must decide for themselves what it is they will offer up for sale in order to earn the incomes they will spend.

And here too there is a balancing act required.

- there needs to be an understanding of the role that decision making at the margin plays in economic analysis – why economists put such emphasis on the relationship between costs, properly understood, and benefits, properly understood;
- some idea of the nature of the market mechanism is needed so that there is at least an appreciation of the relationship between the market in full and the actions of individual producers;
- also needed is some idea of market structure – that there are different possible outcomes depending on the relative size of sellers compared with the total level of sales;
- there should be some idea of the role of innovation and change in the development of economies;
- also required is some idea of the difference between the short and the long run and how such considerations temper almost every economic decision;
- finally, there is a need to understand the nature of market failure – why it is impossible to leave all economic outcomes to the market – which is supplemented with an appreciation that not all failures that take place in the market are forms of market failure.

Being *marginal* means that the moment of calculation is NOW in the present. The past is unalterable and must be taken as a given. It is what it is. The present is merely the baggage that has been deposited by everything that has come before.

These residues from the past include the stock of all machines and forms of capital, and not just what they are but where they are. It includes all of the labour with all of the skills that that labour force might have. It includes all of the technical knowledge available at the time, which is either embodied within the workforce and capital stock in ways that can be put to use, or might as well not even be there at all. It includes the cultural, historical and ethical values of the population. It includes the abilities of its entrepreneurs and of its politicians and public servants.

In essence, the legacy from the past includes everything there is.

From that initial point, any decision brings with it benefits (which are all of the reasons, financial or otherwise, why the decision might be made) and costs (which are the reasons why that same decision might not be made). If the expected benefits exceed the expected costs, that is, if taking some action is expected to provide a net improvement in one's circumstance, then the decision is taken.

These net benefits may or may not be calculated in terms of money, which is why the notion of 'utility' was introduced into economics. It is only when the change will add to one's satisfaction, one's total 'utility', that an action will be taken.

Everyone is seen as the captain of their own soul, the decision makers in their own lives. Each person is expected to make decisions that, at least in their own opinion, add the greatest net addition to their own level of utility.

What other people think, what their family thinks, what society in general thinks; all of these are important considerations that will weigh in on every decision. But when all is said and done, in a free society it is each individual alone who is given the right to choose what actions to take that will lead to the highest possible level of personal 'utility'.

THE ENTREPRENEUR

The single most important character in the drama of economic activity, growth and prosperity is the entrepreneur. Who is the entrepreneur? The entrepreneur is the ultimate authority and decision maker in a business. The entrepreneur guides an enterprise in whichever direction it is to go. The entrepreneur runs the show. All decisions are ultimately determined by this one person who carries the responsibility for the success of the entire enterprise.

Entrepreneurs are people who have the following characteristics:

- they run and often personally own private sector firms;
- they make decisions on what to produce, how to produce and where to produce;
- they are dependent on the success of the businesses they run for their own personal livelihoods.

It is entrepreneurs, taken collectively but acting individually, who assess community needs, secure the necessary finance, buy or rent premises, put capital in place, hire labour, buy inputs and pay the bills.

They are a self-selected group of people who have decided to make their living by operating a firm. No one in a market economy chooses who will run our businesses. They choose to do so themselves, either by starting a firm on their own, or by being employed by an already existing business and rising to the top of the management structure.

It is from the willingness of such people to take on the risks associated with the management and ownership of firms that we have our dynamic growth, the improvements in our standard of living, the real increases in the level of earnings and the continuous and ongoing innovation in the products from which we can choose.

It is the embedding of the entrepreneur within the market economy that causes the economy to become as productive as it is. Without the entrepreneur, we are left with the government to decide what should be produced and the way in which production should take place. It is a recipe for poverty.

UNCERTAINTY AND RISK

At the centre of the mystery of economic events is the existence of uncertainty and the risks such uncertainty creates. The entire economy is wrapped in an impenetrable shroud of unknowing. No one can know the future, the very time frame towards which all economic activity is directed.

Other than for the most trivial examples, production and investment decisions are made in the present but are expected to provide their returns at some later date, often a date many years ahead. All such production and investment are done in anticipation of future returns on productive activity that will take place then. Yet, even while such decisions are being made, the fact that no one can or does know what will happen next makes such decision making extraordinarily difficult.

Think of the world in this way. You are in a foreign land riding on a train with your back to the engine. All that you know about what is coming up ahead you know only from what you can see by looking out of the window. And what you can see is, of course, only what has already gone by. From what is seen, inferences can be made, but there is no certainty that what will come next will be similar to what has already gone past. What is up ahead may be entirely different, but this will not be known until reaching each point along the track. And no matter how much has already been seen, there is always the possibility – the likelihood – that what is ahead is vastly different from what has already gone by.

This is the meaning of uncertainty. The future is invisible and unknown. Yet all decisions of any significance are decisions that must be made in relation to that unknown future.

Business decisions often go wrong because the future did not turn out as expected when those decisions were made. And this uncertainty must be distinguished from risk. Uncertainty pertains to the state of the world. Risk is the potential loss borne by every decision maker in making a decision about what to do.

Because uncertainty is pervasive and continuous, risk is therefore a fact of life for every decision maker. Since the future cannot be known, every decision carries with it various consequences for having been wrong. These are the risks, and in the commercial world they are often enormous. Those who make decisions in an uncertain world are thereby taking on risks in which money, reputation and self-esteem are at stake.

Because of the nature of uncertainty, which forces us to make inferences about the future based on what we know from the past, there are risks involved in every decision. There are no facts about the future. Everything is a matter of judgement as different possibilities are assessed. There are no probability tables available as there would be for tossing a coin, since the past can only be an imperfect guide to what will happen next. It is all judgement about how things will be in a future that is not yet known.

A business deciding whether to take on some investment that might take five years to construct and be expected to repay its costs over the subsequent ten years is in many ways taking a leap of faith since there is no method of knowing the state of the world 15 years ahead.

There is, in fact, no way of knowing the state of the world one day ahead, but the farther out a decision's implications will reach, the less they can be known.

The economist Frank Knight published one of the great works on this issue in 1921. In his *Risk, Uncertainty and Profit* he discussed the impossibility of calculating too far into the future. He wrote: 'Business decisions . . . deal with situations which are far too unique, generally speaking, for any sort of statistical tabulation to have any value for guidance. The conception of an objectively measurable probability or chance is simply inapplicable.'

Each decision is one decision amongst tens of millions that are made day after day. Each decision is dependent for its success on the state of the world, the actions of other businesses, legislative and other changes made by governments, the desires of buyers, the discovery of new inventions and innovations, the prices of inputs and so on and so on. How little anyone knows even of what is taking place right now in the present as a decision is being made, never mind what will happen in the future, about which nothing concrete is known at all.

How much can possibly be known about the world 15 years from now? Five years from now? One year from now? Who will govern and what decisions will be made? Will there be recession? Will the economy continue to expand? Will consumers even need or want the products that are being contemplated by these new investments?

The relative calm in economies is deceptive. Moment by moment the actual circumstances faced by any business are shifting. Each day decisions must be made; some small, some momentous. But each such decision changes the character of the firm and either makes it better able to compete with its rivals or takes it closer to its own demise. Firms that have been around even for a hundred years or more may one day just go under through the relentless competition of the marketplace.

There is no grid, no crystal ball, no map of the future that can eliminate the need for making decisions in the darkness of the unknown. It is for this reason that the entrepreneur, the person whose own capital is often at stake, is the person best placed to organize our productive efforts. Because it is entrepreneurs, often with their own capital on the line, who can be expected to take into consideration as many factors as possible in assessing what to do next.

Nor do all such decisions turn out well. They do not. But what does happen is that those who make successful decisions, for whatever reason, are rewarded with profits and allowed to continue, while those who make decisions which turn out to have been wrong, often a mere matter of luck, are less likely to be entrusted with the capital needed to run another firm.

PRODUCTION IS IN ANTICIPATION OF DEMAND

Only by appreciating the existence of uncertainty and its consequences can one understand the nature of recession and the fluctuating fortunes of business.

The production of all goods and services is in *anticipation* of demand. An item bought on any particular day has become available for sale only because of a string of production decisions that go back in time, often well back.

Everything available for sale exists only because someone had formed the belief at some stage in the past that it could be sold at a price that would cover all of its production costs. This is a conclusion that is often right, but frequently wrong.

A business that loses millions of dollars on some project has not done so on purpose. It is never the intention of a business to lose money. Money is lost because at the time the production decision was made, the way in which events would later unfold was incorrectly foreseen.

Because decisions must be made before their consequences can be known, and because events occur that no one had foreseen, no business can be assured of a profitable outcome. Individual losses and sometimes bankruptcy in a firm occur because mistaken decisions had been made.

This, of course, happens all the time in even the strongest economies. Mistaken decisions and poor judgement are not uncommon, but looked at individually they cannot be seen as the cause of recession and large-scale unemployment.

Economic decisions are made before anyone can tell whether the decision will lead to a profit or loss. The motivation is always gain, but the outcome is only sometimes profitable. It is only in understanding that some economic decisions turn out in hindsight to have been the wrong decisions that a proper theory of recession and unemployment can be built.

Recessions occur where losses are made by many firms at one and the same time. The theory of the business cycle was designed to explain why large numbers of firms have made such wrong business decisions at the same time, why they have failed to anticipate correctly the structure of demand.

TIME AND SEQUENCE

In thinking about an economy, time and sequence are of immeasurable importance. Recognizing at each moment what can and cannot be known is essential if one is to understand how difficult it is to coordinate all of the economic decisions that go into the production of almost anything at all.

Production is a process that takes place through time, where every stage of production must be preceded by earlier stages of production that are the necessary foundation for what comes after.

And it is important to understand such things in order to understand the consequence of poor decision making in regard to what is produced. Poor decisions in one part of the economy have consequences at many other stages of the production process.

A cotton shirt bought at a retail establishment, looking backwards into the past, has required, amongst many many other things, all of the following:

- the planting of cotton;
- the spinning of cotton into yarn;
- the conversion of yarn into cloth;
- the use of the cloth to make a shirt;
- the tailoring of the shirt requiring designers, cutters, tailors;
- the construction of a building which can be used as a shop;
- the rental or purchase of a shop of which one particular purpose will be the sale of shirts to others;
- the purchase of an inventory of shirts;
- the employment of sales staff.

Each of these required an entrepreneurial decision by someone. Someone had to decide to grow the cotton, for example, while someone else had to construct the shop and employ the sales staff. All of these decisions not only had to be made well before the buyer finally bought the shirt, but they had to be made in the proper sequence by individuals who were, for the most part, entirely independent of each other.

This entire matrix is only one small part of the entire *structure of production* of an economy. How all of the necessary elements fall into place for the final production of the millions of items now sold worldwide is the basic mystery that economic analysis sets out to explain.

STRUCTURE OF DEMAND AND SUPPLY

The important consideration in understanding how an economy works is the *structure* of demand, not the *level* of demand. Yet it is the level of demand that in modern macroeconomic analysis is considered the determinant of the growth rate in output and the level of employment.

Nevertheless, it is the structure of demand relative to the structure of supply that is the central issue. Economies grow, employ and continue to prosper so long as the structure of demand – that is, the precise goods and services that individuals wish to buy – is the same as the structure of supply, the set of goods and services put up for sale.

Now, it needs to be understood that the structure of supply continues to change because of changes on the supply side alone. Technological change by itself changes how production is undertaken. The relative costs of inputs change, new production techniques are introduced and innovation brings whole new products into the world.

But the structure of supply must also change in response to changes in what buyers want to buy. It is this which producers must anticipate because it is only the goods and services that others wish to buy that can be sold. Tastes can change, average incomes rise (and occasionally fall), population levels can increase, while the demographic mix can shift. But the major reason for such changes in the structure of demand comes from the introduction of new products.

No market is ever free from change. In the world as we know it, there is a continuous flow of improvement and novelty. Better versions of what has already existed join with entirely new products that had never before been seen. The result is a shifting in the pattern of what is bought, which means there must be a continuous change in the pattern of what is produced.

Suppliers in this kind of world do not respond to what buyers wish to buy, but in fact lead buyers into whole new areas of expenditure.

Moreover, while the typical concentration is on the market for the goods and services bought by final consumers, in reality most of what is bought in an economy is the goods and services used in the production of other goods and services. And every one of these inputs is subject to the same forces of innovation, product development, cost adjustment and redundancy. Every one of these inputs has the potential to be replaced in the volatile markets of a normal economy.

In an economy nothing stands still, and any business that believes it can stand still will soon be out of business.

THE NATURE OF THE MACROECONOMY

An economic world seen in this way is one in which there is a continuous mutual accommodation taking place between those who buy and those who sell, remembering all the while that those who produce are both sellers of what they create and buyers of the inputs sold to them by others.

Each producer of inputs is typically selling their products to a range of buyers. Amongst those buyers are businesses that are growing larger and others that are growing smaller, but all of them may have a different level of demand for the products they buy as each day, month and year goes past.

Each and every one of these businesses must remain completely alive to the commercial world in which they are engaged. They must be aware of the prices they pay, the prices they charge, the demands of their customers, the actions of their competitors, along with having some notion of the state of the economy they are operating within.

This interlocking maze of commercial relationships constitutes the structure of production. It is designed to accommodate the structure of demand that is itself in part determined by the structure of incomes paid out by those who produce, to those who participate in the various economic activities that are ongoing across the economy.

RECESSIONS AND THE STRUCTURE OF PRODUCTION

It is when the structure of demand moves out of alignment with the structure of production that economies slow and unemployment goes up. Thinking about economies in terms of their structure, in terms of how all the parts fit together, makes it possible to understand the nature of economic activity and why it goes wrong.

To look instead at these issues in terms of aggregates is utterly mistaken. Although aggregate economic analysis is the standard approach in macroeconomics today, there is an older tradition that took a more microeconomic approach. It is this approach that actually sheds light on the nature of economic activity and the causes of fluctuations in economic growth and employment.

But all of this leaves out what is more to the point. It is the relationship between the various parts of the economy that makes the important difference. Understanding the macro side of the economy means understanding that it is the structure of the economy that is all-important.

In following the contours of the macroeconomy, measures are needed that will allow policy makers to judge whether genuine problems actually exist in each of these areas.

Yet to repeat, while it is the structure of the economy that will determine how well an economy operates, near enough all of modern macroeconomic theory and policy is built around questions that related to the *level* of activity, not the economy's *structure*.

At the centre of the modern approach to macroeconomic management is the notion of aggregate demand failure. Embedded in this approach is a set of instructions which show why the aim must be to stimulate aggregate level of demand when economic conditions slow.

The aggregates are, however, not in themselves actual components of the economy. They are a summation of actions taken by millions of individuals which are added together to give an overall total. These aggregates do not have a life of their own.

Moreover, the level of aggregation is at such a high level that almost nothing that is actually going on inside the economy is visible. No entrepreneur is visible, nor are entrepreneurial decisions. None of the microeconomic elements of the economy are properly reflected in the aggregates as described. The problem of the microeconomic foundation of macroeconomics has been discussed almost since the first introduction of modern macroeconomics in the 1930s. It is a problem that has not been solved.

THE THEORY OF THE CYCLE

Prior to the revolutionary arrival of modern macroeconomics, the swings and roundabouts of economic activity were explained by the many theories of the cycle that had then existed. Almost all such theories have disappeared into history and are seldom referred to.

What has remained as the last vestigial trace of this once huge body of knowledge is a diagram which is still a staple of the textbook. It shows a rhythmic wave, with the level of activity on the vertical axis and time on the horizontal axis.

There is then a low point in each wave which is called the trough. Following the trough, the wave moves upwards and is variously labelled as the recovery, upturn, expansion or whatever, with the words indicating that conditions are getting better.

There is then an upper limit reached which is typically called the peak of the cycle, after which there is a downward movement, variously described as a recession, downturn, contraction, or again whatever else might indicate that economic conditions are worsening.

The wave-like pattern is shown recurring time after time with more or less the same period shown from peak to peak and the exact same horizontal amplitude of each of the successive individual cycles. And with that the typical understanding of the cycle ends.

Why the cycle is by nature cyclical, why there are variations in the length of each phase, why the depth of the downturn or the height of the upturn vary in each cycle are no longer even hinted at. Yet these are the crucial issues. No discussion of the contours of economic activity can even remotely be discussed without some idea of the nature of the problems economies must confront, how these affect the level of activity and how they need to be dealt with when they arise.

The theory of the cycle was based on understanding how, in an economy where businesses produced for profit, production errors would occur across an economy. All economic activity was based on businesses being able to anticipate demand.

Production would occur before the goods were bought. A service would be offered before others had decided to purchase. All of the expenditure that went with being in business, purchase of capital, hiring labour, renting a premises and the rest, would occur before any sales took place.

In every economy mistakes in production decisions would inevitably be made. Firms would fail to earn profits and either contract or disappear. This is how the economic system works in taking resources out of the hands of those who are unable to use them in a productive (that is profitable) way. Businesses are always failing. But this is not in itself a cause of recession.

Recessions are the result of systematic, economy-wide errors in production decisions which are caused by factors that lead large numbers of businesses into productive activities that turn out not to have been profitable after all.

The kinds of factors that can have these effects include large and unexpected changes in interest rates, a major fall in the availability of credit, a shift in government policy and a large increase in input costs, such as the price of labour or the price of crude oil.

And even though such mistakes may only initially affect a relatively small proportion of the economy, in the right set of circumstances the effects can spread farther and wider as each industry contracts and therefore reduces its demand for the products of other industries. The downturn, which might start anywhere, thus becomes cumulative and eventually affects the entire economy, with some industries harmed to a greater degree than others.

The subsequent upturn reverses the downward spiral. Some industries begin to recover and the increased production in one area leads to increased demands for the products of other industries. The slow return to better conditions continues until there is again a peak in activity at which point the entire structure turns down once again. And so on and so on, ad infinitum.

EXCHANGE RATES, INTERNATIONAL TRADE AND INTERNATIONAL CAPITAL FLOWS

There is finally the nature of international economic relations. It is the part of economic theory that in many ways remains closest to the original free market concept of the classical economists, most likely because it is the most difficult area of an economy for a government to influence.

Not that governments don't try. At every turn there have been efforts made to affect exchange rates, the level of imports, the growth in exports and the escape of financial capital from the domestic economy.

Yet the theory stubbornly refuses to move very far from what is basically a market-driven view of the world, for the most part because every
intervention, especially in the modern world, has spectacularly tended to
reduce the economic welfare of the domestic population.

Even so, there is a large degree of misunderstanding about the importance of free trade. Everyone is a natural protectionist unless they can
learn to see the harm protectionist measures cause.

Some understanding of the importance of free trade in raising domestic
incomes and evening out economic instability (the reverse of the common
perception) provides a minimal requisite for understanding how markets
make individuals better off.

Moreover, persistent downward movements of the exchange rate are
signs of economic mismanagement and are a useful means of keeping
track of how well a government is performing in the arrangement of a
nation's domestic economic affairs.

And the flight of capital from insecure economies towards economies
showing greater stability and potential growth helps explain why governments so frequently try to bottle up such capital flows.

Trade in goods and services encourages efficiency in the domestic
economy because whatever may be the case locally, across the world there
are always others who will take markets away if given the chance. Local
producers are therefore much more diligent in open economies. They do
what is required to keep the competition away.

COMPARATIVE ADVANTAGE IN TRADE

Trade also restructures production in every economy towards the production of what each country is better able to produce *relative* to what
competitor nations are able to produce. It is the relative efficiency that
is important. Even where one country can produce everything at a lower
total cost than a second country, they will still be able to trade because
each will have some things they are relatively better at producing.

What does 'relatively' mean in this case? If one country can produce
shirts for $5 a piece and bottles of wine for $10 each, then in that country
each bottle of wine is worth two shirts. If in a second less efficient country
the costs are $10 for shirts and $50 for wine, then each bottle of wine
is worth five shirts. Trade will ignore the fact that the first country can
produce both items more cheaply and focus on which country is relatively
cheaper at producing which product.

The first country is therefore better off buying between two and five
shirts with each bottle of wine instead of continuing to produce any shirts

at all. Meanwhile, the second country should give up on wine production, since each shirt can buy half a bottle of wine from the second country while in their own country that same shirt will only buy a fifth of a bottle. The actual exchange relationship is likely to shift under trade, but both countries end up better off, with each having more shirts and more wine.

This is known within economics as the law of comparative advantage. It is a theory that demonstrates what everyone already knows. Consumers are better off where international trade can take place. Where no one gets in the way of trade, trade is guaranteed to expand. It wouldn't happen if those engaged in trade were not being made better off.

3. Value added

Possibly the most difficult area to understand about economics is one that you would think would be amongst the easiest and most commonly understood. This is the area of value and value added.

If economics were going to provide an understanding of anything, it would have to be, you would think, an understanding of what value is and where it comes from. And while economists do have such theories, they are relatively obscure and are almost never discussed at the introductory level. Value in economics is a very difficult idea.

Yet for all that, it is not possible to have a clear understanding either of economics or economic policy unless one has a reasonably clear idea about what value is and how it is created. And unless one has this reasonably clear idea about the nature of value, it is almost impossible to make judgements about almost anything done in an economy, from its very organization to the finer details of individual decisions.

The fact that the aim of economic activity is to create value is obvious and straightforward for all the difficulty in knowing just what value actually is. And the point is this. *Something has value to the extent that a person is better off with it than without it.* In economics we frequently say that a good or service has value if it is able to provide *utility*. Economic activity is aimed at providing individuals with increased levels of personal utility.

But it is also true that in almost all cases to obtain something of value, it is first necessary to give up something else that also has value. Nothing comes from nothing.

Value added is therefore, at its base, an understanding that there is the plus that comes from having something from which the negative of losing something to get whatever it is must be taken away. Value added is the excess above the loss. The value that is added is the value over and above the value that has been used up as part of the production process. Only where value is added, that is, only where there is more value at the end of the production process than when it began, can growth occur.

Value is also subjective. There was a period in the early history of economics where it was thought value was an embodied measurable quantum found in goods, such as the amount of labour that went into their production. Eventually, but only after a century of dwelling on the nature of value, was it fully appreciated that value is the personal valuation of an individual in relation to some good or service.

In exchange, this is typically quite easily seen. I want a shirt which it can be seen is something that has value for me, and this is known precisely because I happen to want it. In my opinion, having that shirt would make me in some way better off in comparison with not having it.

But to obtain that shirt I typically must hand over something in exchange, and in the world in which we live, almost invariably what is handed over is a sum of money. Buying something means that there is a valuation put on having the product or service relative to the value put on the money that is paid out. The value of the money lies, of course, in the other goods or services I might have bought instead.

Money is the measuring rod of value. It is the medium of exchange which individuals receive in exchange for what they produce and which they give to others in exchange for what they buy. When people freely spend their own money in buying goods and services, there is no question that in their own view they expect to be better off for having made the purchase.

But in understanding that, it is only a very small step on the way to understanding what value means within economics.

VALUE ADDED IN PRODUCTION

Value is not generally about buying, but about producing. And it is not entirely about the payment of money, although money valuations almost always come into it. It is instead about the transformation of one set of goods and services into another set of goods and services through the production process, where the second set is expected to provide at least as much, if not more, value to their owners in comparison with the first set, with that first set being normally referred to as 'inputs'.

It is an old cliché in economics to state that nothing comes free. It is the kind of statement that everyone hears as it goes in one ear and out the other. Unless one understands in one's bones what this old cliché actually means, it really is a meaningless set of words that gets you nowhere.

So to understand this principle take a very simple example. I own wood, nails and lacquer. I have a hammer, a saw and some time. All of these have value. These are transformed into a table, which also has value. Value has been added if the value of the table to me is greater than the value of the inputs that went into its construction.

Or take a shirt. At some stage it was nothing more than some cloth, thread, dyes and buttons. There were also sewing machines, labourers and buildings in which all of the necessary ingredients for creating a shirt were brought together (by whom?).

Each of these had value on their own. And each of the produced inputs at some earlier date had in turn been a product of some other set of inputs. The cloth, for example, may at some stage have been cotton growing in some field before it went through the many different stages before being turned it into the piece of material ready to be turned into a shirt.

And all of these different inputs into the shirt, and the inputs into the various inputs and so on going backwards to earlier stages of production, were all inputs that could have potentially been used for something else. All had value in that they could have been used elsewhere to make other things.

Nor should it be thought as we move to earlier stages that we are moving to less sophisticated stages. The cloth may have been shipped by air. The labour involved in building and maintaining the various forms of capital equipment might have required years of education and on-the-job skills development to reach the point of being able to undertake the technical tasks required.

THE PRODUCTION PROCESS DESTROYS VALUE WHILE IT CREATES IT

At every stage in the production process there are valuable, often highly valuable inputs that have been required to allow that production to take place. As it happens, in this case all of those inputs were put together to produce a shirt. And clearly, that shirt could not have been produced for only a single person but was one of possibly millions of such shirts that were produced but which initially absorbed all of the required inputs along the way.

In paying for the shirts that were eventually produced, every one of the inputs used in the chain of production had to be paid at least enough to cover every one of the costs involved. If their production costs are not covered, the inputs will not be produced. If the inputs are not produced, the final product can never come into existence.

But what validates the final production of those shirts, that is, what allows it to happen? There is only one thing, and that is the payment of enough in total to the shirtmaker to pay in full for all of the inputs into the production of those shirts.

This, then, is the meaning of value added. In the production of those shirts there was a certain sales revenue earned. At the same time, there was the value used up in the production of those shirts by the shirtmaker and then in turn by all of the businesses in that chain of production that led up to the production of that shirt.

There is therefore the value of the output which must be compared with the value of all of the inputs.

Value added occurs when the total receipts in producing *and selling* those shirts is greater than the value of those goods and services which have been devoted to the production of that end product.

The various inputs have disappeared into the production of this shirt. Each shirt may have only been responsible for an infinitesimal part of the whole of the costs involved. But each shirt must carry its weight.

What is true for this shirt is true for everything produced across the economy. Value is generated when the revenues earned cover all of the costs involved in creating just that structure of production that allowed this tiniest bit of the totality of economic activity to be carried on.

But in looking at the products and services at the end of the production chain it is absolutely necessary to understand that all along the way value has been destroyed so that each product can come into existence or some service performed. That value had existed – the labour, the transport networks, the capital equipment, the factories, and the thousands of other inputs, all of which could have been used in different ways – of this there is no doubt.

That value which had existed has now disappeared – the labour involved, for example, has already been used in one particular way and in no other – of this there is also no doubt. And in the place of all of the inputs used are the products and services we see before us in the present.

Economic activity, in all of its different forms, should be recognized as attempts to create value by using up existing goods and services at one end of the production process to produce other goods and services at the other end of the production process.

VALUE ADDED AND ECONOMIC GROWTH

In an economy that wishes to remain viable, all of that previously existing value must be replaced with products at least as valuable as those that were used up.

If an economy does no more than replace the value used up, that is an economy that stays exactly where it was. If there is more value created at the end of the process than existed when it began, then we are looking at an economy that is growing. And where the amount of value created is less than when the production process began, then this is an economy that is less well off than it was before.

Yet even this does not quite get us there. Value as described is equivalent to covering the costs of production. It is the product of the purchase and sale that go on through each national economy and indeed across the world. Profitable businesses are the strongest evidence that value has been created.

But beneath even this is a hidden assumption that businesses are responding to the wishes and desires of buyers. They are producing what other people wish to buy.

VALUE IS SUBJECTIVE

Value is subjective. It is a personal evaluation of the benefit that will be accrued in adding something to one's life, whether a dinner, service or an addition to one's saving. Whatever adds to one's life satisfactions is seen to add value, that is, to provide them with *utility*.

The reason for the choice of this word was to take away the notion that everything one receives gives actual pleasure or even some kind of satisfaction. Many goods or services one might pay for – a filling in one's tooth, for example – are bought and paid for, not because there is some intrinsic pleasure in the purchase, but only because of some necessity. Reducing 'disutility', as it is said.

The value received is personal in that the amounts paid out are in exchange for some good or service which is chosen in preference to having the money that has been spent. There is some utility received in the purchase.

But how do we know that such utility has accrued? We assume it because a person making a free decision to spend money in one direction rather than another is demonstrating that this is where the highest level of utility can be found.

This is one of the normally unstated assumptions of economics: that the individual is the best judge of what will provide utility. No one else can be a better judge than single individuals taken on their own making decisions for themselves about where to spend their own money.

In such an economic environment, using business profitability as the proximate measure of value added, allows the commercial world to be shaped by the individual decision making of the entire community. It is only in this kind of economic structure that it can be said that the consumer is sovereign.

VALUE ADDED AND UTILITY

There are thus two forces. There are the businesses run by entrepreneurs who are constantly trying to work out what would give people utility. And there are buyers who are continuously sifting through all of the products offered for sale to decide which ones to buy.

These are, generally speaking, the same people looked at first as producers who earn incomes, and then as consumers who use their incomes to buy those goods and services they believe will provide them with the highest possible level of utility.

What is being described here in what is a generally abstract manner is nothing other than the normal activity of everyone. As producers, we are trying to work out what others would be willing to buy from us. As buyers, we are continually trying to work out which purchases would provide us with the largest net satisfaction.

It is why businesses and consumers are always looking for new products; one to sell and the other to buy. The changes in the market are due overwhelmingly to the discovery of products that will provide higher levels of utility. Producers are continuously trying to put up for sale better products at lower prices, while buyers are making their own assessment of which products will more completely satisfy their needs and wants.

STRUCTURE OF PRODUCTION

It is important also to be fully aware of the phrase *structure of production* and what it means. Within an economy there is at every moment in time an actual, existing, deeply layered texture of economic relationships between all its different producers and all of the different buyers of everything that is being produced.

There is a shape given to an economy's productive efforts by the value-adding activities of all of its producers in combination. Each of those producers, those entrepreneurially run businesses, is making a decision about what will be bought, not in the present but in the future.

Each business, in response to its own estimate of where profitable sales activities will occur, makes decisions about what to produce, and from that initial decision flow subsequent decisions on what capital to install, which workers to hire, what buildings to rent and all of the other decisions that have to be made before anything at all can be produced.

Beyond that, there are very few firms which actually have only a single customer. Virtually all producers sell to a wide assortment of buyers, whether final purchasers or other producers.

Cloth is produced, but not just for making shirts. The shirtmakers buy cloth from suppliers who are supplying woven cotton for any number of other uses, whether fabrics for chairs or bandages to dress wounds. Each one of these uses might create higher prices in the short term but may, over the longer haul, create economies of scale that tend to bring down the price for all of its users.

Moreover, each producer almost certainly produces more than a single good or service. Every firm offers a range of products. We tend to speak of supply and demand as the core concept of the microeconomy, and there should be no doubt of how centrally important it is. But in doing so, supply and demand must always be put in the context of the many other goods and services that any single business entity can be expected to produce.

So to picture an economy as it actually is, rather than seeing it merely as suppliers supplying a single product one at a time to a set of buyers buying single products one at a time, it is instead necessary to see all of the overlapping and multidirectional criss-crossing of purchase and sale that is going on.

A convenience store that sells one person a loaf of bread at 11 o'clock at night will only do that because it is selling someone else a carton of milk at 10:30. The airline that flies someone half way round the world will only do so because it can sell other tickets to all of the other passengers on the same flight and on other flights that day, that week and that year.

In some very important sense, everything in an economy is related to everything else. The loaf of bread and the bottle of milk are trivial in their own way, and each sale changes nothing.

But as you build out from all of the sales and all of the producers and all of the relationships between one firm and another and between firms and the final demanders at the end of the process, there is a very large and intricate network that is in place. This network is difficult to picture, but should be seen in its totality to grasp some idea of where the goods and services we buy originally come from.

In some sense it is a quite delicate apparatus and in a more important sense it is quite robust. But it is a series of relationships that is forever changing under the shifts in demand that are a constant, the new products that come onto the market, and the new forms of production that become routine.

And then there is an overlay above all of that of the decisions made by government. These decisions change the regulations under which businesses work and the taxes that are paid by everyone at every stage of the production process through to the consumers whose incomes are always changing.

The structure of production continuously reconfigures itself almost moment by moment. Old firms disappear. New firms arrive. Existing firms change what they do and how they do it, either because they come up with some innovation themselves, or more often because the pressure of competition will pronounce a death knell on any firm that thinks it can continue into the future without changing what it did in the past.

But it is the pathways that lead both backwards and forwards from the productive environment of an economy. The connections for the production of anything are so dense that they cannot possibly be traced. No one can even remotely know how the entire organic structure of an economy fits itself together.

One business might have a list of all of its own suppliers, but who supplies those suppliers no one can possibly know. And so on throughout the whole of the economy. All of the relationships are spontaneously made by individuals and businesses who see products and prices and know generally very little else about how any of it came into existence.

WHY CENTRALLY PLANNED ECONOMIES CANNOT WORK

It is why centrally planned economies are an impossibility. For central planning to work, someone must know all of the inputs into all of the outputs and then know where each must go. And all of this must be known almost instantaneously if any of the millions of adjustments that go on in an economy are to be made as circumstances change.

Central plans are made under the assumption of one set of circumstances, but those circumstances never remain unchanged. In a market economy, there is a shift as sales either increase or fall for some things and there are then adjustments made with suppliers and the workforce.

In a centrally planned economy, none of that can happen because there is no mechanism for the instant response to changes in economic conditions.

How does the market respond? It responds by changing production decisions that affect conditions either in a small circle of businesses or, in some instances, across the entire economy.

An increase in the demand for shirts leads to an increase in the demand for cloth and perhaps there is some overtime for the workforce or even some new employees hired. We never think twice about such things because that is how we now expect them to happen.

Similarly, but more profoundly, if there is an increase in rates of interest, change will occur which will affect pretty well all businesses at once. There are changes which ripple through the economy as each firm accommodates itself first to the change in interest, and then, secondly, to the changes in all other firms that have occurred because of those changes in rates of interest. And then there are further changes as businesses react to the second set of reactions, and then so on and so on and so on and on.

The changes can be pretty drastic for something like a large increase in rates. Some firms may contract their production levels and may even shut. Other firms will find they cannot sell as much as they did and will respond in their own way to the cut in sales, and may themselves reduce their number of employees.

EQUILIBRIUM

The notion of an equilibrium in economics is, therefore, a concept that tends to have very little relevance to an actual functioning economy.

Equilibrium is a concept that indicates that all of the forces at work more or less balance, so that so long as conditions do not change, everything will simply continue into the future as it has done in the past.

When the forces of supply and demand balance, prices do not change, nor do the amounts bought and sold. In an economy taken as a whole, everything just continues, with production and employment remaining as they had previously been.

If one wishes to think of equilibrium in the sense of growth rates, then an equilibrium is said to exist when everything continues to grow in the next period at the same rate it has grown in the previous period.

One of the best definitions of equilibrium is that it is a condition in which all expectations are met.

But however one might define the concept, what is absolutely clear is that no economy, indeed almost no market within an economy, will ever be in equilibrium in any of the senses in which the term might be used.

CETERIS PARIBUS: ALL OTHER THINGS BEING EQUAL

Nothing ever stands still. Everything is always in flux. The concept *ceteris paribus* is central to thinking about economic issues. *Ceteris paribus* is a Latin phrase which means 'all other things being equal'. It is a phrase that helps us isolate individual factors that affect an overall outcome.

In almost all imaginable circumstances, for example, having a factory across the road will lower the value of a home. What a statement like that means is that a house across the road from a factory will tend to have a lower selling price than a house that is not across the road from a factory if every other factor happens to be exactly the same.

All other things being equal is the condition that all of the other factors are exactly the same except for this one particular feature. Using this *ceteris paribus* condition allows you to look at the effects of particular conditions one by one. It does not pretend that everything does stay the same. Everyone knows that the underlying conditions of every market are under constant pressure to change. Nothing stays as it was, and the longer that time goes by, the more changes one can expect.

REACTING TO CHANGE

Nothing is ever in equilibrium. Everything is always in disequilibrium. But that is not the same as chaos. It is because everyone is acting with their eyes open and is alert to change that the proper accommodation to new circumstances takes place.

There is no doubt that sometimes things happen so quickly that the ability for everyone to accommodate everything that has happened is swamped. Businesses fail, people lose jobs, the future becomes even more clouded than usual. Rather than only a small proportion of those engaged in economic activity having to work out what's taking place and needing to think through what to do next, a much larger proportion find themselves in the same boat in that same storm at the same time.

There are at such times no ready answers that can be provided by anyone as all of those affected try to work out how to accommodate the changes taking place. Each person will understand only a very small part of the whole. But as each of the individuals caught up in the tempest begins to work out what to do to save themselves, things become clearer, first for some and then for all. And eventually, the clouds begin to pass and economic conditions settle.

What returns is what passes for equilibrium, which is change that takes place at a relatively sedate pace. But that an equilibrium meaning everything that happens has been expected in advance, that never happens and cannot happen.

That is why private ownership of the means of production is the optimal means of organizing an economy. The owners of private firms, and usually their employees as well, have something personal at stake. They make the effort to overcome problems and achieve the best possible outcome given all of the circumstances that fate has thrown in their way.

4. Governments and the market

Economics is a sub-branch of politics. Governments are not a 'necessary evil', as it has sometimes been said, but are simply necessary for our well-being. Historical experience has made it abundantly clear that governments can be and often are the greatest problem plaguing a population or nation state. Government economic mismanagement is only the start of the many problems that a government can cause to individuals and the societies they govern.

The requirement for any community is to ensure that its government is responsive to its needs and that the government has as little control over individual lives as possible. While this is an extraordinarily difficult task for any community to achieve, and to maintain over time once achieved, being able to restrict the role of government is necessary if individuals outside the political class of their countries are to live in freedom and prosperity.

Economies are embedded in the political process. The identification of an independent, self-guiding process in which goods and services are produced, priced, distributed and sold without any active role of government was a momentous discovery. But an economy always finds itself in operation within some nation state and subject to the laws, customs, rules and regulations imposed by the legal authority of the nation.

How well or how badly an economy will run is to an important extent dependent on the actions of government, but that is only the start. There are always the moral beliefs, values, prejudices and attitudes of the population of a nation that must be considered. If the views of a population are hostile to the operation of a market economy, or if envy or ignorance drive community decision making, once again a market economy can be expected to operate poorly. Market activity will never cease totally, since production for others is part of how humans behave. But the market will not operate to its full potential and the community will be less well served by its economic activities.

FREE MARKETS AND THE 'MIXED' ECONOMY

There are, in theory, only two ways in which a highly technologically sophisticated economy can be managed. It is either through the market mechanism, the price system and dependence on the forces of supply and demand which determine what gets produced and the prices paid. Or an economy can be run from some central point, in which there are decisions made about what to produce and how to produce without reference to market-determined prices. This is referred to as central planning, often called a 'command economy'. A command economy is run through some kind of central plan in which the blueprints for the coming year or for five years ahead are mapped out. Entrepreneurially determined market prices play no serious role in such an economy.

It is sometimes said that we live in a 'mixed economy' in which there are elements of both market behaviour and central planning. This is almost entirely untrue. There are many activities taken on by governments in market economies but almost invariably their actions are undertaken through the market rather than through central direction.

Understanding the dangers that governments pose in the modern world is almost entirely unrelated to concerns that governments will take over major industries and try to run them by political edict and through central planning. This has been tried and it has failed. Virtually all economies are now run using self-directed enterprises of some sort to generate market prices. It is these self-directed enterprises which determine the direction in which resources go and activity will take place.

THE ACTUAL PROBLEMS OF GOVERNMENTS AND THE ECONOMY

The problem of governments is not that we live in a 'mixed' economy where governments run some things by ordering resources to be used in certain ways. The problem is now quite different. The problem now is that governments can and do spend immense amounts of money that they gather through the tax system, borrow from the public and even print up when the other options are closed.

Beyond that, government regulations now attempt to fix economic problems by creating regulations that may be fine as some abstract principle, but that are unrealistic when applied in an actual commercial setting. The lack of genuine understanding of the needs of industry that affects many governments in what are supposedly free market economies is a growing menace to prosperity.

Governments now see themselves as capable of making major expenditure decisions that direct resources into uses that are politically determined with little regard for the value-adding potential of what is produced. There are certain activities with which governments are keen to associate their activities, infrastructure, health and education being amongst the most common. Governments are also pleased to be seen as the bearers of welfare and social services of various kinds. In all of this, they seek recognition as the providers of the good things in life.

There is a case of some sort to be made for many of these but there is also a far far better case for governments to leave what can be achieved through market activity to the market.

Moreover, the role of the private sector in government activity is almost always understated and underappreciated. Governments decree the construction of hospitals and schools and allocate funds to those ends. But the actual inputs – the lumber, nails, paint and glass – are produced by private firms. It is only the end products that are determined by a government. The rest, made up of virtually all of the inputs, is provided by private sector firms operating through the market.

GOVERNMENTS AND MARKETS

Some of what governments do is value adding, some is not. In fact, some of what governments do is essential to the smooth running of an economy. This should not be thought of as some kind of throwaway line where it is market outcomes that ought to prevail with only the occasional exception.

Markets will not work without governments. But what are needed are governments attuned to the needs of the market even when those governments are pursuing objectives other than those that businesses or consumers might have preferred. There are market outcomes that, if left without government involvement, would be socially undesirable. Governments play an absolutely necessary mediating role.

There are quite clearly forms of market behaviour that can endanger some and harm others. These are often best controlled by government decisions that forbid particular actions where there are larger social purposes involved.

But in no sense should this be seen as warranting some kind of open-ended government involvement in economic activity. If anything, given the abysmal record of government involvement in economic decisions and regulation, the clear rule should be that as much as possible should be left to the market. When in doubt, leave it to the market to sort things out.

The fact that governments too often are not in doubt when they take on their regulatory role is a major problem. Governments can and often do much damage in taking the actions that they routinely do.

Governments acting to improve the economic well-being of a community have done almost as much harm in ruining lives and destroying wealth as even the most destructive wars.

Government activities aimed at improving the well-being of a population are inevitable. You may be sure that governments will do things, and they will do things with the expressed intention of improving economic outcomes. But the fact of the matter is that unless they understand their limits, the harm they do can be almost limitless.

Understanding the role of markets and how they work may be the single most important attribute of a government if economic prosperity is the ultimate intent.

What then is the economic role of government?

Legal and Administrative

There is, first, the legal, administrative and enforcement side of what governments do. These, along with national defence, are the historic roles of government found as far back as history itself. From the smallest tribal bands to the most complex and extended empires, putting rules in place and ensuring that the rules are followed has been the primary and most necessary part of what governments do.

Anarchy is literally the opposite of government. A society without laws, courts and effective enforcement will not function. In such surroundings, wealth-creating activity will disappear. The most important contribution governments make is to create a space for civic peace in which individuals can go about their value-adding economic activities.

Beyond that, governments contribute to economic activity by its administration generally; not just through law enforcement but through managing the community's affairs in ways that improve the economic environment. A community is an intricate social network that requires management. The general administration of a community's affairs are activities that governments, and only governments, can undertake.

Regulation

What is best for any individual in a market may not necessarily be what is best for society as a whole. Regulation of economic activity is essential if communal welfare is to reach its highest level.

Zoning laws, which prevent the construction of intrusive manufacturing plants in the midst of residential housing, are an example of a general case. Some activities, even though potentially profit-making, are incompatible with personal well-being for others. Government regulation of economic activity, which attempts to reconcile the needs of the market with the health, safety and well-being of the members of the community, is essential. This is not only essential for individuals, but it is essential for the proper operation of a market economy. Not all economic issues can be resolved through the market system and price mechanism. There are frequently 'externalities' in market transactions, where third parties beyond the buyer and seller are affected by the production and sale of goods and services (individuals affected by polluted streams due to industrial waste, for example).

Government regulation to balance the losses against the gains, to ensure that the harm caused to third parties is taken into account, is required. Getting the balance right is often difficult, but what is required is recognition that there is a balance between the positive value of whatever has been produced on the one side and the cost of these externalities that affect others outside the transaction.

Importantly, recognizing that balance is required not because there is a market but because there is production, production which would occur in any economic system, will help decision makers in crafting regulations that provide a compromise between the harm done by particular activities and the good achieved by living in a prosperous economy.

Infrastructure

Governments also provide infrastructure. These are the capital works that are the major connecting rods of economic activity. Transport, wharves, harbours, roads: all provide economic benefits and these have been traditionally, but not necessarily, supplied by governments.

In some instances infrastructure is provided by governments because no one else can be expected to undertake such projects. In others, it has almost just been history and custom that have determined in one economy that it is governments who provide the service while in others it is the private sector.

Welfare

Governments have also taken on some of the responsibility of providing at least a minimum of welfare for the poor and indigent going back centuries. 'Bread and circuses' might have been a catchphrase of the Roman empire, but it did suggest that the government had taken on the task of ensuring that the population did at least have something to eat. Governments have throughout history sought ways to assist those who could not fend for themselves.

One of the biggest differences in the modern world relative to the past is the wealth now available for politically motivated redistribution. The temptations for governments are enormous, as are the political demands. But every increase in welfare payments means a loss somewhere else. Someone has to pay; someone else's income must be reduced so that welfare payments can be increased.

Taxation Levels and Structure

In undertaking all of their tasks, governments have depended on the tax revenues raised. Whether as tariffs or tolls or taxes in general, the principal source of funds for governments has been the monies collected from the population it governs.

Taxing lightly and in ways that do least damage is important, but governments have not always been fastidious about how they raised their revenue, nor about the amounts that were raised. The theory of public finance had to wait until the eighteenth century even to have its first rudimentary discussions. But in choosing how and how much to tax, governments, both then and now, have played an important role in encouraging industry and promoting value-adding industry.

Government Businesses

And then beyond that there is a possible role for governments in running businesses of their own. The most common form of government business has been natural monopolies.

Natural monopolies are industries whose initial capital costs are extremely high but the additional costs of servicing one more customer so extremely low, that the first firm to enter the industry ends up being the only firm.

This is why public utilities, such as telephones, power and water, were in many places once typically owned by governments. Post offices and municipal transport are also frequently publicly owned. Whether governments are the best qualified to manage even such natural monopolies is a serious question, but given the suspicions that often attach to private monopolies, specially natural monopolies in goods and services, this arrangement was until recently generally accepted.

Schools are the other area that governments have almost universally taken on. In almost all countries, schooling, at least to a certain level, is almost entirely financed and managed by governments. To what level, and whether there should be competition for publicly owned schools, are matters of debate. But the fact that governments own and run the largest part of the elementary education infrastructure is now almost universal.

In most places, medicine is to a varying extent a state-run enterprise, and

for the same sorts of reasons. Something as important as health, it is sometimes said, should not be run as a profit-making enterprise and, however
managed, should not be allowed to price anyone out of receiving the health
care they need. That they will 'need' more health care when the effective
price is zero is what anyone running such a system must always expect.

There are then what is known as 'public goods'. These are products and
services for which 'free riding' is a problem. The provider of the service is
unable to receive payment from all those who benefit. Once the product
is in existence, everyone can receive its benefits with the result being that
it is in no one's private interest to provide the service or to contribute to
its revenue stream. These are rare, with national defence being the most
typical example, but this is anyway never going to be part of the market
economy. Radio and television signals are also potential examples.

Governments, in addition, do run other sorts of businesses. There is
almost no form of business that governments have not run somewhere, at
some time. Marxist theory demanded that governments own and run the
'commanding heights of the economy' and in some places there was no
private sector activity of any kind whatsoever permitted.

Yet the record shows that where governments have owned and operated businesses, these businesses have seldom been managed well and have
frequently run at a loss. Governments have run profitable enterprises, but
usually they are public utilities of the natural monopoly variety.

And even then, as with public transportation systems, possibly because
governments have imposed on themselves a public service obligation so
that even unprofitable parts of the business are allowed to continue, such
enterprises are not just unprofitable, but often lose substantial amounts of
money. They cannot be made to pay their own way. Many techniques have
been attempted to force government enterprises to operate in ways similar
to private sector firms, but these have been almost invariably unsuccessful.

Governments do not have the knowledge to manage businesses successfully, and their agents are public servants, whose expertise is seldom
related to managing firms and for whom the personal costs of failure are
typically very low. Beyond that, the disciplines that a private sector firm
has imposed on it by the market are often not there with public sector
firms, which can usually draw on taxpayers to make up the losses incurred.
Government enterprises have a very poor record of achieving economic
success and adding value to the resources being managed.

Government Spending in Recession

But the final justification for government spending has been the advent of
economic theories that suggest that public spending, especially in times of

economic distress, is an appropriate counterweight to an economic down-turn in the private sector. Moreover, the theory almost totally discounts the need for such spending to add value. Any spending will do to start the wheels of exchange turning.

This is the use of government deficit finance to 'stimulate' the economy, to 'prime the pump'. Putting purchasing power into the hands of individuals, even if what they are doing creates no value in itself, will have them spending, and their expenditure will cause other activity and then other activity after that, in what is described as a 'multiplier' process.

It is the belief that unproductive public spending can cause overall economic growth that is the largest fallacy in the realm of government. Unproductive spending is unproductive. It does not itself, by definition, contribute to value-adding production and cannot induce value-adding activity overall, since at the end of the expenditure chain no net value has been created.

SUMMING UP THE GOVERNMENT CONTRIBUTION

In sum, governments can in theory contribute to value-adding production, but just because they theoretically can does not mean that they necessarily do. Incompetent economic management, grossly inflated expenditure on non-value-adding forms of output, and inept regulation impede growth and prosperity rather than enhance it. But where governments improve things, they do so by providing:

1. good economic management;
2. sound public administration;
3. the development of a commercially appropriate legal system and enforcement network;
4. appropriate infrastructure (roads, harbours, airports);
5. the provision of welfare to those seen to be in need of public assistance;
6. value-adding production in industries with positive externalities that cannot be captured by the supplier and which can usually be expected to run at a loss if a fully extensive service is to be provided (public transport, education);
7. the production of goods and services that have a natural monopoly industry structure (telecommunications, gas, water).

The emphasis should be put on the fact that governments *can* create value with such activities but they do not necessarily do so. Governments need to know their limits.

Sound economic management and public administration are necessary. Direct government activities are potentially value-creating but are problematic all the same. As much of such government production is not tested by the market, or in the case of natural monopolies there are no genuine forms of competition, there is also no in-built gauge, such as a market test, to indicate whether too much has been spent and whether what has been spent has been spent productively.

There is therefore a tendency for governments to pay more for such forms of output than is warranted by the value created relative to other economic activities that could have been undertaken in their stead. It is very difficult to constrain such expenditure and, in the end, the main part of the restraint is provided by the community's tolerance for being taxed.

Unlike with private sector activity, buyers cannot direct their spending towards those forms of output that give them the greatest satisfaction. With political decision making, it is typically all or nothing, and usually there are many other considerations besides economic management that determine the nature of the government.

But then there is this, the last area of public activity:

8.   public expenditure to lift an economy out of recession and stimulate growth.

This is, in many ways, a warrant for public sector waste. If it can be properly fitted in under any of the previous categories, then so much the better, although normally it is not.

Outlays as a means to minimize the impact of recession are generally the least well targeted, least properly based, least productivity-enhancing forms of expenditure. But because such spending is typically introduced during the down phase of the cycle, when economic conditions are in retreat, when enterprises are closing down and job losses high, it is typically the least well monitored. The result is often a far higher level of national debt with almost nothing to show for the money that is now collectively owed.

PRODUCTION POSSIBILITY CURVE

The production possibility curve is typically drawn to provide a basic understanding that in any economy there are limits and that choices need to be made. Basic though this analysis is, it can make clear a number of issues of genuine importance.

To understand the curve properly, it must be understood that it

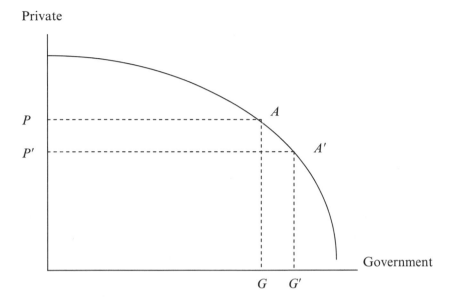

Private

P

P'

A

A'

Government

G   G'

Figure 4.1   Production possibility curve

represents combinations of forms of output that *completely* exhaust the resource base of the economy. On the curve itself, the available labour and technology are not only being fully utilized, but they are being used as efficiently as possible. It is not physically possible for that economy to produce more than it does. An example of such a curve is shown in Figure 4.1.

In the example, and it is only an example of one possible use of production possibility curves, an economy can either produce goods and services wanted by the private sector or it can produce goods and services sought by government. This is the trade-off. And if we are at some point on the curve itself (*A*, for example), then there is a particular amount of private sector goods (*P* in this case) and a particular amount of public sector goods (here shown as *G*).

In a static economy, to have more of one set of goods can occur only if there is less of some other. More public sector goods and services can only be had by having fewer private sector goods and services. The cost, known as the *opportunity cost*, of more of one good or service is the highest valued goods and services that have to be given up to get what one ends up with.

To have more government goods it is necessary to have fewer private goods. The extra government use of resources in moving from *G* to

Private

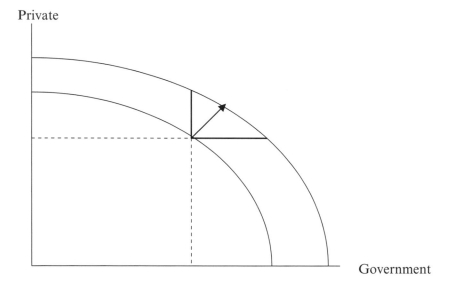

Government

Figure 4.2   Economic growth

G' means that there is less for the private sector to put to its own uses, whether as consumers or investors. The amount of resources used by the private sector falls from P to P'. The extra government use of resources comes at the expense of private sector use.

Economic Growth

In the longer run, as growth takes place, a community can have more of both private and public sector goods but the ability to have more is still constrained by the limits imposed by the economy. As shown in Figure 4.2, the production possibility curve moves out, representing an increase in the productive capabilities of the economy, but it remains as an absolute barrier. Beyond it, the levels of purchases by the private and public sector together remain impossible. The maximum possible remains the various combinations found on the line itself.

Unless the economy has grown, to have more output taken up by governments means that there is less available for private individuals, either as consumers or producers. It is possible, indeed likely, that some of what is provided by governments is wanted by most of the population. Where to draw the line between private and public spending is always a major political question.

Growth occurs when the economy is capable of producing more of all

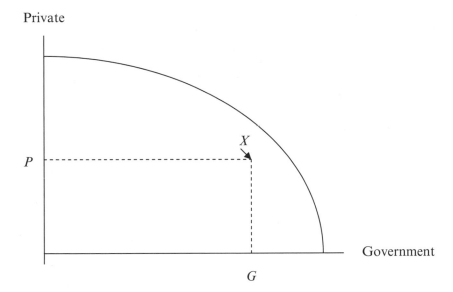

Figure 4.3   An economy not reaching its potential

kinds of goods and services and is shown on Figure 4.2 by the second production possibility curve that is further out from the origin in comparison with the first. With growth, it is possible to have (1) more goods and services going to the private sector without any loss of the amount going to government; or (2) to have more goods and services available to government without any reduction in the amount that goes to the private sector; or (3) it is possible to have more of both. The arrow between the two darker lines shows how, with growth, it is possible to have more of everything.

Unemployment and Inefficiency

Production possibility curves are also useful for explaining how economies do not reach their full potential.

The point X in Figure 4.3 represents the production of P units of private sector goods and services and G units of public sector goods and services. Because it is inside the production possibility curve, it means that more could be produced of either one or both with the available resources and technology.

Not as much as could have been produced was produced. What might the reason be?

a) Unemployment

The most obvious and straightforward reason is due to unemployment and underemployment, usually thought of as relating to labour, but which can just as well occur with all other kinds of resources. Some of the resources that were available were not put to work. Why this is the case would require more investigation, but it is well known that this happens. Unemployed labour is a particularly well known social phenomenon, always one of the major issues in any economy.

For the individual, unemployment can range from being a nuisance to an absolute personal disaster. Unemployment can simply be a brief period without paid work, and in other circumstances can ruin an individual's life. Economic policy is designed to ensure that there is as little unemployment as possible, and when it does occur, that the duration of unemployment is as minimal as possible.

b) Inefficiency

The second reason an economy may be inside the production possibility curve is because of the inefficient use of resources. This is a reason that may over the longer term be more important and is often much more difficult to deal with than with unemployment, as difficult as that is to deal with.

Resources are wasted when they are not used to produce the combination of goods and services that would have created the highest level of value added within a community, even though they could have done so had they been used in a different way. They may be employed, but they are just not employed in their most efficient way.

Efficiency is, however, related to purpose. In most cases, using an ambulance as a taxi is very inefficient since the cost of an ambulance is very high relative to the cost of a taxi. Using an ambulance in this way is, therefore, usually a very bad misallocation of the resource base of a community.

But there are possibly instances when taxis might be urgently needed while ambulance services are not. In such circumstances, using an ambulance as a taxi turns out to be the most efficient use of resources.

Given the intent, an efficient allocation of resources takes place when, whatever the desired output might be, it is being produced at the lowest possible cost. Keeping costs to a minimum, that is, using as little of our resource base as possible to produce each of the goods and services we want, means that production is efficient. But where resources are being wasted on output of lower value than might otherwise have been produced, or where more resources are used than are needed to produce goods and services, production has been carried out inefficiently. We could have had more, but because of how we used our resource base, we ended up with less.

As far as the production possibility curve is concerned, the result is that the community is producing at a point inside the curve. It is not producing as much as it might have, and if resources were better deployed, more could be had.

It is one of the most important roles of market competition to drive resource use to its highest valued form of utilization. Competition is designed to lower the profits of firms not using the resources they are buying to the maximum advantage. If another business can do it better, either by being better able to work out what buyers want, or being better able to provide what they want at a lower cost, that firm will lose customers, and will ultimately disappear.

Market competition pushes firms towards the most efficient form of production. Because every firm in a competitive economy is driven to be as efficient as possible, it pushes the economy as a whole towards producing as much as it possibly can with the resources that it has on hand.

A NOTE ON DIAGRAMS

The final reminder about this and other diagrams drawn in economics is that they are just for instruction and not in any way an exact representation of anything at all. They are drawn to provide an understanding of concepts, not to be seen as a scale model of some underlying actual reality which almost invariably no one ever knows. It is the concepts that are important. In this case, production possibility curve analysis shows that:

- there are always limits on how much can be produced from available resources;
- in a fully employed economy, to have more of some goods and services it is absolutely necessary to have less of others;
- not producing at the maximum possible is either due to some resources being unemployed (and unemployment here includes more than just labour) or it is due to resources not being used as efficiently as they might have been;
- economic growth means more goods and services can be produced and this is either because the resource base has expanded or there has been technological or human capital improvements that have improved productivity.

Each of these is useful to understand. But the diagram itself is merely a vehicle to help understand the various concepts.

MAKING SENSE OF DIAGRAMS GENERALLY

There will be more diagrams throughout the remainder of this book. For some, it may be a barrier to understanding the points being made, but this need not be the case. They are a means to bring a point across that would otherwise take many more words but with less precision in the meaning. Diagrams really do help and they are not hard to understand.

They are basically if–then statements. They state that if this is the case, then that is the case. With the production possibility curve shown above as an example, it states that **if** this is the level of private sector production **then** this is the maximum level of government goods that can be produced. It then indicates that **if** the desire is to increase the level of public sector production, **then** the level of private sector production must diminish.

This can be stated in words, as it has just been stated. But once you understand how to use diagrams, the rest is easy. And so many seriously important points can be explained that otherwise would have to remain relatively obscure. If you are interested in understanding economic issues, even if you are unsure about the use of diagrams, make the effort. The rewards are worth the minimal time involved in mastering this generally simple technique.

5. Factors of production, finance and the role of the entrepreneur

It is something of an established tradition in the instruction of economics to discuss early on and briefly the 'factors of production' and then to go on to discuss what appear to be more important analytical kinds of issues. Yet it is only here, in a proper discussion of the overall relationship between output and the various inputs that go into the production process, that a true understanding of the underlying dynamics of an economy can be found.

The traditional trio of factors are listed as land, labour and capital. Everything produced needs some combination of the three, and having said so the caravan typically moves on to other things. In many ways this rudimentary discussion is a holdover from early nineteenth-century economics where one of the major questions was how income was shared out between owners of land, workers and capitalists. Yet in spite of the way such discussions have diminished over time, the roles of the various factors, and how they are brought together, are essential to understanding how an economy works.

The factors are traditionally referred to as land, labour and capital. This time, however, we will dwell on these three and introduce a fourth, which is often brought into the story but just as often left out. That fourth factor is what is known as the role of the entrepreneur, which is actually the utterly indispensable element whose absence leaves the rest completely without direction and purpose. We will even introduce a fifth factor of our own, but that is for later.

The first two of these factors, land and labour, are generally straightforward and relatively easy to understand. Capital and the role of the entrepreneur, however, are much more complicated both in their origins and in the roles they play in an economy's success.

LAND

'Land' is a metaphor for all of the natural resources used in the production process. Land thus includes water, as well as any and all other inputs which come as 'gifts' of nature. Refashioning and relocating resources to put them in a form and at a location that can be used by others is what economic activity almost entirely is.

In a farm community, land is just that. It is a piece of ground in a particular place upon which crops are grown or animals raised. Even then, it is seldom, if ever, the case that land can be used without other productive factors preparing the groundwork.

But in using natural resources, almost never are they where you want them in a form in which they can be used. Coal and iron ore, oil and trees may in some sense have been provided by nature. But in their natural state they are very very far from being usable for productive purposes; coal is not heat and trees are not lumber. They are a potential which can only be made into an economic resource by being mixed with other productive inputs.

Moreover, farmland requires preparation and fertilizers. Land in its raw state is very seldom available for productive use without some form of preparation.

Even air and water are far from available for anyone to use in any way they please. Although air was once thought of as the one and only example of a free gift of nature, such times are long gone. Air has a scarcity value, and its use must in many circumstances be parcelled out amongst those who wish to use it.

Some people, for example, would like to have air to breathe while others, as part of some industrial purpose, would like to use that same air to dump poisonous gases. How to allocate the uses made even of air is an economic problem of the highest order.

LABOUR

To land must be added labour. Labour represents the human effort in the production process.

Labour, of course, comes in the widest variety of forms. There are vast ranges in age, talent, skills, abilities, experience, knowledge and application. Different people are located in different places, either near to or far from where the particular work that needs doing is located.

There are, moreover, different combinations of such personal characteristics embodied in every single individual making each either more or less suitable for each and every particular kind of work.

The bringing together of different workers who bring different abilities to a productive process is one of the major tasks of a properly functioning economic system.

CAPITAL

Capital is a more complicated matter. Capital is made up of the inputs into the production process that have themselves been an output from the production process. They are comprised of that part of value added that is used not just to produce goods and services for consumption, but they are also used in the production of inputs into the production process and even for the production of other forms of capital.

The production of capital is a drawing down of the productive capabilities of an economy in the present for the purpose of adding to the economy's productive capabilities at some later stage in the future.

Capital is made up of plant and machinery, shops and office building, roads and railways, pens and paper. It includes the stocks kept on hand by manufacturers and retailers.

Capital is any and every form of production that is used by its owner to earn an income. It is the decision to use an item in some form of commercial activity that turns some tangible good into an item of capital. A car is a car, but what makes it into capital is the decision by its owner to use that car to earn income.

A car can be used as a taxi, or to transport goods for payment, or in any number of ways that are part of some enterprise's productive efforts. Non-profit organizations and governments also make use of capital, so that, for example, a car may be used by a charity or by the police.

Capital items, to repeat, are items that have themselves been produced which are then, in turn, used in the production process. But it is how they are used that matters. If they are used to produce other goods and services, then they are capital. If they are used by final users in creating the satisfaction that material well-being can provide, then they are not.

Money most emphatically does not count as capital. Since money as notes and coins cannot actually be used in the production process directly, so far as economics is concerned, it does not form any part of an economy's capital base. Money can certainly be exchanged for items of wealth that can be used productively, but money as money is not capital.

Nor does capital include stocks, shares or bonds. Although often referred to as capital in financial circles, they are only titles to an income stream or to partial ownership of an enterprise. They are in themselves not part of the productive apparatus of an economy. They are therefore not part of an economy's capital base.

Capital is made up of those produced inputs which can be used in creating additional value. Think of capital as technology and machines as the perfect examples of a capital good and you should not get it wrong. But in so doing, bear in mind that much that is part of the capital of a nation is the intangible technological know-how embedded in the physical capital used. An aeroplane is a capital good, but the increasing sophistication of its embodied technologies is what causes its increase in productivity.

It might also be noted that *human capital* is now seen as a produced input in the production process.

Human capital is now also included as part of an economy's capital stock. They are the developments that each individual undertakes to increase their own ability to add value during the production process, and not incidentally to earn a higher income in so doing.

But when all is said and done, capital should be seen as everything that has been developed and produced to be used within the production process.

MILL'S FUNDAMENTAL PROPOSITIONS ON CAPITAL

John Stuart Mill provided four 'fundamental propositions respecting capital', whose validity remains as intact today as when first written in 1848 (Mill, [1878] 1921). But for all that, economics has sailed away from these fundamental propositions much to the cost of our understanding of how economies operate. Without their guidance, it is difficult to understand how an economy works.

The first three of the four propositions are universally accepted by economists even though seldom explicitly taught. The fourth is now explicitly taught as being false, even though it remains perfectly valid. But the loss to our understanding of the disappearance of this fourth proposition has had devastating consequences for economic theory and policy alike.

Industry is Limited by Capital

The first of his fundamental propositions, Mill noted, was so obvious as to be taken for granted but, as he also wrote, 'to see a truth occasionally is one thing, to recognise it habitually, and admit no propositions inconsistent with it, is another'.

This first proposition is that industry is limited by capital. You cannot produce more output than the amount of capital in existence will allow you to produce.

There is only so much that can be produced at any particular time, and that amount is kept within its certain limits by the amount of capital available. It is entirely true that an economy may at various times not expand to the full extent that its capital permits. But more important than this obvious statement is its corollary. In Mill's very nineteenth-century words, 'every increase of capital gives, or is capable of giving, additional employment to industry; and this without assignable limit'.

To translate: it is not possible to produce so much capital that production would overwhelm the willingness of the community to buy every last bit of the extra production the additional capital allowed an economy to supply.

Mill wrote in support of the necessity in understanding this doctrine that 'there is not an opinion more general among mankind than this, that the unproductive expenditure of the rich is necessary to the employment of the poor'.

Today that same doctrine would be stated as, there is not an opinion more common than this, that the expenditure of governments on just about anything at all is necessary to create employment, especially during recessions.

The basic form in which economic theory is taught today specifically teaches that if the community increases its level of saving, the level of economic activity will fall along with the level of employment.

There was a time when this modern view of things was seen as utterly false. Today it is seen as the highest truth, a core belief amongst economists. To quote Mill again, whose meaning in spite of his now-archaic mid-nineteenth-century language, should be crystal clear: 'The limit of wealth is never deficiency of consumers, but of producers and productive power. Every addition to capital gives to labour either additional employment, or additional remuneration; enriches either the country, or the labouring class.'

This cannot be emphasized enough: the limit to wealth creation is *never* the result of a deficiency of consumers, it is *only* a consequence of the limits imposed by the existing availability of producers and productive power.

To produce more does not require additions to consumption: it requires additions to the productiveness of an economy. And these never occur on the demand side of the economy, but only on the supply side.

Ignorance of this simple proposition has led to some of the worst mistakes in economic policy ever made.

Capital is the Result of Saving

The second of Mill's fundamental propositions was that if capital is to be produced, saving must take place. Without saving, the stock of capital cannot grow.

Saving is the feedstock of investment. Capital comes into existence only because saving has taken place. To return to Mill, 'all capital, and especially all addition to capital, is the result of saving'.

There are only two possibilities so far as production is concerned. Either what is produced is used up in the present, or what is produced is directed towards becoming part of the store of productive items that can be used in the production process. The first of these possibilities is consumption, and the second is investment. It is from investment that capital is created.

Economists know this, yet the way in which macroeconomics is often taught is to portray saving as a villain, since if you think of the most important driving force in an economy as its level of demand, then saving, because it supposedly reduces demand, leads to a fall in consumption and therefore in the level of activity.

That is the fundamental core proposition embedded in the way macroeconomics is taught today.

In reality, only if those who earned incomes do not spend all they receive on current consumption but save at least a portion is something left over to improve the productive capabilities of an economy. Investment comes from not using up everything we produce in current consumption but through saving.

What is Saved is Spent

Mill's third fundamental proposition is to point out that what is described as saving is actually a form of expenditure.

The words Mill uses do, however, require some explanation, since they are not the modern way in which these words are used by economists. But to understand what Mill wrote is to move to a deeper understanding of how economies work.

In Mill's words, this third proposition states that capital 'although saved, and the result of saving, it is nevertheless consumed'.

Today the word 'consumption' merely refers to purchases made for personal use by final buyers in the chain of production. To Mill, to consume meant to put something to use, whether by consumers or investors. Consumption meant 'to use up', as we might still say how a house was 'consumed' by a fire.

So in an economy, if electricity has been consumed, then the electricity has disappeared. It has been used up while being put to use in producing something else. If it is machinery or a building, then that machine or building has had the resources used in their production transformed into some specific shape for use in further production.

But one way or another, the use of our productive resources in production has deprived society of all the other ways those resources might have been used. Whatever else, those resources did not lie idle.

Mill was perfectly aware of how difficult it was to get this principle understood. He wrote:

The principle now stated is a strong example of the necessity of attention to the most elementary truths of our subject. It is one of the most elementary of them all . . . Yet no one who has not bestowed some thought on the matter is habitually aware of it. Most are not even willing to admit it when first stated.

Mill goes on to describe how these things are looked at by those who have not considered the issues properly and more deeply. To them, he wrote,

it is not at all apparent that what is saved is consumed. . . . Saving is to them another word for keeping a thing to oneself; while spending appears to them to be distributing it among others. The person who expends his fortune in [personal] consumption, is looked upon as diffusing benefits all around. . . . The eye follows what is saved, into an imaginary strong-box, and there loses sight of it; what is spent, it follows into the hands of tradespeople and dependents.

Those who save have limited their current purchases of consumer goods and services to less than what they have earned, and allow the remainder of those resources to be transferred to investors.

The very fact that incomes had been earned means that something had been produced and sold to the market. Saving allows the earnings not spent unproductively to be spent on financing productive activity either by themselves or by someone else. It is this which enables the economy to grow. Unless there are decisions to transfer purchasing power to those who intend to spend on building productive assets – that is, unless there are decisions to save – the economy cannot and will not grow. This transfer of savings is what the financial system is for.

Whether it is personal consumption taking place or it is investment, resources are being used up in the production process. They have disappeared and been reformed into the products being produced. But in the first case, with consumption, there is nothing to show for it so far as future productivity is concerned, while in the second case, with investment, the economy has been more than compensated for the resources that have been used up.

This is the kind of choice that individuals might face in their own lives. They can choose to take a prolonged international holiday or they can instead decide to build an extension on their home. In both cases the resources of the community have been drawn down, but only in the second is there anything productive to show for it. It is this choice which every community must face; how much of its resources to use up in day-to-day living and how much to use in adding to its productive capabilities.

To explain what Mill had in mind, look at the production possibility curve in Figure 5.1. On one axis is current consumption (*C*). On the other axis is investment (*I*). Where the production possibility curve meets either

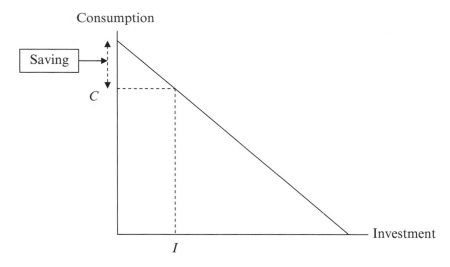

Figure 5.1   Production possibility curve in an economy with only consumption and investment

axis represents the total productive capability of the economy if either one or the other constituted the total level of production.

If all output is consumed, there is then nothing left over for investment. Only by not consuming all of our incomes – that is, only through saving some of our incomes – are there any resources available for investment. That saving is shown on the diagram as the difference between the level of total potential output on consumer goods and the actual level of consumption at *C*.

The existence of saving allows output to be redirected into investment. Without that saving, no investment could ever take place.

Saving is not an absence of spending, it is a decision to transfer one's ability to spend to someone else. But whatever those who have received those savings choose to do, saving does not represent an absence of production, a void to be filled in. Saving actually is production, just as Mill said.

To believe anything else is as wrong as it is possible to be wrong about economics. Yet it is this very error on which modern economic analysis has chosen, as we shall see, to base its understanding of macroeconomic issues.

The Demand for Commodities is Not Demand for Labour

Mill's fourth proposition was once considered the touchstone of economic thinking, 'the best test of a sound economist', as it was once said.

If you could not understand why it is true, you were seen as incapable of understanding how an economy works. This proposition has, however, now grown so far from present usage that it would be a very rare economist who has even heard this statement, let alone who even accepts what it says. Yet for all that, it remains as valid today as the day it was first penned.

Mill's fourth proposition states that 'the demand for commodities is not demand for labour'. Its meaning: when you buy goods and services you are not hiring labour. This is how it was put by Mill: 'To purchase produce is not to employ labour; . . . the demand for labour is constituted by the wages which precede the production, and not by the demand which may exist for the commodities resulting from the production.'

What this means is this. When someone buys goods, they are not themselves employing the labour or paying the wages. By the time the good is bought, the work has already been done and workers have already been paid. The employment of labour is an entrepreneurial decision made in advance of production and sale. It is not the consequence of someone finally having bought the product.

In explaining what he meant, this is how it was expressed by Mill: 'Almost all [economists] occasionally express themselves as if a person who buys commodities, the produce of labour, was an employer of labour, and created a demand for it as really, and in the same sense, as if he bought the labour itself directly, by the payment of wages.'

About this view Mill makes this very dark statement: 'It is no wonder that political economy advances slowly, when such a question as this still remains open at its very threshold.'

That this view – that the demand for goods and services is equivalent to the demand for labour – is now accepted across the economics profession with virtually no dissent is a matter of some considerable interest. A very great deal depends on whether Mill was right or wrong.

What then did Mill and the classics mean? This is how, in modern language, Mill explained why the contrary is so nonsensical.

If it is the case, he argued, that it all comes to the same thing so far as working people are concerned whether someone entirely consumes their own income – buying cars for themselves and overseas trips, let us say – or instead uses up resources on productive activities or on charitable contributions, then what sense is there in having their money taken from them in tax revenue to fund welfare expenditures?

For as Mill wrote, 'since my unproductive expenditure would have equally benefited them, while I should have enjoyed it too', why bother removing the purchasing power from their original owners if their spending it themselves on themselves would amount to the same thing?

The conclusion that should never be lost sight of in understanding how economies work is that buying things creates no value. To purchase is not to produce. Demand of itself creates no value and cannot put people to work.

To lose track of this fundamental proposition will render useless any and every economic judgement based on the belief in its opposite. Stimulating demand with non-productive forms of spending can only slow an economy. Only productive activity – genuine value-adding activity – only this can create growth. That was Mill's message, a message that has all but disappeared from economics as taught in the modern world.

THE ENTREPRENEUR

The last of the traditional factors of production is the most important one of all, the entrepreneur, the factor which rents, hires and purchases the other three and then directs them towards their productive use.

What makes a market economy work, what makes any modern economy work, is that often ignored fourth factor of production. Economies do not, cannot and will not work in anything other than the most primitive way without free, private, individual decision makers who make their living based on the success of the businesses they own and run.

It is, of course, possible to have some clunking assemblage of enterprises and business entities run by employees of the state. It is always possible to try to mimic free enterprise and the private sector by surrounding decision makers within a supposedly productive enterprise with a series of financial constraints and incentives.

All this has been tried time and again with tragic results that impoverish any nation that puts such a pseudo-market framework at the centre of its economic structure.

It doesn't work because as soon as the people at the controls of businesses are employees of government, rather than being self-selected individual members of the community who have chosen to run their own particular businesses in their own particular ways, the very process that drives production onwards instantly disappears.

An entrepreneur should be understood as the ultimate decision-making authority in a business enterprise. Entrepreneurs take on the risks that come from being unable to make a business profitable. Someone must be the final decision maker on all of the major production decisions in an enterprise, and its success or failure is seen as being in the hands of the entrepreneur.

ENTREPRENEURIAL EXAMPLES

To understand the role of the entrepreneur as one of the factors of production, think of a symphony orchestra. There, in miniature, we see the factors of production in operation.

There is first the 'land'. The piece of turf on which the concert hall sits has a location and a series of other uses, which means that it has value of itself. Labour then consists of the various members of the orchestra, each with their own specialized roles to play and each of whom embodies skills which have taken many years, often many decades to learn properly.

Capital then comes in the form of the various instruments as well as the music stands and sheet music. These are all produced means of production. Indeed, the concert hall itself is an item of capital, along with all of the seats in the auditorium. Capital consists of all of the previously produced items that are part of the apparatus that enables the concert to go ahead, as well as the human capital embodied in the musicians themselves.

Finally there is the entrepreneur. But just who is the entrepreneur in an orchestra? Most assuredly, the entrepreneur is not the conductor of the orchestra. The conductor, so far as this example goes, is an employee, often a very highly paid employee, but an employee all the same. The entrepreneur was the person whose role was to ensure that the concert took place at all.

In any enterprise, such as a symphony concert, there is someone who takes the ultimate responsibility for deciding that a concert will take place, ensures that an orchestra, including its conductor, is hired, and then undertakes or organizes to have undertaken, all of the steps along the way to ensure that a concert finally takes place. In virtually every circumstance of this kind, almost no one knows who the entrepreneur has been. But the certainty is that there has been someone, because unless there was, nothing would have ever happened.

Another example is film making. Land in a film is typically called 'the location'. Labour consists of all of the actors and the rest of the production crew. Capital is made up of all of the various items of equipment that turn the actions of individuals on a set into the finished product that ends up within a cinema. But when it comes to the entrepreneur, the director is only an employee and has not been the person in charge. A director is hired by someone else, and is not typically in charge of the entire film-making process.

In film making, the entrepreneur is called 'the producer', someone often unknown by name to almost anyone in a cinema audience. But behind every film there is someone who has been responsible for bringing together all of the elements that have eventually wound up in the film, from the finance, to the actors, to the equipment and so on down. Someone is in charge; someone makes those final decisions and ultimately pays the bills. And unless such a person exists, the film will never be made.

RISK VERSUS UNCERTAINTY

The essence of the business world is uncertainty and it is to deal with uncertainty that is the primary task of the entrepreneur. No one can know what is going to happen next, which makes every business decision a risk of one kind or another. Uncertainty is in the nature of the future. Risk is the willingness to make a potentially loss-making decision where nothing about the world as it will become can be known with certainty.

About the future, only conjectures can be made. Business decisions must be made in a world where no one can be sure about what will come next.

It is the role of the entrepreneur, even in the face of such uncertainties, to decide what to produce, how to produce, where to produce and what prices to charge. The fact that in a large enterprise there are managers who make such decisions does not diminish the crucial significance of the entrepreneur. It is the entrepreneur who has that final responsibility, and on that judgement the entire enterprise depends.

It is the entrepreneur who takes on these risks, and risks exist because the future is uncertain. If the future were known in advance with perfect clarity, there would be no risk-taking required in running a business. It is only because outcomes are unsure and the future is uncertain that entrepreneurial judgement is so valuable to an economy.

COMPETITION AND THE ENTREPRENEUR

Such willingness to take on this organizational role comes with many motivations, the desire for personal gain being only one. In the commercial world, however, where production for profit predominates, the role of the entrepreneur is guided not only by personal gain, but also by the forces of competition whose pervasive presence guarantees there is very close attention paid to ensuring costs are contained, and the products sold are as good as can be found at the prices paid.

It may not work out that way, but that is the aim. Those are the pressures that come from the existence of other competing businesses who would like nothing better than to take for themselves the customers of the firms with which they compete. Business leaders, the entrepreneurs of a free enterprise economy, reach the top by having made decisions along the way that have rewarded their firms with sufficient profitability to ensure that they have paid their way in the world. Anyone may start a business. Anyone may enter a business as an employee.

But whichever may have been the case, success has been registered in the profit and loss statement of the firm. The commercial world is a proving ground for success in business.

And this is true irrespective of the size of the firm. Whether businesses are run by a single person, or are structured as partnerships or limited liability companies under the management of boards of directors, it is only because the firm is directed by those whose allegiance is to the success of that particular business that there is any prospect of the firm remaining viable and itself contributing to economic growth.

Loss-making firms also draw down on the resource base of the community, but ultimately, because they are unable to pay their way, they must let those resources go to others who will then try to make a better use of the capital and labour that the managers of such loss-making firms had been directing.

The market system succeeds by a process in which resources are placed under the direction of those who are able to cover all of their costs through sales revenues received, while it takes the ability to direct resources from those who cannot. Whether through bad management or bad luck, if a firm cannot pay its way, it will either contract in size or completely disappear.

It is precisely here that the role of the entrepreneur comes into view. The major decisions of an enterprise are determined by its management, with the aim of commercial success as the crucial indicator of success. It is entrepreneurs who make the major decisions of deciding what, how and where to produce and sell.

Every major innovation which you might think of as just part of the world we live in – whether the telephone, computer or kitchen sink – is the product of entrepreneurial decision making by someone. Goods and services do not end up in our possession through magic, but are the result of business decisions made by individuals trying to earn a living by working out what others would be willing to pay high enough prices for, and in high enough numbers, to cover every single one of the many, many costs of production that have been incurred along the way.

FINANCE

It is possible to think of a fifth factor of production which is in many ways different from the others. Finance is not normally thought of as part of the underlying factors of production, but without the ability to pay for productive activity before there are any returns on the outlays made, productive activity on the scale to which we have become accustomed could not occur.

So although money or various financial instruments should not be thought of as forms of capital, there are strong reasons to include these as one of the necessary ingredients in the overall structure of business activity.

A major part of what an entrepreneur does in organizing a business is to secure lines of credit so that in conjunction with normal business cash flows, payments can be made as bills become due. And far from being a minor part of this process, it is often amongst the most important. Without an ability to cover production costs as these become due, a business will fail.

Finance is often ignored because, unlike the other factors, it is more abstract. It is not visible in the way the others are, and there would have been times and places in history when finance played almost no role in productive activity. But these were, generally speaking, more economically primitive communities.

Once commercial activity began to grow, the need for financing activity became immediately evident. Someone or some group was often needed to provide the financial backing to allow purchase to occur before any receipts had flowed into the business. Even if the entrepreneur provided the finance, this was a separate function, in the same way that working proprietors might provide their own labour even while being the entrepreneur within their own businesses.

The finance role is a very specialized area of the economy. What finance does is transfer, during some period of time, purchasing power from those who wish to save part of what they have earned to those who wish to spend but do not, at the time, have sufficient earnings to cover all of the spending they wish to undertake.

But what must also be understood about finance is that it often comes in the form of debt. Debt is a wonderful servant but a dreadful master. For an individual business, keeping debt levels under control is crucially important. But for an economy taken as a whole, however necessary it is to its operation, debt during times of economic stress can be an anchor that pulls an economy down, turning a mild downturn into something more savage.

THE NATURE OF INTEREST

Those who lend money to others do so to earn interest, which is the name given to these payments for the savings of others. There is a vast economic literature on the reason that interest is actually paid, but here we will only provide the most basic. Interest is the payment made for the use of part of one's property, and can thus be seen as a form of rental. One lends out one's savings in the same way one might rent out one's house. But at the end of the rental period, the aim is to have the full amount lent out returned, in the same way that one intends to reclaim one's house when the tenant moves out.

It is always easy to find others who wish to borrow. It is far more difficult to find borrowers who will be able to repay the funds they have received.

Business Loans

There are three general classes of recipients of such transferred savings. The first, and economically the most important, are businesses which intend to repay their debts with the receipts from the business enterprises which they manage, and often own.

From the lenders' perspective, what they are looking for are enterprises that will be sufficiently profitable that the money they lend will be returned. To assess and make proper judgements on the various applications for the use of funds is one of the most difficult tasks in the business world. That is what banks and other such financial institutions do, and it is from successfully discriminating between *potentially* successful businesses and those which are less likely, and even unlikely, to succeed that a bank will earn a profit of its own.

But it is only through this process that an economy is able to prosper. It is only by ensuring that funding reaches potentially profitable businesses – that is, that funding reaches those who will be able to repay their loans while being steered away from the unprofitable – that an economy grows.

Saving, and a sound financial system that allocates savings to the potentially most productive users of those savings, is amongst the most crucial determinants of whether an economy will itself succeed or instead remain impoverished and unable to genuinely prosper.

It should finally be noted that there are other forms of finance for business besides direct lending, but all of these are forms of saving which are transferred to a business from those who do not wish to spend at the present time. These include the purchase of shares, corporate bonds and other financial instruments that are designed to finance the activities of firms.

Savers in each of these instances are again likely to take whatever steps are needed to ensure that their savings are protected and will continue to grow over time. There is often more risk, but there are also often greater rewards. But from an economic point of view, the issue is the transfer of purchasing power from those who wish to save in the present, to those who wish to spend.

Personal Loans

The second class of borrowers do not intend to use the funds in a money-making operation but intend to finance their loans from other income-earning activities. The most common form of such loans is the housing loan, where individuals borrow to buy a house but do not intend to use the house to generate the income that will repay the loan. Instead, the payment of the loan will come from other sources of income, usually from working in some business from which an income is earned.

Again, the financial system is required to ensure that those who receive the savings from others are able to repay the loans they have received. Whether it is to finance a house, a car or an overseas trip, the role of the financial institution is to ensure that the money is likely to be repaid.

Government Borrowing

There is then a third area of borrowed savings, and this is by governments. Some of what governments borrow is used productively, some is used unproductively but to fulfil some social purpose, and some is wasted. But irrespective of how the funds are used, where the government is in charge of the money creation process, the money will almost certainly be repaid to those who lent the funds.

That is why lending to governments is often preferred, but it is also why interest rates paid by governments are usually the lowest on the market. It is because governments can borrow so easily that problems are often created for business. The more funds a government wants, the less there is for business, and the greater will the cost of funds be.

Governments are also more likely to waste the funds they receive, which means that savings are used less productively than they might otherwise have been. In an ideal world, government spending will add so much to the productivity of an economy that tax revenues will rise naturally to allow the debts incurred to be repaid. But even if this does not occur, taxes can be raised, and as a last resort the government can print more money to repay its debts.

FACTORS OF PRODUCTION

Each of the five factors of production are necessary components in the growth of industry and the commercial world. They are the components that make up the totality of an enterprise, with the entrepreneur at the very pinnacle of the process.

It is the entrepreneur embedded within the private sector of the economy that coordinates the other factors in a profit-making productive enterprise. The private sector entrepreneur is the keystone of the entire edifice of productive activity. Without the entrepreneur, who is freely able to operate within an environment which is regulated by those who understand the crucial contributions the entrepreneur provides, an economy cannot be expected to prosper.

It is also perhaps noteworthy that each of the factors of production has an associated name for the income generated, except for capital. As the list below shows, aside from capital, each of the others has a form of payment used in everyday discourse:

land → rent
labour → wages
capital → ?
entrepreneur → profit
finance → interest, dividends.

Although the roles of the entrepreneur, the providers of capital goods and the providers of finance can be embodied in a single individual, they do not have to be and often are not. Capital goods can be rented and finance borrowed but what cannot be farmed out is the entrepreneurial role itself. Someone must be the ultimate source of responsibility and the final place of authority in a business.

The entrepreneur is the linchpin for all of the other factors of production and while entrepreneurs may provide any or all of the other factors as part of their business operations, they must each be seen as separate.

The entrepreneur provides direction and focus. Without the entrepreneur embedded within private sector business activity, individual firms cannot on their own succeed, and an economy is guaranteed to flounder.

6. Supply and demand

An economy is a perfect storm of activity buried inside the ongoing activities of a nation. It is not something separate but is entirely all of a piece with the whole life of a community. There is hardly a thing any of us do that does not involve some kind of economic activity, even if not by ourselves, then by someone else.

Even our recreational activities are part of the market. It is hard to think, even amongst our leisure activities, what could occur without there being someone else whose job it is to make sure it takes place. Not the movies, not a sporting event, not a trip to the beach; just about nothing at all can be done without there having been some kind of commercial transaction somewhere.

Our lives are surrounded by the products of the market, which means they are surrounded by the generally invisible forces of supply and demand.

PRODUCTION AND SALE

Supply and demand is the conceptual meeting place between sellers and buyers. It is, first, where entrepreneurs meet up with consumers. It is where the goods and services that businesses have put up for sale are confronted by consumers who are trying to achieve the highest level of satisfaction from using the incomes plus various forms of credit they have available, never forgetting that some of their income might be saved.

But it is not just where entrepreneurs meet up with consumers, it is also where entrepreneurs meet up with other entrepreneurs. Most of the purchase and sale that goes on in an economy takes place between businesses. Businesses sell inputs to other businesses and all of that is regulated by supply and demand.

The most fundamental of all diagrams in economics relate the supply curve to the demand curve. The supply curve incorporates what sellers are expected to do in response to the economic environment in which they operate. The demand curve does the same for buyers. It outlines how those who buy particular goods and services are expected to behave, given the circumstances in which they find themselves.

But understand this. No one has ever actually seen supply and demand curves outside of an economics text. They are like the fundamental particles of physics. In physics, we posit the existence of various sub-atomic particles with certain properties to account for the structure and behaviour of the visible world. In economics, sense is made of the behaviour of people in buying and selling through conjecturing the existence of these two forces which cause goods and services first to exist and then to end up in the hands of particular individuals and not in the hands of others.

A supply curve is intended to show how sellers will behave if prices are changed. A demand curve is designed to show how buyers will behave when prices are changed. The central question being asked is how many units of whatever happens to be up for sale will be bought by buyers and sold by sellers at different prices.

And beneath it all is the ancient *ceteris paribus* proviso. All other things must be equal if the simple relationship between price and production is to hold good.

The theory underlying supply and demand is designed to explain how the particular price and the particular volume of sales is eventually arrived at through the competitive forces of the market.

The very existence of goods or services to buy is the result of a decision by someone or some group to produce and put such goods and services up for sale. The market is another name for human will as applied to the production process.

In a market economy, it is the individual members of the community who set businesses up and make their decision to sell. It is thus very important logically and in actual fact to recognize that the words 'supply' and 'demand' represent not just two separate words, but are in the natural order in which events occur. There is first supply, and only then is there demand.

In almost every textbook presentation the ordering is first to teach about demand and then about supply. This reverses the logic of what really happens in causing goods and services ultimately to find their way into the world before being put on their way to the individual buyers.

THE MARKET

The market is neither a place nor a moment in time. It is a notional concept which provides a frame of reference in which transactions take place. A transaction occurs when a good or a service is exchanged either for money directly, or for a promise to pay at some time in the future.

To this transaction is brought either an existing good or service or a promise to provide some good or service at a predetermined moment in the future.

Producers, to be in a position to supply, have had to have created in the past a production chain that has led them to the particular moment in which the transaction has taken place.

Buyers similarly have had to have put themselves in a position to buy whatever they are buying either by immediately paying the price or else by being in a position to convince the seller that they will be able to complete their side of the exchange when the payment they have agreed to make becomes due.

The entire process of economic exchange is based on expectations. There is, first, the belief held by producers that there are a sufficient number of buyers who will in total pay a sufficient amount of money to repay every single one of the costs incurred along the way.

There must then, simultaneously, also be a belief held by sellers that buyers will be able to pay the full price for whatever has been bought if they are not doing so immediately at the time the transaction takes place.

On the production side, every economic decision, except the most trivial, is directed towards the future. Every economic outcome, again except for the most trivial, is based on a long history of decisions that have preceded the moment at which a transaction takes place.

It is in thinking about market activity that supply and demand become relevant. It is in this context that the process by which total strangers are able to exchange one set of goods for another through the use of money takes place.

Understanding the dynamics of supply and demand is the starting point for understanding how an economy operates.

SUPPLY

Start with supply. In fact, the only place to start is with supply, since it is only with the decisions made to supply that anything can ever be bought. And in starting with supply, we are starting with the entrepreneur.

For something to come to market, someone must make a production decision and in most instances put a price on the goods and services that have been put up for sale. There is an actual human will that exists behind the actual actions that are taken. And it is in recognizing this that an understanding of the information available to the seller needs to be appreciated first.

What every seller is thinking about is how to fulfil the need of someone else. For final consumers, it is to provide utility. For other businesses, it is

Price

Quantity

*Figure 6.1   The certain information available to a firm introducing a new
product or service*

to supply a needed input. But one way or another, it is to put up for sale
some good or service that can be sold at a profit.

The structure of supply and demand curves shows the price of the
product on the vertical axis and the number of units that will be sold at
different prices during some period of time on the horizontal axis.

In thinking about supply, the business has to think through, at its most
primitive, how many units will be demanded. The relevant information
available to the business in introducing a new product for sale is shown in
Figure 6.1.

For a new product or service, what is shown is what is known with
certainty. That is, nothing is known with certainty. Prices are a guess.
The level of sales is a guess, even if an educated guess based on plenty of
market research and intensive review. The kinds of certainty a business
would like to have simply cannot be charted.

In setting up, a business is taking a step into the unknown. The business
failure rate for new start-ups is high, and the survival rate for firms making
it past even the second year is depressingly low.

With supply and demand, however, it is only a single product that is
being examined. For a firm putting that product up for sale, there is simply
no reliable information that can let a business know ahead of time how

well that product will sell. There is no scientific way for the firm to determine the price to put on the item. All of what takes place is often no more
than a matter of judgement and experience.

PRICE AND VOLUME OF AN INDIVIDUAL PRODUCT

But let us get to the next step and think about a product that has been put
on the market. In this case, something is known, and what is known is
shown in Figure 6.2.

What does a business know about any of the products it has put up for
sale? It knows the price it is charging, and generally has a pretty fair idea
about the volume of sales in each period of time. It therefore knows *P* and
it generally knows *Q* but, so far as this diagram is concerned, not necessarily all that much more.

And here it might be emphasized that the point in question is on the
firm's supply curve, since that is what the firm is supplying. The point
may also be on the demand curve, since that is the number of units being
bought at that price. It is, however, possible that more could have been

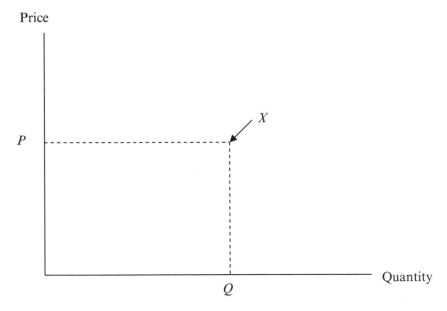

*Figure 6.2   Information available to a business about price and volume of a
good or service it is already selling*

sold at the price if they had been put up for sale, so that the actual level of demand may be greater than that shown by the actual level of sales.

Of course, aside from the information shown on this graph, what this business almost always also knows is what others with the same sorts of goods or services are selling, and the prices at which they are being sold. There is for most goods, in most places, an active market where there are substitutes for everything being put up for sale.

The marketplace is typically a crowded square. There are often many other sellers of identical, similar or closely related goods and services. Even distantly related goods and services can affect each other, such as the way that the demand for restaurant meals might be affected by the relative attractiveness of other forms of evening entertainment (as in, shall we go out to dinner or to a film instead?).

EFFECT OF AN INCREASE IN PRICE

But knowing the level of sales at a particular price is a very limited piece of knowledge. Start with the question of what would happen if the price were to rise or fall, even assuming that all of the other underlying conditions were fixed (which they never are for very long).

What would be the effect of raising the price? Any business thinking about a higher price immediately considers the effects on two groups: its customers and its competitors.

Raise the price, and every business will assume that the level of sales will fall. Higher prices reduce the number of units customers will buy, and that would be the case even if all of the competing firms raised their own prices at the same time by the same amount.

But then, suppose the other competing firms in the industry chose not to raise their prices. The effect on the level of sales would be even greater. The loss of customers to other producers would be larger, often much larger, than if all firms raised their prices at one and the same time.

So there the business is at point X in Figure 6.2, and it is thinking of the consequences of a price rise. What doesn't exist for this business is a nicely presented, already worked out demand curve that sets out what will happen to the level of sales if the price happened to be higher. All that exist are different possible reactions from customers and competitors, all of which will affect the level of sales either hardly at all or to a very great extent, but which can only be guessed at. All this is conjecture. Nothing is known for sure.

This is the reality of business decision making at its most basic level. The product has already been developed. It is on the market and is selling

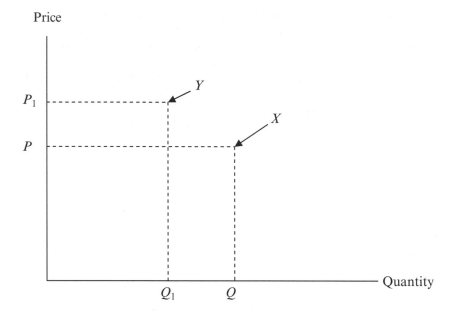

Figure 6.3   Effect of a price increase on the number of units sold

Q units at price P in each period of time. The business has views about its customers, it has views about the products produced by its competitors. It also knows its level of sales and is very conscious of how rapidly this product is selling relative to the past. It knows its costs and presumably has a reasonable idea about the costs facing other firms in the industry. It knows what is happening to the prices of similar products elsewhere. There are many, many such facts which are known. What is not known is what will happen to the level of sales if the price is increased.

Anyway, suppose the price is raised from P to P_1. The effect on the number of units sold is a fall in sales from Q to Q_1 (see Figure 6.3). Thus, in a sense *but not actually*, we have traced out part of the demand curve for this one particular business selling this one particular product which would be found in drawing a line from X to Y.

It is not necessarily a true demand curve since between two time periods it is not necessarily the case that the underlying *ceteris paribus* conditions are being met. A true demand curve shows all the prices and quantities during a particular period of time when every one of the *ceteris paribus* conditions have not changed. In this example, however, when changing the price we have moved to a different time period, since two prices for the same product cannot be charged at the same moment in time.

Moreover, all kinds of other things might have changed, including the prices charged by competitors. But nevertheless, in some simple way, the increase in price and subsequent fall in sales may have given this business some idea of the shape of the demand curve it faces.

THE FIRM'S SUPPLY CURVE

Now it might be noted that for the firm no 'supply curve' independent of the demand curve has been traced out. At each price there is a maximum amount that would be put up for sale in each period of time, which in some sense might be known to the firm.

This is a notional supply curve that exists in a somewhat more concrete way than the presumed demand curve. Individual firms do have some notion of how many units of a product would be supplied to the market at different prices during some particular period of time.

There is a level of sales, and the organization is scaled to meet that level of sales. With the capital and labour available, there is an absolute maximum that could be produced, but no one really thinks about it except during those rare occasions when sales come up against capacity constraints.

Nevertheless, there is a notional amount that is the maximum, and this maximum would tend to increase as the price increases. The fact that with the higher price, fewer units would be sold, tells nothing about the productive potential of the firm. At the higher price, if more could be sold than the original number of units, Q, more would be produced.

At price P in Figure 6.4, the most that might be produced is Q, but at the higher price, P_2, the number of units of output that would be produced per unit of time would rise to Q_2. In this way, by connecting X and Z, a rudimentary supply curve for the firm can be traced out. It slopes up, and indicates that the higher the price, the more that producers would have been willing to produce. Or at least, that is what those who run this business believe, since all of the businesses in the industry haven't tried to increase their production levels together at the same time. If they did, all may find shortages of labour and raw materials that they thought would be available, which in that hypothetical situation turns out not to be the case.

Nevertheless, there is a notional supply curve for each firm that is, at its most concrete, the tacit belief by each producer of what would be produced were the price to rise or fall by different amounts. And there are even some firms who are not producing this product who would enter the market if the price rose high enough.

The supply and demand curves for individual firms are in a sense the

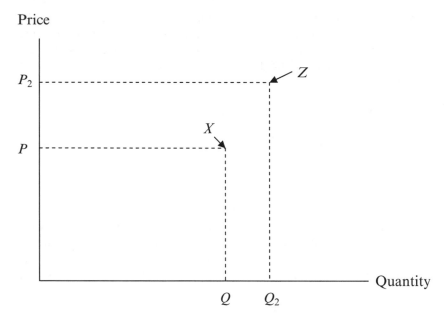

*Figure 6.4   Maximum number of units that would be produced at each
             price in each time period*

individual components of the supply and demand curves for the market
as a whole. If they are all added together, they provide the totals for all
buyers and all sellers, actual and potential, all other things being equal.

And as much as the supply and demand curves for individual firms
constitute merely a conceptual notion with no possibility of calculation,
the data for the market as a whole is even more phantasmagorical. They
have no existence other than as a conceptual tool for understanding how
markets work.

COMPETITION

The term we use for what happens in markets is 'competition'. It therefore presents what is taking place as a form of contest which, as normally
conceived, suggests that someone must win while someone else must lose.

So it is important to think very carefully about just who is engaged in
whatever this contest is, and who really are the winners at the end of whatever competition is going on. How does one tell at the end of the contest
who has actually won?

To the extent that it is a competition, the winner is the business that is able to provide buyers with whatever it is that those buyers prefer from amongst all of the alternatives presented. The contest is between sellers. The winner is determined according to which of those sellers buyers prefer to buy their goods and services from.

Thus, the judges in this competition are the buying public. The laurels are given in the form of sales and profitability. And the result is a structure of production made up of just those businesses which have been able to satisfy buyers more completely than any of the other businesses which had offered their goods and services up for sale.

Of course, at any one time, there is usually more than one supplier of any particular product. But there are also usually many more who had tried to supply that product but had been forced to leave the market because they did not provide whatever it was that buyers were looking for.

This jostling amongst sellers to make the sale is the essence of the market system, and it is this that continues to ensure – so long as markets are free, open and contestable – that the products on offer continuously improve in quality while falling in price.

In understanding what takes place, it is the supply side where all of the true action happens. It is on the supply side that decisions on what to produce, how to produce, where to produce and what prices to charge are made. Demanders really do no more than choose amongst the different possibilities that have been put before them. It is the producers who make all of the decisions of consequence right up to the moment when buyers confer their decision to purchase on one set of products rather than another. Until that moment, everything that has taken place has been under the direction of a string of entrepreneurs from the producer of the first of the inputs to the final decision to put some item or service up for sale in some retail establishment.

Until some good or service has been sold to its final purchaser, every step along the way has been the outcome of a series of decisions made by the owners and managers of various firms, from the producers of the most minimal inputs to the retail shop where it is ultimately bought.

It is this that is embodied in the market supply curve. It is the summation of all of the previous decisions to transform various inputs into final output put up for sale.

MARKET SUPPLY

And again, with the market supply curve the first place to start is with the blank market supply and demand open space (see Figure 6.5). It is on

Price

Quantity

*Figure 6.5   Market supply and demand space before the decisions are
made to supply some product*

this empty field that actual decisions will be imprinted by entrepreneurial
decision.

Name the product: it is not available for sale until someone has decided
to produce it.

Having decided to produce, with only some very odd exceptions, the
price found in the market is the result of a business decision.

And finally, however many units there might be available for sale, those
units are available only because some entrepreneur has made the decision to bring those to market, either from new production or out of some
inventory that has itself been the result of earlier decisions to produce.

In thinking about the market situation, beneath it are the various considerations made by each of the potential sellers. All have applied their
judgement in one way or another to decide how many units to put up for
sale. And the kinds of supply-side considerations that are of most concern
to such entrepreneurs in making such decisions include:

- the cost of inputs, including the cost of labour;
- the capital stock available;
- the kinds of technologies available;
- the skills available within the workforce;

- expectations about the future;
- government taxes and regulations.

And then there are the demand-side considerations that each seller must bear in mind:

- how many can be sold;
- what will the competition charge;
- what innovations might affect my sales.

Each of these is based on the expectations held within the firm. There are no concrete facts the firm can depend on to tell it how many units it will be able to sell. Its decisions to sell will depend on the business judgement exercised within the firm.

Having factored in all of these matters, a decision will be made on how many units to produce and what price to charge. These are the *ceteris paribus* factors. The price and quantity decision that is finally made is based on some assessment made of all of these. And when each of these changes, the prices charged and/or the number of units produced might also be changed in response.

'SUPPLY' MEANS THE WHOLE CURVE

But the notion of supply in economics refers to more than just about the decisions that each of these entrepreneurs has made about what quantities to sell and at what price. It also goes further, much further, and asks how many units would be put up for sale if the price were higher or lower.

Supply is *all* of the different volumes that would be sold at *all* of the different prices that might realistically be charged where all of the underlying factors remain unchanged. Supply is not an amount. Supply is a relationship between price and quantity (see Figure 6.6).

Supply to an economist is that whole line. It is a schedule showing how many units would be supplied to the market at each price.

A supply curve should be seen as an **if–then** statement. It states that **if** the price is at some particular level shown on the vertical axis, **then** the number of units that will be supplied to the market will be some number shown on the horizontal axis, and that if the price is something else, then the number of units that will be supplied will be the number of units shown on the horizontal axis for this new, different, price.

Price

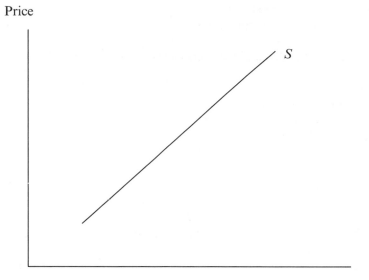

Quantity

Figure 6.6   Supply

SUPPLY VERSUS QUANTITY SUPPLIED

People often do talk about supply as if it is a specific amount and it is therefore important to make sure that when someone is talking about 'supply', one is aware of which meaning they have in mind.

Compare these two statements:

1. if the price goes up supply goes up (and who would deny this is so?)
2. if supply goes up the price goes down (and similarly, who would deny this?)

This becomes the following conclusion if the two statements are run together:

3. *if the price goes up* [supply goes up; if supply goes up] *the price goes down*.

That is, if the price goes up the price goes down. A higher price is the cause of a lower price. Obvious nonsense, but it comes from using the word 'supply' in its two different meanings.

In (1), this is using the word 'supply' to mean a movement along the supply curve when the price happens to rise. In (2), this is using the word 'supply' to mean a shift of the entire supply curve when one of the underlying factors has changed.

It is therefore essential always to make sure which meaning of supply is intended. You can usually tell from the context of what is being said, but the words here are slippery and can lead you into trouble.

And the same cautionary note is applicable to demand when we come to it. The words 'supply' and 'demand' have two separate meanings, one meaning the whole curve and the other as a point on the curve. Knowing which one is meant is important. Not being aware of this distinction will lead to endless confusion.

The supply curve is in a particular position *all other things being equal*. But these other things change, as they always do. And when they change, the supply curve changes along with them.

MOVEMENTS OF THE SUPPLY CURVE

When any of the underlying *ceteris paribus* conditions change, in fact, when anything changes that affects the willingness of businesses to put a good or service onto the market, *other than the price of the product itself*, the entire curve will shift.

If the change makes entrepreneurs willing to produce greater amounts at each price, we say supply has gone up, which is represented by the supply curve shifting to the right. In Figure 6.7, it moves from S to S_1. So if costs go down, technology improves or business taxes fall, then the response of businesses would be to increase the amounts they would be willing to provide to the market *at each price*.

If, on the other hand, whatever has changed has made businesses only willing to provide a reduced amount at each price, then we say that supply has fallen, and this is represented by a shift of the supply curve to the left, in this case from S to S_2. This might occur because of an increase in business costs, higher wages let us say, or expectations of a slowdown in the economy. Whatever makes businesses less willing to go to the expense of producing for the market will cause the supply curve to move to the left.

The movement of the supply curve is merely the application of common sense to economic events. And never forget that beneath the curve are entrepreneurs making business decisions about what they should do.

Price

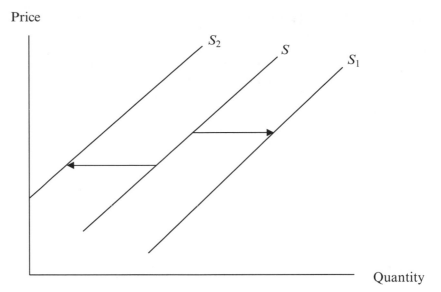

Quantity

Figure 6.7   Changes in supply

MARKET DEMAND

Then we come to demand. Demand represents the actions taken by the buyers of all of the products that entrepreneurs have put up for sale. And this is not just the final goods found in shops, but includes everything that is sold by one business to another. Iron ore is never bought by consumers, but there is a very large demand for iron ore all the same, by businesses that make steel, for instance.

Those who buy are almost invariably choosing amongst products that have already been produced and in any event are known to exist and can be brought to market. For demanders, supply and demand is not an empty space. There are, instead, all kinds of goods and services that have already been made available and in virtually every case already have a price attached.

Demand curves, like supply curves, are a relationship between a range of realistic prices and the number of units that would be bought at each of those prices. Demand is not an amount. But again, beneath the position of the demand curve there are a host of *ceteris paribus* assumptions about all of the other factors that are assumed to remain constant while the price and quantities are being varied. These factors include:

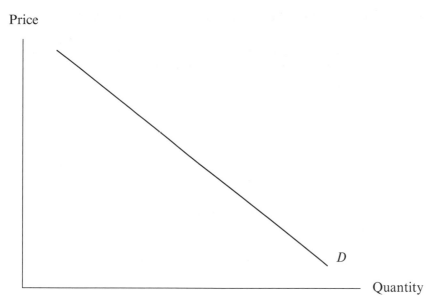

Figure 6.8   Demand

- incomes;
- tastes;
- the prices of alternatives (substitutes);
- the prices of goods or services used in conjunction with the product (usually referred to as 'complementary' goods or services);
- technological changes that have caused a shift either towards or away from the product;
- government decisions, regulations and taxation;
- expectations about future prices or future availability.

Demand is influenced by anything and everything that makes a product either more or less desirable to buyers.

The demand curve is a relationship between the price and the number of units of a product that will be bought during any period of time, all other things being equal. A demand curve has the downward slope found in Figure 6.8.

Demand is *all* of the different volumes that would be bought at *all* of the different prices that might realistically be charged where all of the underlying factors remain unchanged. Demand is not an amount, it is a relationship between price and quantity.

DEMAND VERSUS QUANTITY DEMANDED

Demand, like supply, is often discussed as if it is a specific amount rather than a relationship. And as with supply, it is important to be able to make the distinction between statements such as:

1. the price went up and demand went down

and statements such as:

2. demand went down so the price went down.

Here, too, you can run the two statements together and end up with a complete contradiction:

3. the price went up [so demand went down; demand went down] so the price went down.

That is, the price went up so the price went down. The reason the price went down was supposedly because the price had first gone up. Once again, the problem is that the word 'demand' has been used in two different way. In this example (1) means a movement along the demand curve induced by a rise in price. In (2) it is a movement of the entire demand curve which has led to a fall in price.

With the first meaning, it is often recommended that the movement along the curve should be called a movement in 'quantity demanded'. Yet even economists will regularly speak of demand and mean either shifts of or shifts along the curve. It is just necessary to be able to recognize which meaning is intended because you cannot count on anyone else maintaining the distinction consistently.

MOVEMENT OF THE DEMAND CURVE

A shift in demand, as in a shift of the entire curve, will occur when any one of the underlying factors changes. Then things have not remained equal. The underlying demand conditions have changed and this is represented by a movement of the entire curve (see Figure 6.9).

The movement of the curve from D to D_1 represents an increase in demand. At each price, the number of units of the product that will be bought has increased. Some shift, such as an increase in incomes or a rise

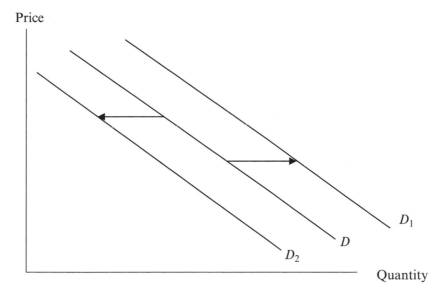

Figure 6.9   Changes in demand

in the price of other similar goods, means that more of this product is desired. The entire curve therefore shifts to the right.

A fall in demand is represented by the shift of the curve to the left from D to D_2. With this reduction in demand, there is a fall in the number of units that will be bought at each price. Some underlying factor, such as the product going out of fashion or no longer being needed as an input into some other production process, has reduced the number of units that others want to buy at each price.

When any of the underlying *ceteris paribus* conditions change, in fact, when anything changes that affects the willingness of buyers to buy a good or service, *other than the price of the product itself*, the entire curve will shift.

And just as it was with supply, the movement of the demand curve is merely the application of common sense to economic events.

EQUILIBRIUM

The supply and demand curves together provide the equilibrium position, which allows for the *simultaneous* determination of the number of units of the product that will be sold in each time period and the price at which those units will be sold.

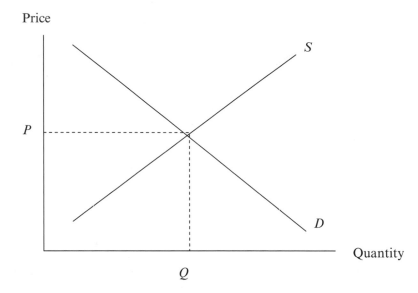

Figure 6.10   Market equilibrium

Bringing the supply and demand curve together on the same diagram shows the mutual determination of the two outcomes at one and the same time (see Figure 6.10).

The point where the supply curve *S* and the demand curve *D* cross is the equilibrium position. It is at this price that the number of units that buyers are willing to buy and sellers are willing to sell are the same. At no other price is this the case.

If nothing else changed, this market for this single product would come to a rest. Nothing else would happen, other than that for time period after time period, the same amount *Q* would be produced and all of it would be sold at the equilibrium price *P*. This is precisely what would never happen in the real world but it is an important place to start if one is to make sense of economic events.

7. Supply and demand: beyond equilibrium

The entire notion of equilibrium is something like a diversion to take your eye away from what is really important in markets, and that is change, and how people deal with such change.

Figure 7.1 shows the equilibrium position where at price P there will be Q units of the product bought and sold in each time period. And this would go on literally forever unless something changed. But since something can always be counted on to change, it doesn't go on forever.

Importantly, change can only come from a change in one or more of the underlying factors that cause a shift in the position of one of the curves.

Start with something simple, an increase in the incomes received by buyers of this good. If it is a normal good, higher incomes will lead buyers to buy more. (If it is what is known as an 'inferior good', an increase in

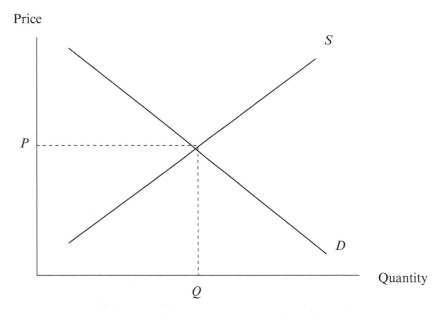

Price

Figure 7.1   The equilibrium from which everything starts

income will actually lead to a fall in the demand for the product as buyers switch to higher quality products.)

Here the assumption is that higher incomes have led to an increase in demand. The question is, how would anyone in business know, first, that there has been an increase in the incomes of the industry's customers and then, secondly, that this increase in income has been followed by a desire to buy more of the industry's output? The one action no one in business can take is to look at what is happening to the demand curve, either for the business or for the industry. There is no demand curve. There is no one to alert a firm. There are only the clues to a changed situation that the market provides.

The supply and demand curves in a traditional analysis are drawn at an equilibrium point but no one in reality knows where these are. The only actual point on either curve that may ever be known to anyone is where price P and quantity Q meet. Even then, the only part that anyone may really have known, so far as the industry was concerned, was the price. The total volume of sales across the industry may not have been known to anyone and may never be known.

If we are talking about the market for black umbrellas, let us say, there would never be a mechanism for knowing the total level of sales, and as far as the market is concerned, no one would ever likely care. But the picture shown in Figure 7.1 could occur for any good or service you might care to name.

HOW A BUSINESS KNOWS THERE HAS BEEN AN INCREASE IN DEMAND

There is that original equilibrium point E. And something has happened, so that rather than selling Q units of output, the same amount that had been produced, the market is now trying to buy Qa units (see Figure 7.2). In that first instance, only the volume of sales has changed and it is setting up quite a disturbance within the industry.

Businesses selling this product are finding they are selling more units than their past experience would have led them to expect. This may or may not have created a commercial opportunity. There may or may not be an obvious reason for this change. There may or may not be an obvious response to the different level of sales.

What has happened, though, is this. More are being sold than on previous occasions and either their stock levels are running out (for a good) or the sales staff are far busier than in the past (for a service). The question then is first to decide whether the change is permanent or just a

Price

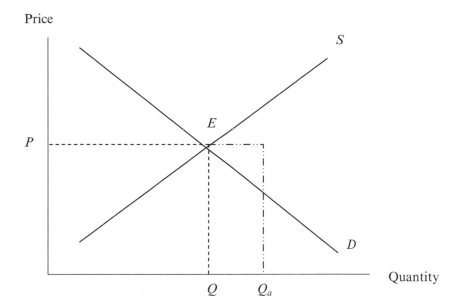

Figure 7.2   An increase in quantity demanded

statistical fluke, and then, if it does seem to be permanent, what action to take.

Because on top of all of the other considerations that go into making a decision, there is the front row question of what the other firms in the industry are going to do. But the one certain fact is that more is being bought than is being produced. There is therefore pressure on businesses all around the industry to increase production levels and possibly raise prices. And if this shortage persists, then the response may well be to increase production levels and push prices up.

This will be the attitude of many in the industry, and eventually, given the unknown supply and demand situation, through a process of trial and error the price will lift, and the quantity demanded will cut back to some extent but usually not to the full extent of the previous increase in sales. Eventually a new equilibrium is established at a higher price and a higher volume in which the level of sales is matched by the level of demand. That is what is shown in Figure 7.3, except that the unknown demand and supply curves are drawn in. *D* has moved to D_2.

Ultimately, the price has gone up from *P* to P_2 while the level of sales has gone from *Q* to Q_2. But it has been a process of market adjustment that required a series of entrepreneurial decisions at every stage along the way.

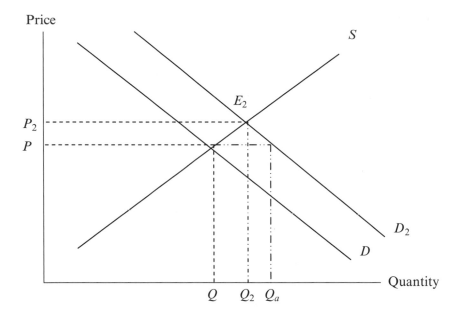

Figure 7.3   Market adjustment with supply and demand

EFFECT ON BUYERS

As we do economic analysis, we state that demand has shifted. This is a short form statement about there being new facts on the ground that those who run businesses must take into account. To leave out the need for business decisions to be made by actual human beings who raise the level of production and who put up the price, leaves out the actual dynamic processes involved.

It also leaves out the decisions that face the buyers of the product. For them, there was a product they bought whose price has suddenly increased. In most circumstances, each customer had bought only a tiny fraction of the total volume of sales. And for no particular reason that they can see, the price has risen and they have to make a decision on what to do.

Relative to the original equilibrium, they are in aggregate buying more. Relative to the intermediate position, when demand had risen but the price had not, now that the price has gone up, fewer units are being demanded. But here too there are real, live people making decisions on how many units to buy, with all of these decisions being finally registering as the total number of units demanded that is also, when everything has worked itself through, the same as the total number of units supplied.

But as for the curves themselves, they will never be seen. It is only a diagrammatic way to explain the shifts in behaviour that are taking place across the entire market for this product which have led to an increase in price and an increase in the level of production and sale.

CHANGE IN SUPPLY

Suppose instead we think about some change that affects the willingness to supply at each and every price. The initial market equilibrium is shown in Figure 7.4, but again no one knows where these curves are.

So far as these diagrams are concerned, a business knows only its price and volume of sales. It would know what price it would need to receive to be willing to put various amounts onto the market, but as far as the market itself is concerned, it would often know very little about the effect of price changes on the level of demand or the reactions of its competitors.

Originally the willingness to supply is shown by the firm's supply curve, *S*. In the vicinity of the equilibrium point, the supply curve represents how sellers would react to a change in price. Although no one can know for sure in advance, it is the kind of information that a firm often believes it has. In general, it would be understood that higher prices would lead to more

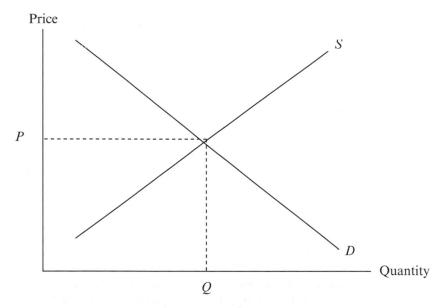

Figure 7.4   Initial equilibrium before an increase in supply has occurred

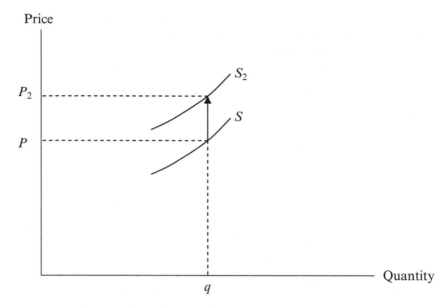

Figure 7.5 What a firm might know

production and lower prices to less. But basically, unless an expansion was in the works, the effect on the firm's level of production of a large change in the price, either up or down, would not be part of the calculation.

But into this setting, suppose there is an increase in costs. This moves the notional supply curve in Figure 7.5 up to S_2. At the level of production, q, the price would have to rise to P_2 to cover the entire increase in costs for that level of production. And that is what you would expect to happen if there were no effect on the level of demand. Production would stay at q (the small q here used for quantity since it is only a single firm's supply).

The higher price, however, leads to a lower level of sales. Behind the scenes is the unknown and invisible demand curve which, if the information could be known, would instantly tell sellers what the new price ought to be if only such a supply curve existed. In reality, there is a process of adjustment businesses must go through in finding their way to the new equilibrium.

The oft-stated lament from business, that they could not pass on their entire increase in costs, is a tacit recognition that they are facing a downward-sloping demand curve. They don't know its shape although they have some sense of it from past experience. But what they do know is that in raising the prices they charge, the consequence is a loss of sales. An entrepreneur does not need to have seen a demand curve to have had this experience in business.

INDUSTRY SUPPLY

Translate these shifts across to the industry supply and demand curves. For convenience, we keep the same supply curve shape that was drawn for the individual firm. Nothing about the underlying analysis has to change.

The demand curve is unknown, but as shown in Figure 7.6, the higher price has a powerful effect on the level of sales across the industry. Prices do not rise to the full extent of the increase in costs. Perhaps with lower volumes, input costs are lower or overtime is no longer needed, allowing costs to fall. Some high-cost producers may drop out of the market.

HORIZONTAL AND DOWNWARD-SLOPING SUPPLY

But it is just as possible that the supply curve may be horizontal over the relevant range or, with economies of scale, perhaps even downward-sloping. Both of these are genuine market possibilities.

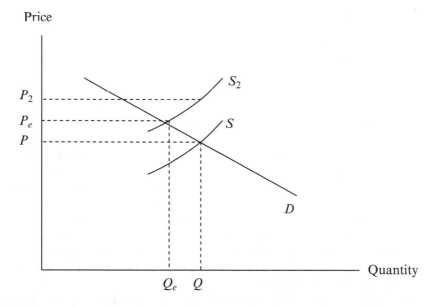

Figure 7.6 Market equilibrium with a fall in supply

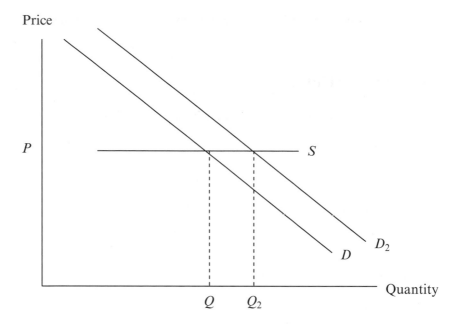

Figure 7.7　Effect on price and volume with horizontal supply

With a horizontal supply curve over the relevant range, changes in demand lead to changes in production levels but not to changes in price (see Figure 7.7). Businesses may even be absorbing higher costs. The supply curve merely traces the response of suppliers to higher levels of demand.

Market demand curves are invariably downward-sloping, which is why the relevant principle is called the *law* of demand. Supply curves can go in any direction, particularly over what might be described as 'the relevant range', which is the output level in proximity to the current level of production.

Horizontal supply curves show that over a broad range of output, given the existing workforce, technical know-how, input costs and any of the other *ceteris paribus* conditions, it is quite possible to maintain the same price irrespective of the particular level of output.

There is also no particular reason why the supply curve might not be downward-sloping in some industries as shown in Figure 7.8. In industries where there are large economies of scale that can be captured, so that as output goes up average production costs go down, it is possible that higher volumes will bring prices down.

But in reality, when the moment of supply arrives it is always the short run since for almost any good or service, during any relatively short period

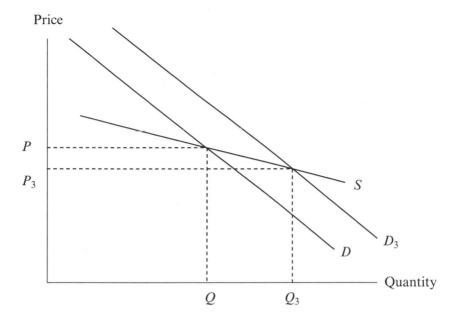

Figure 7.8   Economies of scale and increased demand

of time there is only so much available and no more. Had suppliers known at some relevant stage in the past when the production decisions could have been changed either upwards or down, what the prevailing price would actually turn out to be, or what demand conditions would actually turn out to be, then they might have acted differently than they did.

All that can be said is that the longer the time period involved, the greater the ability of suppliers to change their production level. Demand is more or less a response of the present; supply is the culmination of a long and involved chain of entrepreneurial-driven conjectures, forecasts and decisions that have led to whatever circumstances there are in the present. Whatever one is able to demand today was determined by supply decisions in the past.

In this case, an increase in demand will lead to a lower price for the product. From cars to cameras to calculators to computers, increased volume of sales has brought prices down by spreading overheads over a larger number of units sold.

Moreover, the shape of these curves is to some extent determined by the time period we are looking at. In the short term, extending no farther than the immediate future, supply might in most cases be almost vertical, since for most products there is only so much and no more.

As the time frame is extended, the supply curve may begin to bend forward until in the longest of runs, the supply curve may actually be downward-sloping as the most efficient approaches to production are introduced.

In trying to think past these very abstract supply and demand curves, it is imperative to remember at every stage that there are individuals reacting to the economic circumstances of their lives. These curves provide a short form means to summarize everything that is happening in a generally simple way across a large number of individuals.

But beneath it all, it should not be forgotten that there are individuals on both the supply and demand sides who are making these decisions to produce and buy.

The answers these diagrams provide ought to be powerful reminders of the ways in which free markets, where both entrepreneurs and their customers are permitted to act in ways that provide themselves with the greatest good – the highest utility for consumers, the highest profits for producers – will lead to a continuous improvement in living standards and increased satisfaction with life to the extent that satisfaction comes from an increased command over goods and services.

USING SUPPLY AND DEMAND

The key to the use of supply and demand is to recognize that they are a relationship between price and quantity, all other things being equal. Moreover, so far as economic theory is concerned, *a market price does not change unless there is a change in the conditions affecting either demand or supply, or both together*. If a market price or market volume have changed, one or the other of supply or demand must have changed first. Perhaps both have changed at the same time. Unless there has been some government decree, within economics there is no other valid explanation for a change in prices charged or output produced in any market.

Therefore, if there has been a change in a market price or in the level of sales, an explanation must be given in terms of supply and demand. If a price has gone up, then either demand has increased or the level of supply has gone down. Similarly, if a price has gone down, either demand has fallen or the amount supplied has gone up. When prices change this is where one needs to look.

And with regard to volumes, if the level of sales has gone up, either supply or demand has increased, while if sales levels have gone down, either supply or demand has fallen. It is perfectly pointless to have gone to the trouble learning about supply and demand without understanding that it is precisely when P or Q has altered that supply and demand curves are what are needed to understand why.

THINKING THROUGH PRICE MOVEMENTS

The price of electricity has gone up, let us say. Why might it be? That is where the *ceteris paribus* issues come in to play. On the supply side, we might think that any of the following could have been important:

- the cost of inputs, including the cost of labour, might have increased in price;
- the capital stock available has diminished because there has not been sufficient maintenance of electricity-generating capacity;
- there are expectations that demand is going to increase and more capital will be needed;
- taxes on the industry have gone up.

If, instead, one thinks about the various factors that might have affected the willingness to purchase electricity, then going through the list of demand-side *ceteris paribus* conditions, we might think that one or more of these were part of the explanation for the higher price of electricity:

- incomes have risen and more energy is demanded;
- the population has gone up;
- there has been an increase in the use of products that use electricity;
- the prices of other sources of energy have risen.

These are just examples. For most price movements there are usually readily understood reasons for prices to have moved.

PRICES AND INFLATION

During an inflationary period, it is almost always the case that wages and other labour costs are rapidly rising faster than technological change can produce productivity increases. The supply curves of many products are therefore moving to the left. At the same time, because incomes in nominal terms are rapidly rising, which is the same thing as higher labour costs but from a wage earner's perspective, the demand curves for many products are moving to the right.

As Figure 7.9 shows, the effect on the level of prices is certain to be positive but the effect on the level of sales could be anywhere, either rising or falling depending on whether the supply curve or the demand curve shifts to a greater extent.

It is also useful to be aware that in an inflationary period, the prices

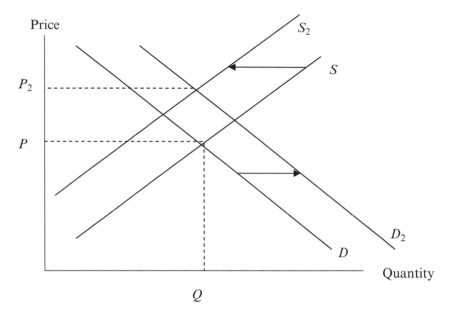

Figure 7.9   Inflationary effects on individual prices

of different products are rising at different rates. Some prices may even
be falling. Thus, while inflation may mean that the 'average' price level
has risen, individual prices for individual products will experience different sets of changes depending on the effect on the underlying shifts in the
supply and demand curves for the products.

USING COMMON SENSE

It is usually a matter of common sense to understand the effect that some
underlying factor will have on the willingness of producers to supply or the
willingness of buyers to demand. The formal use of supply and demand
clouds some people's minds so that what they once understood intuitively
they lose their grip on by seeing it in this way.

Just understand this:

- if producers have become more willing to produce, then the supply
  curve will move to the right – they will supply more at every price;
- if, on the other hand, producers have become less willing to produce,
  then the supply curve will move to the left – they will supply less at
  every price;

- then, amongst buyers of a product, if demanders have become more willing to buy, the demand curve will move to the right – buyers will buy more at every price;
- and finally, if demanders have become less willing to buy, then the demand curve will move to the left – they will buy less at every price.

Understanding this will take you a long way towards thinking like an economist. Not understanding this means that you never will.

PRICE CEILINGS

Governments frequently attempt to influence the prices of various goods and services by imposing prices on the market. It happens less than it once did, partly because the level of economic knowledge has improved somewhat. But the attempts by governments to gain popular approval by in some instances holding prices down, and in other instances holding prices up, are often irresistible. It is always, however, a bad decision economically, no matter how it might be received politically.

A price ceiling is a maximum price imposed by governments below the equilibrium point. The prices of particular goods or services are seen by decision makers as a political problem, and rather than subsidizing the sale of such goods or services (which would move the supply curve downwards at every price) they either merely impose a maximum price on the market or restrict the rate at which such prices may legally increase in the future.

A very popular use of the price ceiling was once the use to control rents, which is still done in some places. Rising rents are often very unpopular and governments have frequently tried to do something about the increased price of rental accommodation by imposing rent controls. The inevitable result is harm to those the decision was intended to help.

This is shown in Figure 7.10. And as in the use of all other diagrams, here too we are trying to show a principle, not some exact situation.

If the market were allowed to find its own equilibrium, the price would be at *Pe*. However, the government, for reasons of its own, decides that the market level of rent is too high so it imposes a maximum rental. Here the ceiling is shown to be at price *Pc*.

Is this good for renters? And, if so, which renters?

According to the diagram, three things are sure to happen: (1) After the price ceiling is imposed, rents are lower than they otherwise would have been. (2) With lower rents, more people try to rent, with the demand for rental accommodation moving up from *Qe* to *Qd*. (3) With lower rents,

Price

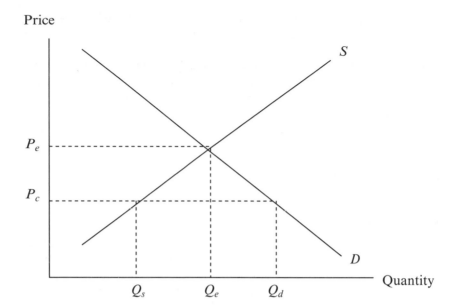

Figure 7.10   Price ceiling

meanwhile, fewer landlords are willing to take on the expense and hassles of renting, and the supply of rental accommodation falls from *Qe* to *Qs*.

In these circumstances, the rents may be lower for those who can actually find a place to rent, but there are not enough places to rent. Even some of these who had been renting before no longer have a place, since the number of rented places falls as houses that had previously been rented out are sold to others as family homes. What's worse, there are even more people looking to rent than before rents were lowered. It looks cheap, if only they could find someone to rent them a place.

The original equilibrium price did two things. It encouraged producers to build and maintain rental accommodation, and it encouraged those with places to rent out to put them on the market. It pulled the quantity supplied up.

But at the same time it made renters economize. They would rent smaller units or share with others to help pay the rent. They might stay at home with their parents. Since there is only so much rental space in any urban setting, allowing the price to adjust will not only ensure that the number looking for a place to live and the number renting places out are the same but will also lead to an increase in the number of rentable dwellings.

If the aim is to have more places for more people, rent control is exactly the wrong way to go about achieving it.

The basic moral is this. Keeping the price of anything below its equilibrium price will create shortages. The evidence from history is overwhelming. Although supply and demand curves are totally invisible, the world operates in just the way we would expect if these curves could actually be seen.

PRICE FLOORS

The opposite of a price ceiling is a price floor. A floor price is the lowest price allowed by law or the price at which the government will buy everything not bought by the market.

The diagram in Figure 7.11 shows a price floor. Examples are the minimum wage, where it is illegal to pay a wage lower than that stated in law, or agricultural price supports, where the government promises to buy up any production not sold on the market at the price established by government.

The equilibrium is *Pe* but the price imposed is at *Pf*. Let us say that this is the market for butter and the government wishes to assist farmers. They therefore promise to maintain the price of butter by paying the higher price, *Pf*.

Price

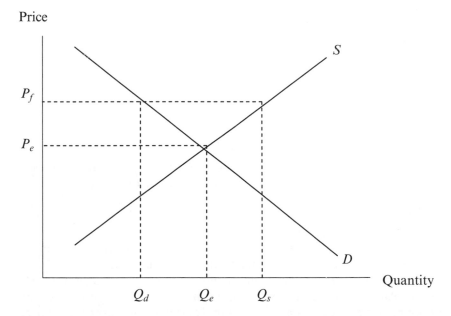

Figure 7.11   Price floor

The result is an excess supply of butter, what became known as the 'butter mountain' in Europe where this was tried. Farmers, responding to the price, produce a quantity of butter equal to Qs. Buyers, however, do not buy all the butter produced at a floor price above the equilibrium price, buying only Qd.

Here again there are three certain results: (1) after the price floor is imposed, prices are higher; (2) with higher prices, there is less of the good or service bought in the market than had been bought before; (3) with higher prices, however, more is produced even though less is being bought in the market.

Price support programmes in agriculture have ended up exactly as the theory of supply and demand has said they would. There have been literally mountains of unsellable products produced. Pushing the price above equilibrium causes more of the product to be produced than the market is prepared to buy at that price.

This is how markets can be expected to work. In a well ordered economy, with prices allowed to adjust as circumstances dictate, output adjusts itself to the willingness to produce on the one side and to the willingness of buyers to buy on the other. This is because behind these adjustments are the individual buyers who are shifting between the various goods and services being put on the market on one side of the ledger and the different amounts of every good and service being put up for sale.

Implementing a minimum wage is less messy since those workers priced out of the market are indistinguishable from the rest of the unemployed who are without work but for other reasons. But for all that, some people are not working because the wage they must be paid is kept too high.

ELASTICITY

Amongst economists, there are specific terms that are used to describe the tilt of supply and demand curves. Rather than describing these curves as 'horizontal' or 'vertical', the words used are 'elastic' and 'inelastic'.

The economic point about elasticity is to gauge the *responsiveness* of changes in one economic variable to changes in another.

Demand, for example, is said to be elastic if there is a large change in the quantity demanded following a relatively small change in price.

A typical economics text will spend quite some considerable time on explaining how such elasticities are measured, which of course, can only be done if there is an actual supply or demand curve that can be drawn.

You cannot calculate the tilt of a line without being able to see the line. Since the line can never be seen, such calculations are beside the point. Other books will teach you how to calculate elasticity. You won't find it here.

DEMAND ELASTICITY AND TOTAL REVENUE

But elasticity is a useful concept, since it is a reminder that different businesses and industries face a different demand response to changes in prices. And in addition, elasticity has an important conceptual point related to changes in the total revenue earned as the price is changed.

The definition of elasticity of demand shows the significance.

$$\varepsilon = \frac{\text{Percentage change in quantity}}{\text{Percentage change in price}}$$

Suppose a price went up 10 per cent, which led to a 20 per cent fall in the number of units bought. That is, at whatever the price was, the response to a 10 per cent increase in the price was a 20 per cent fall in the volume of sales.

In terms of the elasticity calculation, the percentage change in quantity being 20 per cent is divided by the percentage change in price, which was 10 per cent, which comes to 2.[1] So what? So this.

Suppose the price had originally been $20 per unit and the number of units sold was 1000. Total revenue is therefore $20 per unit × 1000 units = $20000. But then the price went up by 10 per cent which meant the price rose to $22. However, the number of units sold fell by 20 per cent, that is by 20 per cent of 1000, which is 200. Thus, there were 800 units sold at the higher price. The total revenue is now $22 per unit × 800 units = $17600.

The price went up and total revenue went down. This might seem obvious, but that is not necessarily how it goes.

Try this instead. The price goes up by 20 per cent, but this time the level of sales falls only 10 per cent. In elasticity terms, the percentage change in quantity is 10 per cent while the percentage change in price is 20 per cent. Elasticity is now 10 per cent divided by 20 per cent, which comes to 0.5.

So to put in a set of numbers: suppose again the price had originally been $20 per unit and the number of units sold was 1000. Total revenue is $20 per unit × 1000 units = $20000. This time, however, the price goes up by 20 per cent, which means the price rises to $24. Meanwhile, the number of units sold falls by only 10 per cent, that is by 10 per cent of 1000, which is 100 units. Thus, there were 900 units still being sold at the higher price. The total revenue is now $24 per unit × 900 units = $21 600.

This time the price went up and so too did total revenue.

ELASTIC AND INELASTIC

In the first instance, when the price went up the quantity demanded was generally responsive to the change in price, with the definition of generally responsive being that the percentage change in quantity was greater than the percentage change in price. The elasticity measure was thus calculated to be over 1.

And where quantity demand is generally responsive to change in price, demand is said to be elastic.

Meanwhile, in the second instance, when the price went up the quantity demanded was generally unresponsive to the change in price, with the definition of unresponsive being that the percentage change in quantity was smaller than the percentage change in price. The elasticity measure was thus calculated to be less than 1. And where quantity demand is generally unresponsive to change in price, demand is said to be inelastic.

Where the effect on the number of units demanded is greater than the effect on the price, demand is said to be elastic and total revenue will move in the opposite direction to the movement in price.

On the other hand, where the effect on the number of units demanded is smaller than the effect on the price, demand is said to be inelastic and total revenue will move in the same direction as the movement in price.

And what is interesting is that the very same demand curve will typically shift from being elastic at higher prices to becoming inelastic at lower prices. That means that as the price comes down, at first total revenue will go up and then, having reached a maximum, total revenue will come down. This will not always be the case but would be the effect for any straight line downward sloping demand curve.

ELASTICITY USUALLY CHANGES ALONG A DEMAND CURVE

The numerical example in Table 7.1 shows a fall in price in the first column and a corresponding increase in the quantity that would be purchased at each of those prices. As the price falls from $14 to $7, total revenue rises from $0 to $49. This is because the percentage change in quantity is greater than the percentage change in price. We are in the elastic part of the demand curve.

Table 7.1   Price–quantity demand relationship

Price	Quantity	Total revenue	
14	0	0	elastic
13	1	13	elastic
12	2	24	elastic
11	3	33	elastic
10	4	40	elastic
9	5	45	elastic
8	6	48	elastic
7	7	49	unit elastic
6	8	48	inelastic
5	9	45	inelastic
4	10	40	inelastic
3	11	33	inelastic
2	12	24	inelastic
1	13	13	inelastic
0	14	0	inelastic

However, from a price of $7 per unit down to a price of $0, as the price gets lower so too does the total revenue, until when the price goes to zero, total revenue goes to zero as well. This is because the percentage change in the fall in output is greater than the percentage change in the fall in price. Here we are in the inelastic portion of the demand curve.

Now it should not be forgotten that this process works in reverse. In the inelastic range, a rise in price will lead to a rise in revenue. However, from the moment that the demand curve moves from the inelastic portion to the elastic section, the rise in price is associated with a fall in revenue. This is shown in the diagrams in Figure 7.12. As price goes down, total revenue rises until there is a point at which revenue reaches its maximum level. From then on as price descends, total revenue descends as well.

And once again it should be emphasized that no business knows what the demand curve for its products looks like so cannot make decisions based on any of this.

But even then, what should not be thought is that the point of maximum revenue is the point at which business decisions will drive output levels if only they knew where this level was. Missing still is the level of cost at each level of output.

The point of maximum profit is the point at which the total level of revenues exceeds the total level of costs to the greatest extent. This is the level of output that firms are directing their activities towards.

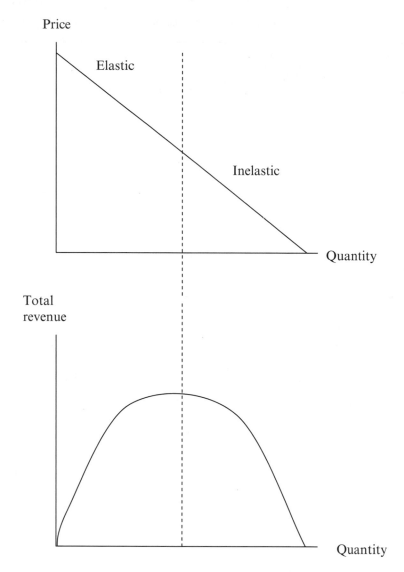

Figure 7.12　Effect of elasticity of demand on total revenue

NOTE

1. Arithmetically it should be –2 since the fall in demand was –20 per cent, but we leave out the minus sign for convenience.

8. Marginal analysis

Marginal analysis, the very core of economic thinking, is based on an understanding that every decision takes place in the present. The past was once the present when all of the decisions were made that affect the world as it is today. Today's decisions will affect the future, cannot alter the past, and in reality cannot alter the present either.

What's more, decisions are made without certain knowledge about what will happen in the period ahead. There is always a degree of uncertainty about every decision, and the farther into the future one must be forced to look, the more uncertain that future becomes.

In regard to an economic decision to invest, there is normally reasonable clarity looking forward a month or two. Looking forward a year, issues become more opaque and are even more difficult if one projects forward two years or five. Looking ahead ten years or twenty, there is no mechanism to determine how the world will look then, and therefore to determine how sensible today's decision will turn out to be.

Yet decisions do have to be made with these kinds of time frames in mind. Twenty-year-olds make such decisions all the time by choosing which areas they will study. Those decisions made at twenty will often affect the entire direction of their lives as they choose to take on skills in one particular area rather than another.

Businesses, in choosing the shape to give their capital, are making decisions that may require decades for the full realization of the initial outlay. Planting forests, to take a simple and obvious example, requires payments to be made in the present without any chance of repayment for years on end. How do such decisions end up being made?

The framework in which decisions are presumed to be made is referred to as marginal analysis. Decisions are, it is said, made at the margin.

DECISIONS AT THE MARGIN

And here the word 'margin' is used to mean at the edge. And the edge at which marginal decisions are made is at the very end of all past history up until that moment, that being the always-with-us present.

Marginal analysis means that sound economic decisions are not made in reference to anything related to the unchangeable past, but only in relation to what can still be changed going forward. What cannot be changed can never be part of a good economic decision. Only what can be made different are ever included as part of marginal analysis.

That people often do include the unchangeable past in decisions about the future is a psychological fact. If they have already invested funds in some project, the money already spent maintains an added pull in the direction of good money after bad. Proper economic decisions completely disregard what cannot be changed, in this case being money that cannot be unspent.

Time moves in one direction only. Decisions are about the future. Sunk costs are sunk. The only question is, given where someone is, what can be done that will add more to the benefits received in going forward relative to the costs that will be incurred in trying to obtain those benefits?

This is the weighing up that is the basis for decision making in an economy. It can be rules of thumb and back-of-the-envelope estimates of the relative costs and benefits, all the way to the most sophisticated decision making techniques that management science has so far developed. The greater the potential costs involved, the more detailed will tend to be the assessment process.

But whatever the means used to make the assessment is, it comes down to this: to a weighing up of all of the potential costs against all of the potential benefits brought back to the present. That is, brought back to the moment that the decision is made and is to at least some extent, reversible.

COSTS AND BENEFITS

Every time a cost is taken on, it is taken on only with some projected benefit in mind that exceeds the costs being borne. No one will make decisions that are expected to make them worse off (unless becoming worse off is seen to provide some kind of net benefit).

People may be wrong about outcomes. That happens all the time. But at the moment of decision, so far as economics is concerned, the expectation is that the outcome will be a net positive. The return will be greater than the costs.

That is what is meant by rationality in economics. The decision maker alone decides what the benefits to be had are. More money, prestige, fame or whatever; benefits can be both tangible and intangible. But before the decision is made to achieve some end, the *expected* costs are compared with the *expected* benefits to determine whether the game is worth the candle, that is, whether the return is sufficiently large to repay all of the costs and effort involved.

If the expected benefits are greater than the expected costs, then the first threshold is passed in deciding to go forward. If the expected benefits do not exceed the expected costs, then the project is rejected.

But that is only the first threshold. In many instances, there is more than one possible project with a positive net return. In this case, the project with the largest excess of benefits over costs, as estimated by the decision maker, is chosen.

OPPORTUNITY COST

This is what is meant by opportunity cost. There are almost always alternative possibilities that have to be ranked. In choosing one project from amongst all of the alternatives available, the choice is the one with the greatest excess of benefits over costs.

In a sense this is a roundabout way of saying the obvious. But it is only obvious in the commercial world if we assume that no government is involved in making the choice, either in forcing the hand of a business or through pre-empting the decisions of a profit-making enterprise by taxing away their profits and doing something altogether different instead.

But when the private decision maker, the entrepreneur, is considering all of the alternatives, there is the best alternative and then there is the second best from amongst the full range of possibilities. The opportunity cost is defined as the best forgone alternative. It is this that is considered the cost of going forward with the alternative that is actually chosen.

Suppose there are three projects, the first with a return of $100 million, the second with a return of $70 million and the last with a return of $40 million. The cost of taking up the $100 million project is the lost opportunity to undertake a project that was potentially worth $70 million. That was the project's opportunity cost.

TIME AND ECONOMIC RETURN

But there is yet another complexity that needs to be negotiated, at least conceptually. That is, what is the time frame in which the forecast returns are expected to accrue? It makes a large difference if the returns are expected to be relatively soon, compared with a situation in which they are expected to accrue well into the future.

Using the tree plantation as an example, if it takes 25 years for the trees to reach maturity and become commercial, the cost of planting the trees now must be set against an expected return that can occur no sooner than a quarter of a century later. Meanwhile, there may be another project that might require the same initial outlay in the present that will achieve a smaller return, but sooner.

These are the everyday kinds of calculations everyone in business must regularly make. These are the kinds of decisions that must be made in every economy by someone. Balancing distant gains against an earlier return, where the distant gain is expected to be larger, but because it is farther into the future, is potentially less certain and less attractive requires a great deal of judgement.

The choice of $100m in one year or $200m in five years is a commercial decision that requires some delicate weighing up. The cost of finance, an assessment of the risks involved, time preference and a host of other considerations will be stirred into the decision-making brew. This is the kind of entrepreneurial decision that must, however, be made all the time and for which no hard and fast rules can be made.

There are techniques that have been developed to deal with such problems at the managerial level. Using '*present* value' calculations which try to estimate the costs of a project against the revenues, where the costs and revenues are of different amounts and occur at different dates in the future, is precisely an attempt to bring back to the only relevant moment in which to value a project.

But all such techniques are merely means to deal with these uncertainties, but they can never eliminate them. Such uncertainty is intrinsic because the future is unknowable.

But everyone makes these kinds of decisions routinely. Minimizing costs relative to benefits is a constant process that becomes second nature.

Look at the following example. In Figure 8.1 there are four different supermarket checkout lines, and each is of a different length. Yet no one looking at these lines of different length would have any doubt why that is. It is because each individual person coming to check out at the supermarket would look at the amount of groceries in each of the shopping trolleys in the different lines and make an assessment of which one would take the least amount of time to get to the front. People make mistakes about which lines will take the shortest time, but this they will only know when time has passed and the different lines have moved forward at different rates.

This is a minimalist example of what happens at every stage in the business world, and indeed, amongst both producers and buyers. We make decisions all the time that are intended to reduce costs to ourselves (in this

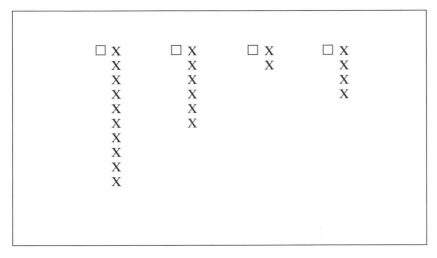

Figure 8.1   *Why are a different number of people in the different supermarket queues?*

example, the cost being the time required to get through the checkout). Whether things turn out as planned is often quite another story.

MAXIMIZING PROFITS

In looking at businesses and what they do, the most basic of the economic assumptions is that firms attempt to maximize profits.

We say this either because the assumption is made that this is in the nature of the kinds of people who run businesses or because the nature of competition is such that if a firm does not try to get as much profit as its circumstances will allow, competitive forces will threaten it with extinction. Profit maximization in this second case is a form of self-preservation.

Again, profit maximization is a notional concept. There are so many considerations, both short-run and long-run, that go into thinking through the course of action to take, that all that can be said is that businesses try to work their way through the minefield of all of the different issues, both large and small, that must be dealt with in order to make as much money as possible.

But the time frame in which this money is being made is impossible to specify. If we again think of that forest plantation, how can any calculation be made about the profit to be earned, when it will be earned and the uncertainties along the way. To use as a catch-all notion that those making the decision are trying to make the most money possible given the possibilities available to them, balancing all considerations including the need to take a more long-term perspective, we are very seldom likely to go wrong in trying to make sense of the economic world we find ourselves in.

It need hardly be pointed out that sometimes profits in the short term will be sacrificed for profits in the long term. It would be normal business practice to accept lower profits in the present to increase profitability over the longer haul.

A retailer, for example, might implement a no-questions-asked returns policy on items sold. And certainly, for any item returned there is a loss, but if the difference can be made up through increased volume, then profits are higher because of the practice. This is how businesses can be expected to operate.

They will choose actions they believe will lead to the largest difference in revenues relative to costs over the relevant time period. The time period they have in mind will, of course, be decided by the business itself.

MARGINAL ANALYSIS GENERALLY

Economists use the concept of marginality at every stage. It is a forward-looking concept. In the traditional analysis, in effect it asks this question:

> Taking all that exists already as a given, what will be the effect on one economic variable if there is a change (usually described as a 'one unit change') in some other economic variable?

Marginal cost, for example, asked what the effect would be on production costs of a change in the level of production. Marginal revenue asked the same question about the effect on sales revenue of an increase in quantity demanded.

There is then marginal utility. We cannot even measure total utility so there is nothing in actual fact that is being measured when marginal utility is discussed. But the notional concept is, what is the increase in total utility that follows from a one-unit increase in the possession of some good or service? That is, how much does utility rise for some individual through the purchase of one more shirt to go with all of the other shirts already owned?

Marginal product asks the effect on the level of production that occurs through the addition of one more unit of some input while holding all other inputs constant. Here again, as an example, it is supposed to show the effect on total output that would occur if one additional worker were added to all of the other workers already employed. This would be the marginal product of the last worker. If you don't know which one was the 'last worker' that is not the point. And if you think that each worker is different and has different capabilities, again that's not the point.

The concept is notional and tries to focus attention on the decision maker in each case. With utility, the focus is on the buyers of final goods and services. With marginal product, the focus is on producers who must decide whether to add more employees to the payroll.

And almost invariably, the marginal measure is used in comparison with something else as part of a decision making process.

For a consumer deciding whether to buy one thing rather than another, the question is which will provide a higher level of marginal utility, that is, a greater improvement in personal welfare as decided by themselves.

Looking at the marginal productivity of labour, the same kind of question underlies the concept. The comparison is typically made with the wage that has to be paid for the additional employee added on. If the expected money value of the addition to output is greater than the money cost of employing one new person, then the person is employed. If the expected value is less than the wage, the person will not be employed.

In general, though, the use of marginal analysis is based on understanding the process that anyone making a decision must go through as they, embedded in the present as they must necessarily be, compare future states of the world with one decision having been made rather than another (with the decision to do nothing at all always a realistic option).

Marginal analysis concerns itself with making a decision in the present while trying to make judgements about the future consequences of that decision. It is what people generally do. It is how most people normally behave when faced with uncertainty. They weigh up the options and choose one course of action in preference to all of the others. That things seldom come out as planned is just the way of the world.

MARGINAL REVENUE AND MARGINAL COST

The notions that lie beneath the decision making process as understood by economic theory are bundled under the names 'marginal revenue' and 'marginal cost'. When the two are equal within a firm, profits will have reached their highest level. It is therefore said that 'profit maximization' occurs when $MR = MC$. There is then quite an elaborate discussion on these concepts, both with figures and with charts (and in more mathematical treatments using calculus) to show that this is so. The appendix to this chapter covers the material as it is typically discussed.

But to understand the issues properly, it is actually preferable to first understand the aim and intent. Once the purpose of the analysis is understood, the technique becomes much easier to follow.

Reduced to its essentials, the argument is basically this. A business will continue to increase its production levels so long as every time it produces more output it can add more to its revenues than it does to its costs.

The trick is in understanding that a business faces a demand curve that slopes down. Therefore, if it is selling every unit at the same price, if it tries to sell one more, it has to lower the price for all of the units that it is already selling. To sell more it must lower the price per unit. So even on the revenue side there is a trade-off. A business can increase its level of sales, but it must lower the price to do so.

As we saw, along a straight line demand curve, as prices fall, total revenue first goes up and then after some point begins to go down. Meanwhile, the more is produced, the higher is the level of costs.

For a while, in a profitable firm, as more is sold, revenues rise faster than costs are rising. But at some level of production and sales, there is a crossover where costs begin to rise faster than revenue. It is at this crossover point that profits reach their maximum level. It is at this level of output that the firm will produce, and the price it will charge will be the price associated with this level of output.

PROBLEMS WITH TRADITIONAL MARGINAL ANALYSIS

The problem with this analysis is that it assumes too much knowledge on the part of those who own and manage firms. It first assumes they know the shape of the demand curve they face. It assumes that they can tell what would happen to their own revenues if they adjusted the price. It assumes that costs are generally static and can be foretold for each level of production.

And what it leaves out is time. There is no sense in this analysis of the considerations that any business gives to the trade-offs it might accept in the present to increase its profitability over the longer term.

It makes it seem that business decision making is a mechanical exercise in looking at marginal revenue on the one side and marginal costs on the other and then setting a price while producing the relevant volume.

It almost completely assumes away the fact that virtually every product sold is a 'joint product' with other goods or services produced and sold by the same firm at the same time. It ignores cross-subsidization of every good or service sold as costs are spread over many different products.

But what is really important about marginal analysis is buried. Because what is really important is that decision making in a firm takes place within an environment surrounded by radical uncertainties. Those who make the decision cannot know, at the time those decisions are made, whether the outcomes will in reality add to profitability or lower it. This no one in business can ever know before the fact.

But what is possibly the largest problem with the marginalist approach to business decisions is that it has traditionally discussed the effect on some entity caused by a shift in a *single unit* of some other entity. It therefore takes the entire notion to the point of utter vacuity. Production of one more unit of anything, unless we are discussing aircraft or some such, is not a decision but is a matter of routine. It just happens.

But if marginal analysis is seen as it ought to be seen, as a step into the dark of the future where *conjectures* about what will happen to revenues are balanced against *conjectures* about what will happen to costs, then it brings home just how difficult it is to find that point of maximum profit. Indeed, it underscores just how hard it can be to earn any profits at all.

MARGINAL ANALYSIS IS ABOUT DECISION MAKING AND NOT ABOUT PRODUCTS

And there is this. Marginal analysis is about making a decision. Marginal analysis is useful in understanding the nature of entrepreneurial decision making. It helps explain the process that people in business (in fact, people generally) go through in reaching decisions.

They weigh things up. They look at the pros and cons. They look at different time perspectives. They wrestle with a host of unknowns and recognize the existence of unknown unknowns.

Marginal analysis is about actively deciding what to do in a situation of uncertainty. It is *not* one unit of this or that being discussed. It is about the expected effect on revenues and costs of moving in one direction rather than in another. It takes the entire situation into account, not some infinitesimal increase or decrease in the production of some individual product.

Traditional marginal analysis studiously ignores what is actually interesting about marginal analysis.

APPLYING MARGINAL ANALYSIS TO THE THEORY OF THE FIRM

To look just a bit further into what is wrong with the traditional theory, we examine what is described as the theory of the firm in economics. The business firm in economic theory is a very abstract entity. It is a series of costs related to a series of potential revenue streams in which the level of production for a single product is determined in isolation from every other product a firm might in fact be producing. The standard microeconomic theory of the firm corresponds with no actual existing firm found in the real world.

The concentration in the theory of the firm is on the product, and not on the business itself. It is supply and demand writ large. But if one is to understand what firms do, it needs to be seen that they do not concentrate on any particular good or service, but once in existence, they do whatever will earn them a profit.

Could one seriously go into a department store and then use a form of analysis that focused on the price and quantity relationship for single products? Could one think of the supply and demand for 'shirts' when the variety of actual shirts in the market must mean that at any one time thousands of different products could be described as a shirt?

The point of marginal revenue and marginal cost analysis is fundamentally sound but it takes much too narrow a compass in how it looks at things. Firms do act so that they will maximize profits, but they do so not by selling one product but by selling many, and not by staying with whatever original line of production they were in, but through a willingness to seek opportunities wherever they may open.

They also try to maximize those profits, not in some kind of immediate term, but they are always thinking strategically as best they can where there is a trade-off between earning as much money as possible in as short a period of time, as against taking a longer-term perspective by earning less in the present than might have been possible, so that more might be earned over the longer term. Considerations of time are a very large part of how businesspeople think.

The production costs of a firm are often difficult to allocate to any one good or service. Adding one more employee is a decision that will depend on a host of considerations but it is seldom related to the sales potential of any one particular product. Are all costs in the very short run fixed costs and therefore able to be evenly spread across the entire range of output? Or is there something that needs to be added to our economic conception of what businesses are and how they make decisions?

MARGINAL ANALYSIS IS A THEORY OF DECISION MAKING

Generalizing beyond a single product to the way businesspeople think about everything is necessary. Broadening $MR = MC$ into a theory of decision making in general is what is required.

This is in fact a major aspect of economic technique. What is called cost–benefit analysis (CBA) is a short-form name for the application of *MR* and *MC* to a vast range of questions, and not all of them economic.

At the core of CBA is the need to bring the value of the flow of future benefits (usually quantified as the receipt of sums of money at different dates in the future) and compare these with the value of the costs incurred (also usually quantified in money terms). A project gets past at least the first threshold if the expected flow of revenue as quantified in the present exceeds the expected flow of costs, also quantified in the present.

This kind of technique is applied to all manner of projects from the smallest to the most immense, projects which can often take many years before they even reach a stage where they are breaking even. The assumptions made are guaranteed to go wrong and projects often miscarry for any number of reasons. But the technique itself is an attempt to think through questions about whether some project is even worth consideration.

And when cost–benefit analysis is finally reduced to its essence, the technique itself turns out to be a question of the expected additions to revenue of taking some decision, balanced against the expected additions to costs as perceived at the moment when the decision is being made.

USING MARGINAL ANALYSIS

Marginal analysis comes down to this. A decision is to be made, and in the economics of the firm, it is a commercial decision. Some entrepreneur must decide what to do.

The decision, like all decisions, is to be made in the present. The consequence of that decision will unfold in the unknowable future.

In this circumstance, marginal revenue means the entire additional flow of benefits that are expected to accrue from making this decision. Since the flow of benefits will take place at different dates in the future, some means of bringing the value of such benefits back to the present needs to be found.

But the essence of the decision making process is to have some means, whether rule-of-thumb or highly sophisticated mathematical technique, available to make these revenue projections and return those projections to a figure that relates to the present moment.

There are then the marginal costs. Marginal costs are the additions to costs that the decision will entail. To achieve the benefits – the revenues that will be earned – various costs must be borne, and in most economic decisions the costs come before the revenues.

Some means must be found to estimate what those costs will be and then to bring those costs back to some form of money valuation that can be compared with the expected present value of the revenue stream.

The fact that there are far more complications in such an analysis, such as just ensuring that every cost can be financed along the way as the project goes ahead, is understood. But when all is said and done, a project will be undertaken when the expected addition to revenue is greater than the expected addition to costs.

Profits will be maximized for a firm where every project is undertaken where the expected revenues will exceed the expected costs, and some kind of equilibrium will be achieved when for the least profitable project being considered the addition to revenues is just equal to the addition to costs. That is, where $MR = MC$.

To think in this way is to think like an economist.

INDUSTRY STRUCTURE

There are many different ways to characterize firms, from the number of employees or the level of sales through to the kind of industry they are in and the type of products produced. The economy adapts itself to the production techniques of the time as shaped by, amongst many other things, entrepreneurial initiative, the capital stock in existence, the availability of savings, the characteristics of the workforce and the regulatory and tax structures that governments have put in place.

In a market economy, no one deliberately chooses in advance how the commercial world will evolve, but at any moment in time it is possible to gather statistics to identify what actually happens to exist. It is what it is, but not because it was planned in that particular way.

Amongst the various industry characteristics that some have deemed of significance is the question of industry concentration. The issue in regard to concentration is how many firms are in the industry and how large each firm is relative to the size of the industry as a whole.

How to decide what actually constitutes an 'industry' is itself never so obvious (for example, is the 'industry' shirt manufacturing, menswear, clothing in general, manufacturing in general or even something else?). There are also issues of geographical distribution. When we speak of industry concentration, that is, when we speak of how many firms there are competing in some industry, the number of firms involved is often dependent on how large a geographical area we are including. Almost nothing is highly concentrated if looked at on a global scale. Narrowing the area over which one is looking increases the proportion of sales any one firm is likely to have made.

So even to determine just how few or how many firms are in an industry is never clear-cut.

Nevertheless, economists have provided a kind of division between different industry structures based around the idea that more competition is better than less. The divisions are generally something like this:

- *monopoly*: where there is only a single seller of a product;
- *oligopoly*: where there are a few sellers of a product which may or may not be differentiated, that is, which may either be identical to the products sold by all other competitors (think iron ore production) or may instead be highly individualized (such as with car manufacturing);
- *monopolistically competitive*: where there are many relatively small sellers of a generally differentiated product (such as restaurants);
- *highly competitive*: where sellers are very small relative to the size of the market and where each seller sells what is for all practical purposes a product which is indistinguishable from the products sold by competitors (such as with milk producers).

Each industry structure is to an important extent driven by the nature of the products sold. The largest determinant of structure is the efficient size of an individual firm. In some industries, the most efficient size is very large relative to the market, so that only one or a few firms may be in operation. In other industries, such as with barber shops and bakeries, an efficiently sized operation may be quite small in comparison with the size of the market as a whole.

The tendency for some to worry over industries where a few large firms dominate seems excessive, to say the least. There are genuinely anti-competitive practices but they are not particularly associated with the size of firm. These practices are attempts to get round market competition where private side agreements are reached with other firms which are supposed to be in competition with each other.

Such side agreements are designed to reduce the amount of competition by reducing the uncertainties faced by each of the businesses in the market. Most such agreements work against the interests of the buying public, and are almost invariably made illegal.

But a similar kind of process occurs where businesses argue that the forces of competition are so stacked against the efficient operation of individual firms that the government must come in and prevent certain normally fair practices by other firms. A firm lowering its price because it can employ economies of scale and in that way lower average costs and therefore average prices charged is not engaging in an unfair practice, even though some small businesses try to have such price reductions declared illegal.

Whether that is the same as a large firm going out of its way to drive its smaller competitors from the market by keeping prices low until the smaller businesses leave the industry is entirely a different case. But how to differentiate between the two is often difficult to determine in practice.

But this everyone should understand. Market competition is often hard and the risks can be very high. Running a business is not for the faint-hearted.

APPENDIX

Profits are Maximized where *MR* = *MC*

This appendix should be seen as a no-go area for all but the most intrepid. If you want to see how economists look at things, you can find out below. But in looking at this example, beware of getting caught up in the numbers. It is the concepts that matter if you are to understand how economics is taught.

The theory of profit maximization in economics states that in a business profits will reach their highest level where marginal revenue equals marginal costs: $MR = MC$. To understand what the words mean is to understand that this is so.

But the analysis is based on the production and sale of a single item. It says almost nothing at all about how production and sale occur in the real world, where everything is sold accompanied by the sale of something else. In the traditional microeconomic presentation, we see only how the price and volume for a single product is determined. Only in the most abstract way does it discuss what a business firm in general might do.

Marginal revenue is defined as the change in revenue from producing one extra unit of output of some particular product.

Based on the data from a normal demand curve, total revenues will first rise and then fall. As the price falls from the point where the demand curve hits the price axis, since this is the elastic portion of the demand curve, total revenue at first continues to rise.

This is shown in Table 8A.1. As the price falls from $14, where zero units are sold and therefore no revenue is earned, total revenue keeps rising until the price falls to $7, where 105 000 units are sold.

As the price descends below $7, more units are being sold, but as this is the inelastic part of the demand curve, total revenue begins to fall. Eventually, the price reaches zero, where the good is free. Total revenue here is also zero.

Marginal revenue is the *addition* to revenue that comes from selling one extra unit of output. Forget for the time being that no business knows what its demand curve looks like and therefore there is no certainty about what will happen to total revenue if the price is brought down. Here we pretend that we can see the demand curve and that we can calculate what happens when the price falls again. You will see that the marginal revenue data are between the various total revenue figures since they are representative of the difference in revenue for each single unit increase or decrease in the number of units sold. The differences are shown in this way on all of the tables where marginal changes are discussed.

Table 8A.1   Total and marginal revenue

Price $	Quantity 000s	Total revenue 000s	Marginal revenue 000s
14	0	0	
			195
13	15	195	
			165
12	30	360	
			135
11	45	495	
			105
10	60	600	
			75
9	75	675	
			45
8	90	720	
			15
7	105	735	
			−15
6	120	720	
			−45
5	135	675	
			−75
4	150	600	
			−105
3	165	495	
			−135
2	180	360	
			−165
1	195	195	
			−195
0	210	0	

The highest level of revenue this firm can earn comes at a price of $7. There it is capable of taking in receipts of $735000 per time period. But whether this is the price to charge depends on what the business's motivation is. If the aim is to earn as much revenue as possible, then that will be the price. But if the aim is to make the highest level of profits possible, then it is necessary to introduce production costs into the calculation.

Production costs are shown in the hypothetical example in Table 8A.2. The table shows the various forms of costs at each level of production

Table 8A.2   Production costs

Quantity 000s	Total fixed costs 000s	Total variable costs 000s	Total costs 000s	Average total costs 000s	Marginal costs 000s
0	100	0	100		
					30
15	100	30	130	8.7	
					45
30	100	75	175	5.8	
					55
45	100	130	230	5.1	
					65
60	100	195	295	4.9	
					75
75	100	270	370	4.9	
					100
90	100	370	470	5.2	
					110
105	100	480	580	5.5	
					120
120	100	600	700	5.8	
					140
135	100	740	840	6.2	
					175
150	100	915	1015	6.8	
					220
165	100	1135	1235	7.5	
					260
180	100	1395	1495	8.3	
					320
195	100	1715	1815	9.3	
					375
210	100	2090	2190	10.4	

from zero units all the way up to 210 000, matching the possible levels of sales in Table 8A.1.

And whatever else might happen in the long run, over the short to medium term, to produce more means that costs are higher. You have your fixed costs and they cannot be varied (which is why they are called 'fixed'). Therefore, when the quantity being produced is zero, total costs are equal to fixed costs, which are $100 000.

Only in the long run are there no fixed costs, which is the definition of the long run. In the long run, everything can be changed and therefore in the long run no costs are fixed.

However, once output begins to rise, costs keep rising as output keeps rising. When there are no items being produced, total costs are $100 000 and when 15 items are being produced, variable costs rise by $30 000 (as shown in column 3).

The next column shows total production costs for each level of production. They are calculated as the sum of fixed costs plus variable costs. When no units are being produced, the total is $100 000. When 15 000 units are being produced, total costs are then estimated at $130 000.

Average total costs are shown in the next column. They are calculated by dividing total costs by the number of units produced. When this business is producing 15 000 units, the average cost of production is $8700.

The next column shows what is the most important of these calculations. What is shown here is the *ADDITION* to costs of producing extra units of output, which is called the *marginal cost*. It is shown in the final column on the table. Here is shown the addition to total costs of producing 15 000 additional units of output. To go from zero units to 15 000 units adds $30 000 to the total. To go from 15 000 units to 30 000 adds $45 000 to the total, and so on down the line.

Here it might be noted that it is normal to discuss marginal costs and marginal revenue in relation to the addition of a single extra unit of output. This is so trivial as an example of how businesses work or how anyone normally looks at things. Therefore, to add a (very limited) sense of realism to the argument, the gradients have been reckoned in the thousands rather than in terms of a single extra unit of output.

Profit Maximization

From the above, we have, according to economic theory, all the information needed to calculate how many units a business should sell of this product and at what price it should be sold.

The point here is metaphorical but explains how economists think about how economies work. Businesses are in business to make money. And the point at which a firm makes the greatest amount of profit is where marginal revenue is equal to marginal cost ($MR = MC$).

Having said that, however, the danger is that you might get so entangled in the arithmetic and lose the economics. Even as you are looking at the numbers, try to think instead about the underlying logic and not the numbers.

If one is in a situation in which doing something would add more to revenues than to costs, then economists assume that this action will be taken.

Table 8A.3   Profits are at a maximum where MR = MC

Price $	Quantity 000s	Total costs 000s	Total revenue 000s	Marginal costs 000s	Marginal revenue 000s	Profit 000s
14	0	100	0			−100
				30	195	
13	15	130	195			65
				45	165	
12	30	175	360			185
				55	135	
11	45	230	495			265
				65	105	
10	60	295	600			305
				75	75	
9	75	370	675			305
				100	45	
8	90	470	720			250
				110	15	
7	105	580	735			155
				120	−15	
6	120	700	720			20
				140	−45	
5	135	840	675			−165
				175	−75	
4	150	1015	600			−415
				220	−105	
3	165	1235	495			−740
				260	−135	
2	180	1495	360			−1135
				320	−165	
1	195	1815	195			−1620
				375	−195	
0	210	2190	0			−2190

Thus if someone can get $1000 by spending $1, it is assumed that the $1 cost will be absorbed and the $1000 will be earned for a net profit of $999. In this case, *MR* is $1000 and *MC* is $1, so that one would happily make the decision to go ahead with whatever project would produce this return.

A more realistic example is shown in the example that makes up the rest of this chapter.

Reading across Table 8A.3 from a price of $14 down to a price of $9, it can be seen that total revenue rises and total costs rise and total profits rise. As the price moves down, marginal revenue keeps falling, but at each point remains higher than marginal cost until the price reaches $9.

The extra revenue earned selling additional units of output remains higher than the extra costs taken on until the price is $9, when marginal revenue and marginal cost are both equal to $75000. Here the level of profit reaches its highest level at $305000.

Unfortunately, this is not exactly the case. In fact, as anyone can see, as far as this table is concerned, profits reach their maximum at a price of $10, where the business is also earning profits of $305000 per time period.

What is in fact the actual situation is that profits reach their maximum level at a price somewhere between $9 and $10. Therefore, the entire exercise will be done again, this time with the pricing points in 10 cent intervals between $9 and $10. In this way we can see exactly where profits reach their highest point and that this occurs where marginal costs are equal to marginal revenues.

Table 8A.4   How profits are maximized

Price $	Quantity 000s	Total costs 000s	Total revenue 000s	Marginal costs 000s	Marginal revenue 000s	Profit 000s
10.00	60	295	600			305.00
				6.6	7.1	
9.90	61	302	607			305.47
				6.8	7.2	
9.80	63	308	614			305.88
				6.9	7.3	
9.70	64	315	622			306.21
				7.1	7.4	
9.60	66	322	629			306.48
				7.3	7.5	
9.50	67	330	636			306.68
				7.4	7.5	
9.40	69	337	644			306.80
				7.6	7.6	
9.30	70	345	652			306.84
				7.8	7.7	
9.20	72	352	659			306.81
				7.9	7.8	
9.10	73	360	667			306.68
				8.1	7.9	
9.00	75	370	675			306.48

This is all shown in Table 8A.4. We have the prices between $10 and $9 where the number of units sold per time period rises from 60 000 at the higher price to 75 000 at the lower price. At the same time, total costs rise as production levels rise, from $295 000 to $370 000. Revenues at the same time rise from $600 000 to $675 000. All this information is found in the previous tables. What are added are the increments in between.

Also added are the increments for marginal costs which are scaled down because we are adding much less to costs each time since we are not adding as much to production each time. Similarly with marginal revenue. The numbers are lower because the increments are lower.

What we see, however, is the point of maximum profit. It comes at a price of $9.30 per unit when 70 000 units are being sold. There marginal costs and marginal revenues are both equal to $7600. Profits reach a maximum at $306 840 in each period of time.

The economist point is that businesses will keep adjusting what they do so that the level of profitability will rise as high as can be estimated, given how little is known about what conditions are really going to be like when production finally takes place. If some change can be made which is expected to add more to revenues than to costs, then that decision is made. Incrementally, businesses will continue to take those steps that will cause them to reach a maximum level of profits.

But it is not the arithmetic that matters, but the process. It is a step-by-step process in which decisions are made whose aim is to create a business structure that will make more money than any other structure the business might have had. That there are other motivations is understood, but you really cannot go too wrong assuming that businesses act in ways that will make them additional profit.

Where people often do go wrong is in thinking that businesses acting in this way are somehow acting against community interests. It is sentiment and prejudice that often cloud the minds of those who are trying to understand how things work. Profitability is the engine of economic growth, and we are all materially far better off because of the way businesses go about their business.

But there are other aspects of the table which should be noted. First, the level of profit made at the profit maximizing price is hardly different from the profits that are to be made at other price quantity pairings. This kind of exactness is never to be expected from business. There are so many considerations when a business is trying to decide what to do, that profit maximization in this crude, proximate kind of way is never going to be attempted, let alone achieved.

Secondly, we are here discussing a single product. This is not a depiction of how businesses behave in general but is presented to provide a supposed understanding of how a firm decides the price and volume of production for a single product. It is utterly unrealistic to think of business decisions in individual product lines in this way.

Finally, and this cannot be emphasized enough: none of the demand side information can be known other than as mere conjecture about what might happen around the existing price. The information shown in the standard diagrams is unknown in virtually every instance. There is therefore no means whatsoever to derive the marginal revenue figures other than as a rough estimate based on various simplifying assumptions.

The cost data are knowable for a single firm and there are specialists who can estimate the total potential costs at different levels of production, and therefore can estimate the marginal cost.

But this approach is provided not because this is how businesses actually work things out when setting prices. It is provided to explain how an outcome will arise given that there is a level of demand at each price, that there are costs of production, and that businesses are typically trying to make money in a very competitive world in which others will take their customers if they can.

Marginal analysis provides guidance on how businesses, guided by beliefs about the level of demand for their own products and the effect of different pricing strategies of their competitors and customers, will behave. What it definitely does not say is that the decisions will be the right decisions. Businesses make wrong decisions all the time.

But if they are private decisions, in which individuals are putting up their own money, the certainty is that those who make the decisions will do everything they can think of to ensure that the decisions are the right ones. That is, they will do whatever they can to ensure that the decisions will lead to the greatest excess of benefits over costs, however those decision makers might wish to make the calculation.

Graphical Presentation

This discussion would not be complete without including something about the diagrams that are associated with marginal revenue, marginal costs and profit maximization. They are far from intuitive, and are difficult to understand, but every economist at some stage must make the journey.

Let us take, first of all, average and marginal revenue (see Figure 8A.1). Average revenue is the price itself found on the demand curve. If each unit sells for a particular price then the price is also the average amount received per unit of output sold.

Marginal revenue is derived from the average revenue curve and shows

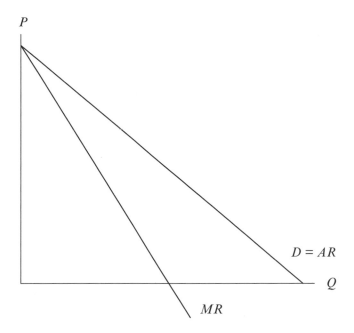

Figure 8A.1   Average and marginal revenue

the change in total revenue for each additional unit of output sold. And the specific and crucial point to remember here is that if one is already on the demand curve, then to sell additional units, the price must be lowered, not just for the last unit sold, but for all of the other units put up for sale.

Where the *MR* curve cuts the horizontal axis is the dividing point between elastic demand to the left and inelastic to the right. Therefore total revenue rises from the point where the demand curve touches the vertical axis and nothing is produced right up until the point where *MR* = 0 as the *MR* line crosses the quantity axis. It will be clear why, if you understand the nature of these two curves.

Figure 8A.2 shows Average Costs and Marginal Costs. The *MC* curve cuts the *AC* curve at its lowest point. If you understand what each of these curves is intended to explain, you will also immediately understand why this is so.

Each curve taken on its own is readily understandable. They are just the two sets of data transcribed onto a chart. Where there is often confusion is when the two sets of lines are brought together so that one is overlaid on top of the other. Yet if we are to use a diagrammatic approach to

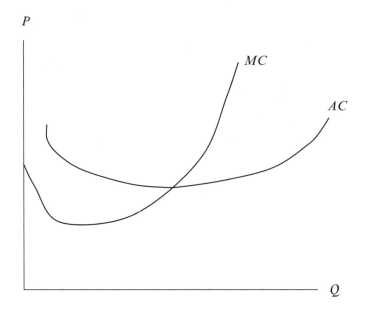

Figure 8A.2   Average and marginal costs

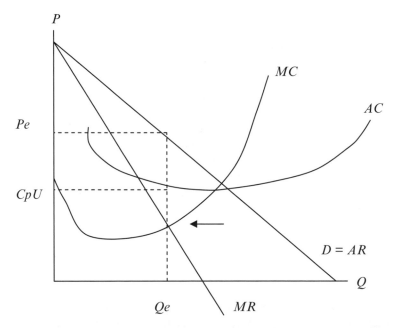

Figure 8A.3   Profit maximization where MC = MR

understanding how profits are maximized, this is what needs to be done. This is shown in Figure 8A.3.

There is an arrow on the diagram to point out where *MC* is equal to *MR*. That directly tells you the number of units of production, simply by looking to the horizontal axis. But for the price it is necessary to look at the maximum price that number of units of output can be sold for. This means running upwards to the demand curve.

In this case, we have an equilibrium quantity of *Qe* and an equilibrium price of *Pe*. This is the point at which profits are at their highest.

The figure for Cost per Unit of production (marked *CpU*) shows what the average cost for each unit of production would be at the profit maximizing level of production. The price shows the average revenue. The difference between the average revenue and the average cost will be the average level of profit for each unit of output. Multiplying profit per unit by the number of units sold gives the figure for total profit.

What this analysis is supposed to explain is how a price is determined for an individual product, but the fact is that no one could seriously believe that it does. In some vague way, it might tell you something about a business that sold only a single product, such as an electricity company. But even there things are far more complicated, since to provide electricity at different times of day or on weekends comes with different production costs and a different level of demand. This would provide no real explanation of how a business behaves.

The analysis is for the most part a study in mathematical logic without really being a study in economics at all. It diverts attention away from what is really useful, which is how businesses reach decisions in the face of uncertainty. Instead, it acts as if everything that needs to be known is knowable and actually known, and then forces an outcome based on the logic that originally went in.

Certainly there are some things that can be picked up mechanically using marginal cost and marginal revenue. The following are some of the more direct lessons that are explained:

- profitability is a process in which changes are made to prices charged and volumes sold and these changes are dependent on management expectations of what will happen to costs and revenues;
- there is a point of maximum profit for every firm based not just on its revenues but on keeping its costs under control;
- firms cannot charge just any old price but are usually well constrained by the market;
- businesses are forever trying to adjust what they do so that profits are as high as possible;

- costs may fall for a while as production levels increase, but in most firms in the short run especially, average costs start to rise rapidly as capacity constraints take effect.

These are certainly worth knowing. This analysis, with $MC = MR$, is found in textbooks around the world. But what remains deeply odd is that to become an economist requires someone to learn how almost no business decision is actually made to enable them to eventually learn for themselves, and only if they are lucky, how business decisions really are made in the real world.

9. Measuring the economy

Beyond individual markets is the economy as a whole. This is the entire network of purchase and sale of all goods and services, plus all of the actions taken by governments in raising revenue and spending their receipts, plus all of the actions of financial markets in taking in savings and allocating funds, plus all of the transactions, both physical and financial, that take place between one country and another.

And in dealing with these questions, the aim of theory is to guide policy so that economies are able to achieve rapid rates of growth, low rates of unemployment, low rates of inflation as well as exchange rate and balance of payments stability.

The branch of economics that deals with these questions is referred to as macroeconomics. It is the area that tends to be of most interest to the community generally since such macroeconomic issues appear to affect them most directly, while the operation of markets seems more distant. Although microeconomic outcomes are the bread and butter issues for each of us individually, the macroeconomic issues still seem to hold the greatest interest.

Yet it is markets that matter most for prosperity, and even beyond that, it is only in understanding the interaction of entrepreneurs, financial institutions, businesses and consumers that the greater macroeconomic questions can be understood and answered.

MEASURES

To coincide with the four major macroeconomic issues of economic growth, unemployment, inflation and balance of payments stability, there are four major measures of economic activity that are essential in understanding the direction in which an economy is travelling. These are:

- Gross Domestic Product (GDP);
- the Consumer Price Index (CPI);
- the unemployment rate;
- the balance of payments.

There are many other forms of economic statistics produced by governments around the world (and there are still others produced by the private sector), but these are the four that matter most. They are the ones that are looked at most closely and it is these that provide the most important guide to policy.

At the end of the day, the question really is, what purpose do the figures serve? Each set of data requires a statistical agency to set down a framework for collecting the underlying figures. The ways in which the final statistics are to be used must determine what numbers are collected and how they are put together.

Most statistical collections are expensive. It therefore does require a good deal of thought to be given to the uses that are to be made of the statistics once they have been structured. Statistics are not naturally occurring numbers that merely require a count, such as with a census. They are highly complex artefacts that occur only at the end of a very long process of thought and methodological refinement.

Every major statistic has gone through a period of evolution to reach its present stage, and it may be stated with certainty that, as time goes by, every statistical series will continue to be improved.

GROSS DOMESTIC PRODUCT (GDP)

The National Accounts is the name given to the most comprehensive group of measures of overall economic activity. They are a drawing together of all of the most important economy-wide data on production within an economy.

Within the National Accounts, the most commonly used measure of the overall strength of the economy is the data on Gross Domestic Product, or GDP.[1] It is an attempt to answer the question regarding how much is being produced during some period of time, and more importantly, it is used as a measure to show how much more (or less) is being produced during some period in comparison with some earlier period.

The figures are also used to make comparisons of one country with another, either in terms of output levels, or in relation to their relative rates of growth.

The problem in estimating an economy's rate of growth is deciding what to include in the composition of a country's output, and then finding some way to add it all up.

A country in one year might produce one set of goods and then a decade later a quite different set of goods. Comparing the value of the earlier set with the later set requires a large number of issues to be negotiated.

Of course, the time frames involved are usually much shorter than a decade. In relation to GDP, the usual periods are between financial years or between quarters, such quarters being the three months ending 31 March, 30 June, 30 September and 31 December. It might thus be said that the growth in the June quarter relative to the March quarter was such-and-such per cent.

But just what was it that was growing? The aim is to have some measure of *production*; in other words, how much was produced in one time period relative either to another time period or in one place relative to some other place.

But in trying to make such estimates, here are a few of the problems:

- There is an enormous variety of kinds of goods and services that are produced, literally tens of millions of items from paper clips to aircraft; how can they all be added up together?
- Some of what is produced is sold on the market for money, while some – such as home-produced or government-produced goods and services – is not.
- Since the only common denominator amongst most of the goods and services produced is the price that has been placed on them by their sellers, where comparisons across time are sought it is necessary to find some means to isolate the change in the level of prices from changes in the level of production.
- The range of goods and services produced changes year by year so that in comparing two time periods one is almost literally comparing apples with oranges.
- The range of goods and services produced is different in different places so it is hard to make comparisons with the production taking place in two different locations.
- Most of what is produced is used as inputs into the production of something else, so the danger of double counting in adding it all up is great.
- Some of what is produced is used as final goods and services which disappear almost immediately after being produced while some, even if produced as final goods, remain in existence and are used for years on end.
- There are different levels of production in different time periods with, for example, a fall in output often occurring during summer months and a large increase in the production of retail items in the period before Christmas.
- Some of what is produced are capital goods used in the production process which last beyond the current time period.

Each of these questions has been a subject of international debate since the 1930s. It became crystal clear during the Great Depression that some kind of measure of economic output was needed. Until then, strange as it may seem, no such measures existed to provide a summary indication of an economy's overall strength.

The approaches used by national accounting statisticians have now become so complex that it would be impossible to explain how what is done is now actually done. But a scale model of the methodologies now used provides some sense of how these figures are produced and more importantly, how they can be interpreted.

Variety of Goods and Services

It is quite clear that an inventory of all of the goods and services produced during some period of time would not provide the kinds of information anyone could possibly use. What is sought is a number which summarizes the whole of the amount produced.

The answer to this was to find the total sale price of all of the goods and services sold during the relevant time period. For goods sold in the market, each item sold had a sale price. Adding up all of the prices paid for all of the goods and services sold provides a total aggregate cost of the goods and services that had been bought.

If one adds up everything bought, in that total must also be included the various government goods and services that had been put up for sale and sold. These might have included public utilities such as electricity and telecommunications, public transport and public housing. If government goods or services are sold on the market, then they are included as part of purchase and sale and dealt with in the same way as the output of private sector firms.

Home Produced Goods and Services

But not everything produced is sold on the market. There are, first, home produced goods and services. A meal eaten in a restaurant is a marketed activity. A meal prepared and eaten at home is not. There is therefore no actual market transaction to provide a valuation. The same thing is found with home made wines or home made anything. There is no market transaction although there clearly has been value-adding activity.

The answer has been to ignore for national accounting purposes the value produced by home production. If an activity is undertaken by private persons but there is no sale transaction, then it is left out of the National Accounts. This may cause some underestimate of the total level of production, but so long as there is not much variation between time periods in the amount of home production, the growth rate between periods – the actual figure that is usually being looked for – will not be much affected.

Government-Produced Goods and Services

Government-produced goods are also often not sold on the market and have no prices attached. Governments provide schools, roads, hospitals and the like, often with no direct payments by any of the users. There is also the vast apparatus of the public service for which no market payments are ever made.

These are forms of production that obviously cannot be left out and yet there is no associated market price for any of them. The answer, therefore, has been to simply include public sector activity 'at cost'.

What does it mean to include these 'at cost'? It is to incorporate the entire non-marketed segment of public expenditure into the national accounts by using the amount that the government has paid as the value added. If the government paid an annual salary to someone of $75000, irrespective of what that person did, it would be recorded as $75000 worth of value. The expenditure would just go in as it stood.

Government investment would be included in the same way, with its full production costs being recorded. The outlays would be recorded as its addition to value.

In that way, while the wages of teachers in the private sector would only be incorporated as part of the income received from private school fees, teachers in the public sector would have their wages included straight in, without the intermediation of anyone actually paying for the service other than through taxation.

Range of Products

One further complication in making comparisons of the level of production between two time periods is the certainty that there will be changes in the composition of goods and services offered up for sale. Between two quarters the differences are minimal, and even over the period of a year, changes are unlikely to be significant.

But as time goes by, the larger the differences become. New products are introduced while older products disappear. Innovation and product development continue at every moment. The wider apart two time periods are, the more diverse the products on sale are certain to be.

There are also shifts in the level of demand for some goods relative to others so that even if there were exactly the same products put up for sale, they would be found in different proportions. Demand for some products increases while the demand for others falls away. This ebb and flow is ongoing.

Beyond even the goods that have come and gone are the improvements in goods and services which now take place routinely. What might have been classified as a 'telephone' in 1950 is a far different device from a 'telephone' today. The national accounts must be able to record not just expenditure, but incorporate quality improvements as well.

Differences in the Range of Products between Geographical Regions

Production statistics are used to make comparisons between regions as well as time periods. And here again it is typical for different regions to produce a different range of products. In fact, it would be unusual to the point of impossibility for two geographical areas to be producing or even purchasing exactly the same goods and services.

Different parts of the world, even different parts of the same country, will have different demands made on their productive apparatus. Even the weather will affect the kinds of housing constructed and clothing worn.

Amongst the most important reasons for the production of different goods and services in different regions is the existence of trade. Some parts of the world specialize in particular kinds of products, and exchange those for the products of other regions. This is almost as true within individual nations as it is internationally. Specialization and trade are certain to cause production to be different in one region in comparison with another.

Double Counting

Most of the outputs in an economy are inputs into something else, either as some product that is almost immediately transformed through production into something else, such as cloth in the making of a shirt, or as a necessary component in value-adding production, such as the fuels in a transport network. These disappear into the productive process and no longer exist as they once did.

Thus, where cloth is used in producing an item of clothing, it would be double counting to include the production of the cloth separately from the production of the shirt. The economy did not produce two separate items, a piece of cloth and a shirt. It produced first a piece of cloth, and that piece of cloth was then transformed into a shirt.

Ensuring that production of the cloth and then production of the shirt are not both added into the production total is absolutely necessary to prevent a vast overestimate of the amount of actual production which did take place.

Consumption Goods versus Capital Goods

There are then the capital goods which are first produced so that they can be used to produce something else. There are machines which are used to produce other machines, such as the capital equipment that is used to build industrial sewing machines. There are then machines which are used as part of the production process, such as these sewing machines which are used to produce clothing.

The production of such capital equipment presents a much larger problem than the production of the various forms of inputs that are totally used up during a period of time. Capital equipment will under normal circumstances survive the period of production and often continue to contribute for years on end.

And, of course, a sewing machine can be bought by a business and can be bought by a final user for the home. The same item, depending on the use to be made of it, can be either a final good or an input into the production process. These two entirely different purposes for an identical item need to be distinguished when calculating the level of production.

Depreciation

The use of *Gross* Domestic Product is a reflection of the fact that the national accounting data are not adjusted for depreciation. That is, they are not adjusted for the effects on the future productiveness of capital equipment that are eaten away during the production process.

The wear and tear on capital equipment is part of the cost of production. Each day that an item of capital is used brings it a day closer to the moment it loses all effective economic value. The amount worn away by use is the depreciation. The fact that GDP is a gross estimate means no adjustment is made for this loss in economic value.

Depreciation is the opposite of investment. It is the value lost in the use of capital equipment. The National Accounts ignores this lost value. The only aspect of capital equipment that is recorded is its first sale to its first owner. After that, since it is no longer part of the production process, its existence forms no part in the recording of GDP.

Seasonality

When dealing with quarterly data, movements between periods will be affected by the normal levels of production that can be expected at different times of the year.

The most obvious shifts in the level of activity related to the calendar are the large increases in production and retail sales which typically occur in the lead-up to Christmas. It can be expected that the December quarter production levels will typically be far greater than the level of production in the March quarter.

If growth statistics do not take this into account, there will in each year be an apparent drop in output that is fully predictable, has no economic meaning, but which will affect perceptions about the actual underlying rate of economic growth, unless adjustments are made to the statistical series.

These factors are described as seasonality, and statistical series which are adjusted for these factors are referred to as the 'seasonally adjusted' data. Most economic series are produced in both the non-seasonally adjusted and seasonally adjusted forms, but no discussion of statistics ever deals with the non-seasonally adjusted series. The non-seasonally adjusted data are almost always used only as a staging post on the way to calculating the seasonally adjusted and trend figures.

Trend

Even within the seasonally adjusted data there are large and frequent movements that cause the data to move upwards and downwards. These are due to irregular changes that are not related to the seasons but, whatever their cause, they can have a significant effect on the data.

There are therefore shifts in statistical data that again can cloud the ability to see into the data and understand their longer-term underlying direction. As a consequence, trend data have been introduced in some series.

What the trend data do is remove the effects of these irregular events so that the statistical series is 'smoothed'. The irregular upwards and downwards jags in the number are taken out, and what is left is a series that is intended to show the actual underlying movement in the direction of some economic variable.

Measuring GDP

So to summarize, in measuring production, what is needed is a means to do all of the following:

- add together all of the immense number of goods and services produced during a period of time;
- find some means to deal with goods and services provided outside the market which are usually those goods produced by individuals for themselves without payment;
- find some means of incorporating changes in the composition of the

goods and services produced between time periods or between different geographical regions;

- bring together both goods that have been sold on the market and those that have not;
- recognize that some goods and services are used as inputs into the production of other goods and services while some are produced for final consumers;
- for quarterly data, incorporate into the data the 'seasonally' different levels of production that can be expected to take place at different times of the year;
- and for the quarterly data, adjust for the irregular events that can distort the pattern of production and disguise the actual direction of an economic statistic.

Clearly, the only common factor that can be used in recording the vast range of goods and services produced in an economy during a period of time is monetary value, imposed on the level of output. Only by providing a valuation can everything be reduced to some measure that is, for most of the goods and services produced, easily found.

GDP is therefore measured as a money value. There is a figure for output that is provided that, at its crudest level, represents the total amount of money that would be required to purchase everything that has been produced and included as part of this measure.

But not everything produced is included. The most important exclusions are goods and services produced by individuals for themselves and which have not been part of a market transaction. A bed made at home is not a market activity and is therefore excluded; a bed made in a hotel by someone else and for payment is included. They are both productive activities, but one is left out and the other kept in.

Adding Together Private and Public Sector Activity

Of goods produced outside the home, there are first those goods and services which have been produced and put up for sale. These are virtually all private sector forms of production as well as some produced by the public sector (such as public transport).

Private sector activity comes with a ready-made price and transaction cost. These can be directly recorded since they are embodied in the sale prices of the goods and services sold.

A great deal of public sector activity, however, occurs outside the market (such as public service activities and public schools) and therefore does not have a sale price since these goods and services are not actually bought and sold. Since there is no price attached, as has already been noted, the convention has become to include public sector activity 'at cost'. That is, whatever the level of public sector outlay, it is included as the value added of these forms of activity.

Thus, at the very core of the National Accounts is a methodology that equates the results of market-directed private sector activity which can only survive where a profit has been earned, with public sector activity which requires no test other than that the government has chosen to fund whatever the expenditure happens to be.

It need hardly be pointed out that governments are not profit-oriented entities but choose to fund activities for a wide variety of reasons, the creation of net value not necessarily being the most important.

Exports and Imports

It is also important that goods sold to overseas residents (exports) and bought from overseas residents (imports) are properly accounted for.

Imports are made up of goods and services that are bought within the domestic economy but that were not produced within the domestic economy. Exports are goods produced within the domestic economy but not bought within the domestic economy.

Therefore, if we are interested in the level of production in an economy, then we have to net out the level of imports. At the same time, we have to include within our production totals, the amount of output that was produced domestically but not purchased domestically. There is therefore a need to add in exports (usually designated by the letter X) and take away the amount of imports (usually designated by an M). Therefore, within the national accounting identities, there is often the expression $X–M$ which means exports minus imports The $X–M$ is often simply stated as NX, which means net exports.

Calculating GDP

There are three methods used to calculate GDP, which in theory are identical but both because of computational problems as well as some conceptual questions never come out exactly the same. The most often referred to methodology is what is known as the 'expenditure' method. The other two are the 'value added' and 'income' approaches to measuring national output.

Expenditure method
The most well-known approach used to calculate GDP is the method most commonly found in public discussion and is referred to as the expenditure

method. It attempts to calculate how much it would have cost to buy everything that was produced. But even though it is the most frequently discussed methodology, because its framework has been adopted into macroeconomic theory, it is in its own way the most confusing to understand properly.

In understanding this approach, it is important to recognize that only final goods and services are counted. Since produced inputs are embedded in the production of other outputs, there is a risk of a massive level of double counting.

The methodology employed is to add together the expenditure on all *final* goods and services *bought*. A final good is classified either as a good or service sold to its final consumer, or as a form of capital (that is machinery, plant and equipment) expected to last for more than one year and not to be immediately used up during production.

In addition, capital is an item of production that has been added to the inventories of a business even if the intention is eventually to sell whatever it is to its final consumer.

The production of capital goods and inventories is classified as investment, with investment listed as a separate category of final goods.

A shirt bought by its final consumer is classified as a consumption item. The cloth that goes into making a shirt, however, is classified as a purchased input. It is left out as an independent item of production since it was not purchased by the final user but was embodied in the production of the shirt which was bought by a final user. The purchase of a sewing machine by a business, however, even though also used in the production process, is included independently as a form of final good and recorded as investment.

There are thus two basic categories of final good in the domestic economy (looking only at the private sector): consumption goods and investment goods. These are typically identified in economic discussions as

$$C + I$$

There are then goods and services produced by governments, whether or not put up for sale. These include the public services and other forms of public outlays not sold on the market (for example road works). The letter used in economic discussions to refer to public sector expenditures is G. The formula can now, therefore, be written as:

$$C + I + G$$

There are then exports, the goods and services purchased by overseas residents. The letter used to designate exports amongst economists is X. The formula for total purchases can now be written:

$$C + I + G + X$$

This is the total of everything bought from domestic sellers *but it is not the total level of production.* Some of what was sold within the domestic economy was imported from other countries. Imports are designated by the letter M.

We thus have everything bought: $C + I + G + X$.

We have everything imported: M.

If from the total of everything bought is removed those parts which were imported, what is left must be what had been *produced.* The expenditure measure of production of GDP is therefore:

$$C + I + G + X - M$$

Or as this expression is often written, since Y amongst economists stands for GDP, production, output or national income:

$$Y = C + I + G + X - M$$

But even in seeing this formula, it is imperative to understand that this is a *definition.* There is nothing about this formula that indicates that the left side of the expression is the direct result of activities on the right side.

The identity sign ($\equiv$) is used below to show that in this expression we are dealing with an accounting definition. It is simply true because that is how things have been defined.

$$Y \equiv C + I + G + X - M$$

So note this. If the level of imports, M, increased and nothing else changed, the level of production represented by Y would fall. But it should be obvious that an increase in imports does not of itself cause a fall in domestic production.

In the same way, GDP does not go up because consumer demand (C) or investment (I) has gone up. It is output that has gone up, and the statistician then makes a decision about under which category to record the increased production.

It is an error many make and few can resist to believe that production (Y) changes because of changes in any of the elements on the right-hand side. In an accounting expression the two sides must balance.

Y does not go up because of decisions to consume. It may go up because of decisions to produce for consumers. Whether a change in C, I, G, X or M leads to a change in Y is a matter for determination by economic theory.

Value added method

The aim of the National Accounts in estimating the level and growth of production is to measure the level of value-adding production. Here what is done is to add together all of the value added at each stage of the production process. If one thinks only of the private sector, and if an economy were made up only of private sector firms, this would be conceptually the most straightforward.

For each firm there are the total input costs and there is the total revenue. The difference between revenues received and all of the costs incurred is the value added created by the firm. Adding up all of the value added created by every producer in an economy provides a measure of total value added.

However, because much production takes place in the public sector, it is impossible to employ such a straightforward methodology. Instead, government spending is included as if all such public outlays are of themselves value adding and growth producing in the same way as private sector value-adding activity.

Income method

The final method for calculating the level of production is what is known as the income method. It is, in a sense, a reworking of the value added methodology. Using value added to measure output, the net receipts are the measure. Using the income method, the distribution of those receipts to their different recipients is recorded.

Businesses receive payments when they sell their products. These payments are then divided amongst a series of groups and individuals. Some go to wage earners. Some go to those who have rented their premises to businesses. Some go to those who earn profits. And some are taken by the government in the form of indirect taxation.

Thus in the income method, all payments received are broken into the different ways in which business income can be distributed. A business receives various amounts of payments from its customers and these payments become the various forms of income received by those with a claim to share in the amounts outlaid. These are:

- the wages, salaries and other forms of compensation received by employees;
- the profits earned by entrepreneurs;
- the rental incomes of property owners;
- the indirect taxes received by governments.

Adding up these payments must come to the same total as the amount originally spent and is also equal to the total value added of the economy. This is the third measure of GDP.

Accounting for Movements in the Prices Level

The total level of GDP as calculated is recorded as a dollar amount. The total is an aggregate of various forms of outlay, whether on goods and services, value added or on incomes. But all are at the price level when the transaction occurred.

But there is little interest on most occasions in the total dollar value of production. What in fact is of interest is the *growth* that has taken place between two periods of time, that is how much more output there has been in the second period relative to the first.

But the total level of GDP as measured in *current* prices of the time can increase because either more output has been produced or the prices charged have gone up. That is, in the first period there is the dollar value of output (Q_1) at first period prices (P_1):

$$GDP_1 = Q_1 * P_1$$

And in the second period there is the dollar value of output (Q_2) at second period prices (P_2):

$$GDP_2 = Q_2 * P_2$$

The answer to the problem, which is fantastically more complex to do than to state, is to calculate GDP in every period at the prices charged during some arbitrarily chosen base period. This is described as the level of *real* GDP. Thus:

$$\text{Real } GDP_2 = Q_2 * P_1$$

The real level of GDP in the second period is calculated as the second period's output at first period prices. So when the *real growth rate* is calculated, prices cancel out.

Numerical calculation

The real data are usually calculated for all measures of GDP but only for the individual components of the expenditure series because these are the figures for which a set of price data can be most readily estimated. It is a very complex process but all a user needs to know is that adjustments have been made for the individual components of the calculation, for *C*, *I*, *G*, *X* and *M* as well as each of the individual sub-components.

But while the necessary price indexes can only be calculated for the expenditure series and its components, the real figures are provided for each of the GDP estimates. But even here the necessary price indexes are usually calculated from the expenditure series.

The figures are published as an amount denominated in the local currency. It will thus be said that GDP was so many millions for the year, and in the most recent quarter the seasonally adjusted level of GDP was also so many million, which is usually a figure around one quarter the size of the annual total, although obviously with seasonal differences.

Growth Rates

In virtually all cases, the interest in the figure produced is not in the level of output but in its rate of growth. There is seldom an interest in the GDP figure itself. The usual interest is in comparing the statistic during some period of time with the same statistic during a different period of time.

Suppose in the previous year that, the annual level of GDP had been $480 000 million and in this year the figure had risen to $510 000 million.

To calculate the annual growth rate, the procedure would be the normal means of calculating a percentage change:

$$\text{Annual Real Growth in GDP} = \frac{501\,600 - 480\,000}{480\,000} \times 100$$

$$= \frac{21\,600}{480\,000} \times 100$$

$$= 4.5\%$$

Thus, the real level of GDP has been estimated to have grown by 4.5 per cent over the previous year.

Growth rates between any two periods can be found in this way and it can be calculated for any of the series produced in the National Accounting statistics.

Usually, of course, the calculation does not work out to some exact whole percentage movement, so that the growth rate must be rounded. The convention is that for almost all economic statistics, only a single decimal point is shown for growth rates for virtually all economic data.

CONSUMER PRICE INDEX

Measurement of price movements in general has a wide variety of uses and is essential to the monitoring of the state of the economy.

At the very minimum, measures of price movements are needed as a measure of inflation, which is now seen as nothing other than the measurement of the rate at which prices are growing.

But possibly even more important is the use of a price index to convert economic indicators, which are shown in terms of *current* or *nominal* prices, into *real* measures of activity.

Nominal wages, for example, are calculated in the price level of the time at which they were paid out. But if the interest is in the purchasing power of wages at different times, they must be converted, using some indicator of price movement, into a measure of the real wage.

Price measures are almost invariably calculated as an *index*, which means that these figures are pure numbers. That is, they have no units associated with them. GDP measures, for example, are typically calculated in terms of the local currency, while a price index will have no units of any kind.

Being just a number, the sole purpose of price indexes is to examine the rate of increase in whatever is being measured. Sideways comparisons with other measures, such as the *level* of prices in different places, cannot be calculated using price indexes. Only the rate of increase in a single place between two time periods can be measured.

An economy produces many forms of price index. Anything that has a price, such as manufactured goods, airline services, imports, can have a price index calculated. However, the most frequently discussed price index is for consumer prices.

The Consumer Price Index (CPI) is calculated in virtually every country and all are based on the same international standard. It is a system that has continued to evolve, as has every other statistic, but the basic outline for calculation is generally clear, at least in concept. Actually creating the index and keeping its estimate relevant is, however, difficult.

The Basket of Goods and Services

To create a price index of any kind, it is necessary to know which prices are to be included. But not only do you need to know which prices, you need to have some idea of how many units of each item to include.

The aim is to mirror the 'average' expenditure of whichever group the prices relate to. If it is 'manufactured goods' then you have to know not just what was bought but also how many units were bought of each item.

With the purchases of consumers, it is not enough to know that a typical household has bought bread, furniture and overseas trips, but also the proportion of total outlays that is spent on each of these during the measurement period.

Therefore, what is whimsically called a 'basket of goods and services' is put together, which is in reality a list of the average amounts bought by the target population of each of the items purchased during the relevant time period.

The first step in making price estimates is usually to conduct some kind of household expenditure survey to find out what people buy and in what quantities. For some items, like loaves of bread and cartons of milk, more than a single item is bought in each time period. But for others, such as personal computers and cars, these are bought only every so often, so that only a fraction of a unit would be bought during the relevant period.

The list would be different in different countries, and even in different locations within a single country. A different mix of products can be expected to be purchased in different places, either because of different income levels, relative costs, cultural traditions or any number of other factors that would lead to a preference for one set of goods and services rather than another.

The list of items in the basket of goods, and there are typically thousands of items included in the CPI of most major economies, is then priced. Employees of the statistical agency go to places where these items are sold and find the price, and these are recorded. If the product is on special offer and the price is lower than usual, the actual sale price, not its normal price, is included.

The total cost of the basket of goods becomes the basis for the Consumer Price Index.

How the Index is Constructed

When all of the items are priced, the cost of purchasing this set of goods is calculated. The total is the basis for the index but is not the index itself.

Suppose in the base year, that is, the year from which all movements are calculated, the total cost of the basket of goods was $850. Because it is the base year, the index is arbitrarily given the value of 100.0. Although there are exceptions, the base year is almost invariably given this value.

But the arbitrary attribution of the index at 100.0 is irrelevant to the purpose that these indexes are for. It is the growth in the level of the index that is important.

In the base year the cost of the basket of goods and services is $850 and the index is equal to 100.0. In the second year, the cost of buying exactly the same basket of goods and services may have risen to $880. This is an increase, after rounding, of 3.5 per cent.

The index number is then raised by 3.5 per cent, in this case from 100.0 to 103.5. The statistical agency then publishes the 103.5 index as the CPI.

One can then calculate the growth in the level of prices by calculating the percentage change in prices in the normal way using the indexes in the two years. What is therefore published is not the money cost of the bundle of goods and services but the movement in the index which reflects the underlying movement in the cost of the basket of goods and services. Therefore in this instance what is published is a new index, which is 3.5 per cent higher than the previous index, which is 103.5. This index can then be used, as shown below, to calculate the growth in prices.

$$\text{Movement in CPI} = \frac{103.5 - 100.0}{100.0} \times 100$$

$$= \frac{3.5}{100.0} \times 100$$

$$= 3.5\%$$

Suppose in the next year, the total cost of the bundle of goods and services rises to $916. This is an increase over the previous year's cost of $880 of 4.1 per cent. But again, the cost of the basket of goods and services is not published, only the index number which is made 4.1 per cent higher than the previous year's index of 103.5. The index thus becomes 107.7, which is 4.1 per cent higher than 103.5.

To calculate the movement in the price level, again a percentage change between the two indexes is calculated in the normal way.

$$\text{Movement in CPI (2nd period)} = \frac{107.7 - 103.5}{103.5} \times 100$$

$$= \frac{4.2}{103.5} \times 100$$

$$= 4.1\%$$

It would then be said that consumer prices had risen by 4.1 per cent.

The movement in the price level can then be calculated between any two time periods. Suppose the interest was in the growth in prices over the two-year period. The means to do this would be to calculate the percentage change in the index over that two-year period, when it rose from 100.0 to 107.7. The calculation, as before, would be:

$$\text{Movement over the entire period} = \frac{107.7 - 100.0}{100.0} \times 100$$

$$= \frac{7.7}{100.0} \times 100$$

$$= 7.7\%$$

That is, the growth in prices across the two years would have been 7.7 per cent.[2]

Real Movements in Economic Indicators

Price indexes are also of immense value in calculating the 'real' movements in economic indicators which are given in current prices. Take, for example, data on wages which show the following changes:

Year 1 $50 000
Year 2 $52 000
Year 3 $53 500

If during this period of time, the price level has also risen, the question then is whether the purchasing power of the money wage has increased. The way to calculate this is to use movements in a price index to estimate the *real* growth in wages.

Using the CPI calculated in the previous section, the means to estimate the growth in the real wage is first to calculate the real wage in each year:

$$\text{Real Wage} = \frac{\text{Nominal Wage}}{\text{Index}} \times 100$$

Therefore, to calculate the real wage in each of these three years:

$$\text{Real Wage Year 1} = \frac{\$50\,000}{100.0} \times 100 = \$50\,000$$

$$\text{Real Wage Year 2} = \frac{\$52\,000}{103.5} \times 100 = \$50\,240$$

$$\text{Real Wage Year 3} = \frac{\$53\,500}{107.7} \times 100 = \$49\,675$$

Thus, in Year 2 the real wage was higher than in the first year, while in Year 3 it had fallen below its real level of both of the previous two years.

It is this technique that can be used to bring any series affected by changes in the price level to a set of base year prices so that changes in the real level of the economic indicator can be monitored.

EMPLOYMENT AND UNEMPLOYMENT

The third measure of economic activity is in many ways the most important. Certainly in political terms it is the most important, since allowing the number of unemployed to rise significantly will create problems for any government that is at all responsive to community concerns.

In purely economic terms, unemployment is a measure of wasted opportunities for an economy. Those who are unemployed could have contributed to the productive potential of the economy. Their being unemployed has deprived the community of the goods and services that could have been produced had they found productive work.

The *unemployment rate* is the most important measure of unemployment. It is the number of persons unemployed as a proportion of the *labour force*. And who is considered to be a member of the labour force? Everyone who is already working plus everyone who is not working but who is officially classified as unemployed. That is:

Labour Force

= Number of Employed Persons + Number of Unemployed Persons

Or to rearrange this expression, we can see that the number of unemployed persons is represented by the following:

Number of Unemployed Persons

= Labour Force − Number of Employed Persons

And to calculate the unemployment rate the following calculation is used:

$$\text{Unemployment Rate} = \frac{\text{Number of Unemployed Persons}}{\text{Labour Force}} \times 100$$

These are the concepts. How is it measured?

Labour Force Survey

In every country there is an official unemployment rate. Where does it come from? How is it possible to know how many people in an economy are working, not working, want to work or are willing to take a job?

The aim is to turn the concepts into a statistical measure, because even if one has a precise idea of what ought to be measured, operationally it is less clear-cut since each term in the calculation must have something that can actually be measured.

Moreover, it is necessary to have a means to actually put numbers onto the items that are to be included. To say that the unemployment rate is a ratio of the number of unemployed relative to the labour force still requires someone to know how many there are in each category.

The means of calculation is therefore preceded by a statistical survey of a sample of households in which individuals are asked whether they are employed, unemployed or not in the labour force. Not all households are in the survey; only a very small proportion of the total population is at any time included. But it is from this labour force survey that the required information is taken.

Someone from the national statistical agency therefore makes contact with those households that have been selected to be in the survey. And it is the answers to a series of questions that determine the number of those who are employed, those who are unemployed and those who are considered to be outside the labour force.

The Employed

The first issue is to separate the employed from those who are either unemployed or outside the labour force. It is also necessary to make a distinction between those who have chosen not to work and those who are deemed too young to work.

The first threshold question relates to who is over the official working age because only those over that age can be considered part of the labour force.

The second question then relates to whether the person had had paid work during the official sample week. It must be in the sample week to keep the survey consistent.

How long does one have to have worked for payment to be considered employed? So far as the official statistics are concerned, someone need only have had one hour of paid work in the previous week to be considered to have worked.

For many of those unused to such statistical definitions, it often appears ridiculous that the division between employed and not employed is a paltry single hour of paid work. The statistic is not, however, intended to differentiate between those who had a full satisfying week of work that will provide an adequate income, but merely to register those who had worked at all.

Certainly as a measure of what we would really like to know there is something lacking. But as a statistical measure of employment, it is seen to be preferable to pick up virtually everyone who was paid for their efforts during the sample week than to leave such individuals out.

The issue is thus not whether they would have preferred to have worked longer than they did, since most of those who work one hour in a week probably would. The only question is whether they have been paid for any work at all, and one hour is the length of time required for statistical inclusion in the paid workforce.

Then, finally, if one has not worked, there are questions regarding whether someone was away from their paid employment because they had been on holiday or sick leave. If they normally worked but were ill or on vacation, they are included in the total of those employed.

The Unemployed

To be unemployed is not as simple as it sounds. It is not enough to have been without work and to have wished to work. There are a series of criteria that must be met that determine whether one is to be officially included amongst the unemployed:

- they must be old enough to be included in the labour force statistic;
- they must not have worked for a single hour during the sample week;
- they must have actively taken steps to find work (for example applied for a job, looked at newspaper ads);
- they must be capable of commencing work in the period immediately ahead (for example not finishing a course, no child-minding problems).

But if the person is old enough for inclusion, did not work in the previous week, actively took steps to find a job and is able to start paid employment, then that person is officially unemployed. Otherwise, they are classified as not part of the labour force. They are then neither employed nor unemployed.

From these survey results, the statistical agency then publishes a number showing the official level of unemployment, employment and the total labour force.

Seasonally Adjusted Data

Even these raw numbers are not sufficient since the figures are often not of much use on their own.

Because there are periods when employment is typically high, for example during the winter months, and other periods when employment is typically low, such as during summer holidays, if there were not some adjustment made for these 'seasonal' differences, the numbers would not be of much use.

There is therefore a calculation made to 'seasonally adjust' the employment data in the same way that is done with the National Accounts, and indeed with virtually every other series produced by national statistical agencies.

With the employment and unemployment data, the raw data are virtually never quoted. The figures most often quoted are those which have been seasonally adjusted. (There are also in many economies 'trend' data, which are unaffected not only by seasonal influences but also by irregular occurrences that affect employment levels.)

Calculating the Unemployment Rate

Suppose that the figures in Table 9.1 are those collected by the national statistical agency on employment and unemployment.

In the first period there were 10 000 persons employed and 500 who were unemployed. The labour force was the total of the employed and unemployed, which is 10 500 persons.

The unemployment rate is found as a simple percentage of the number of unemployed relative to the total labour force.

Table 9.1   Sample data on the employed, unemployed, labour force and the unemployment rate

Period	Employed	Unemployed	Labour force	Unemployment rate
1	10 000	500	10 500	4.8
2	11 000	600	11 600	5.2
3	12 000	700	12 700	5.5
4	13 000	800	13 800	5.8
5	14 000	850	14 850	5.7
6	15 000	880	15 880	5.5

$$\text{Unemployment Rate} = \frac{\text{Number of Unemployed Persons}}{\text{Labour Force}} \times 100$$

$$= \frac{500}{10\,500} \times 100$$

$$= 4.8\%$$

In the table it will be seen that the unemployment rate continues to rise from 4.8 per cent in Period 1 until it reaches 5.8 per cent in Period 4. It then falls to 5.7 per cent in Period 5 and 5.5 per cent in Period 6.

But what is worth noting is that the number of unemployed keeps rising. The higher the number of persons in the labour force, the larger the number of unemployed people it takes to raise the rate of unemployment.

Discouraged Workers and Underemployment

It might have been noticed that to be unemployed it is necessary to be actively looking for work. Some people, however, are unemployed, would like to work but have given up trying to find a job after making the effort but not being taken on.

There is a specific category for such people within a classification called 'discouraged workers'. Such potential workers are not included in the labour force data and therefore are not included in the unemployment data. The unemployment data, therefore, to the extent that discouraged workers are an important group, underestimate the actual dimensions of the unemployment problem.

There are also many who work part-time and who would prefer to work full-time but cannot get a full-time job. The economy is therefore deprived of the additional hours of work they would prefer to contribute while they earn less income than is optimal from their perspective.

Together with discouraged workers, such underemployment is also a measure of the underperformance of the labour market in generating jobs for all who want them.

BALANCE OF PAYMENTS

Balance of payments statistics, given their importance, are the numbers that are of least interest to the general public. And in many ways, this is a reflection of the difficulty in making clear-cut judgements about the figures and what they show.

What the balance of payments data provide are, first, a recording of the purchase and sale of goods and services between the home country and the rest of the world. These data are then combined with a series of measures of the flow of monetary payments that allow the total always to balance. The balance of payments data are literally a series of accounting records.

Since the sale of goods and services to foreign countries (exports) will never precisely equal the purchase of goods and services from foreign countries (imports), which is what is calculated in the *current account*, the *capital account* records the balancing flow of payments and debts incurred that have permitted the flow of exports and imports to take place.

There can, for example, be a deficit on the current account if imports are greater than exports. Deficits have a negative connotation, but the reality is that there is nothing intrinsically wrong with such deficits. It is the way economies work and the fact that there is a balancing item on the capital account is merely how the two sides of the accounts are made to be equal.

Some idea of the economy itself and its strengths and weaknesses is needed to make sense of the balance of payments statistics on their own.

These are accounts as devised by accountants. Therefore here, and only here in this chapter, does the word 'capital' refer to money, finance and credit. Everywhere else, capital means goods and services used in production.

In the days of fixed exchange rates, which meant that the value of a currency in relation to other currencies was specified by every country, the balance of payments data held a deadly fascination for governments. If imports began to grow much more rapidly than exports, leading to larger and larger deficits on the current account as time went by, the probability would grow that the country could no longer finance its imports through its exports and capital raisings. There could then be weeks of political instability until either the currency was devalued (lowered in price relative to other currencies) or the crisis dissipated as evidence grew that no actual problem existed.

In the present, however, with most exchange rates now *floating*, so that the value of the currency moves upwards and downwards depending on trade and financial conditions, such periodic episodes have almost completely disappeared. The balance of payments has therefore become of little interest outside professional circles, and even then there is no consensus on when a problem can even be said to exist.

Exchange Rates

There is still, of course, widespread interest in the exchange rate, which can and does have profound effects on an economy. Exchange rates in the world of floating currencies are determined in the market, with the supply

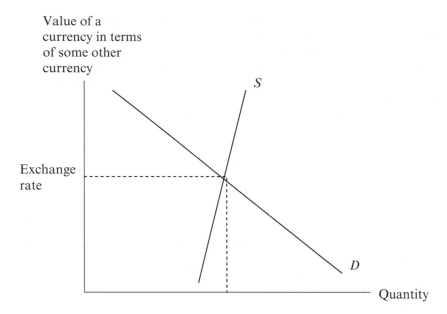

Figure 9.1   Determination of an exchange rate in the market

and demand for a particular currency the subject of the amount of that currency available relative to the desire of others to own that currency, either for trade purposes, finance, travel needs or speculation about the future.

The supply and demand curve shown in Figure 9.1 is for some currency. Its value is determined by the supply and demand for the currency in terms of other currencies.

And as always, it is the *ceteris paribus* conditions that matter most. Whatever causes an increased need or willingness to hold a currency will move the demand to the right, and if there is less need or willingness to hold that currency, then the demand moves to the left.

Since with each exchange rate the price is in terms of the value of every other currency being bought and sold, the underlying complexities are many and varied. But in the market for currencies, expectations play a very large role, with anything expected to cause a willingness to hold a currency immediately reflected in a shift to the right of the demand curve, which causes an immediate rise in the value of a currency. Similarly, a fall in the expected value of a currency will cause the value of the currency to immediately fall, since there will be an immediate fall in the demand for the currency.

NOTES

1. Sometimes the most important measure within an economy is the data on Gross National Product (GNP) rather than Gross Domestic Product. The difference for most economies is trivial. It hinges on whether the output was produced within the country (GDP) or was produced by the citizens of a country with some of that production having taken place in foreign lands (GNP).
2. It might be noted that the growth rate is higher than if the 3.5 per cent were added to the 4.1 per cent. This is not a rounding error but is due to the effect of compounding. Adding growth rates to get the arithmetical total is inaccurate, and the larger the growth rates involved, the larger the error would be.

APPENDIX

Average Annual Rates of Growth

One of the most useful techniques for examining data is the appropriate statistical technique for finding the average of a series of growth rates. If one is interested in the average annual growth in some series over the last decade for example, because of the effects of compounding, merely to divide by ten is inaccurate, and the larger the growth rate the more inaccurate the measure will be.

Suppose that over that decade the growth had been 50 per cent. Dividing by 10 will suggest that the average growth per year had been 5 per cent, when in reality it had been 4.1 per cent (after rounding to a single decimal point).

The proper methodology is as follows:

1. Count up the number of *periods* (n) between two figures.
2. Divide the later figure by the earlier figure.
3. Using a calculator take the nth root of the answer in (2).
4. Subtract 1 from the answer in (3) and then multiply by 100.
5. Multiply the answer in (4) by 100.

Thus, if between 1969 and 1985, some index had risen from 120.0 to 198.0, the means to calculate the average growth rate would be, following the above methodology:

1. The number of periods is found by subtraction: 1985–1969 = 16.
2. Then dividing 198.0 by 120.0 leaves a figure of 1.65 (which by subtracting 1 from this result shows that the growth across the period had been 65 per cent).
3. The 16th root (on a calculator '1.65^(1÷16)') – is then shown to be 1.03179.
4. Subtracting 1 from the answer gives 0.03179.
5. Multiplying 0.03179 by 100 gives 3.179 which rounded to one decimal place shows a growth rate each year of 3.2 per cent.

This technique can be used for any kind of statistical series, whether calculated as an index, such as with the CPI, or as a whole number, as with the data on GDP.

10.   An interlude on the history of economics

In moving from the microeconomic side to macroeconomics, it is a strategic moment in which to have a look at the way in which economic theory developed. An appreciation of how economic theory became what it is, and the steps it took along the way to become what it has now become, will make textbook and mainstream theory easier to follow. Rather than just looking at the theory as if it had been handed down to us as a finished product on tablets, it is useful instead to recognize that it was actual human beings, living in societies in many ways different from our own, who carved out of the solid rock of an underlying reality the way we make sense of the world at the present time.

It is also important, as a matter of general cultural awareness, to know the great economists of the past who have had an influence on the way in which we think about economic matters. For good or ill, these people have influenced our lives more than any other group in the social sciences because it is based on their theories that our economic structures are now organized. This is true irrespective of the kind of economic system one happens to live within.

ORIGINS

People have always fed, clothed and housed themselves, but for most of past history what was done was seen as just how it was done. Alternative ways of going about organizing economic structures and institutions were not on anyone's agenda. The traditional way of managing production was generally considered the only way. Whatever evolution that did take place was slow. Any improvements were generally imperceptible to those living at the time. Most of any writing on economics was undertaken as a form of ethical discussion in relation to what was fair and just. What virtually no one discussed until the eighteenth century was how to make economies more prosperous or how to raise the living standards of a community.

What changed all of this came from a number of directions. The industrial revolution was in its infancy but was effecting real changes in production levels. Rather than all economic and political issues remaining local, the nation state had begun to emerge as the political organizing principle, at least for those nations bordering the North Atlantic. And political theory had begun to point towards individual rights and freedoms as an ethical principle. In England, in particular, the rise of parliament in relation to the monarchy opened up possibilities that had not existed before.

It was in this environment that the first major writings on economics, then referred to as political economy, began to emerge. And while there were many writers at the time, one name emerged which has towered above all others as the first great economist. It was Adam Smith and his *Inquiry into the Nature and Causes of the Wealth of Nations* that changed the entire way economic issues have been conceived ever since. The book was published in 1776 and became an immediate sensation. It has never been out of print (Smith [1776] 1976).

ADAM SMITH AND CLASSICAL ECONOMICS

The aim of this first great work of economics was to demonstrate the power of individuals acting in their own interests as the potential driving force of economic activity. Rather than needing governments to direct economic activity from above, and to make every economic decision a matter for review by government, what Smith argued was that economies were social institutions that could be left to run themselves.

Invisible Hand

At its centre is the argument that individuals, if left to act in their own best interests, will create a world of wealth more efficiently and with more certainty than any other possible way of arranging a nation's affairs. The following passage may be the most famous, most quoted passage in the whole of economic theory. It may also have been the single most influential.

> [A merchant] generally, indeed, neither intends to promote the public interest, nor knows how much he is promoting it. . . . He intends only his own security; and by directing that industry in such a manner as its produce may be of the greatest value, he intends only his own gain, and he is in this, as in many other cases, *led by an invisible hand* to promote an end which was no part of his intention. Nor is it always the worse for the society that it was not part of it. By pursuing his own interest he frequently promotes that of the society more effectually than when he really intends to promote it. (ibid., Book IV, Chapter II: 477–78, emphasis added)

The 'invisible hand' of Adam Smith was a metaphor for the market. In this passage, Smith made a number of points:

- businesspeople do what they do to make money;
- but in going about making money, they actually do a great deal of social good even though it was not their specific intention to do so;
- businesspeople are only trying to create as much value as they can because whatever value they create they can exchange for other things and become more wealthy themselves;
- but, unbeknownst to these businesspeople, in acting in their own best interests, by creating value they are led by that 'invisible hand' to act in ways that often turn out to be very good for society as a whole;
- indeed, had these businesspeople actually decided to do things with the intention of benefiting society, it is uncertain whether they could have done so as effectively as they have by just building their own businesses and running their own firms.

The clear message was that no one had to run the market or the economy in general. The spontaneous actions of individuals seeking to do what is best for themselves would provide the direction and impulse for economic activity. And leaving such matters to the market would create a greater improvement in economic output than any other possible set of arrangements. This is how Smith put this argument:

> As every individual endeavors as much he can both to employ his capital in the support of domestic industry, and so to direct that industry that its produce may be of the greatest value; every individual necessarily labors to render the annual revenue of the society as great as he can. (ibid., Book IV, Chapter II: 477)

Self-Interest and Economic Outcomes

Smith pointed out the motivations behind the production of goods and services by individual businesses. This, too, was a famous and very influential passage in the *Wealth of Nations*.

> It is not from the benevolence of the butcher, the brewer, or the baker that we expect our dinner, but from their regard to their own interest. We address ourselves, not to their humanity, but to their self-love, and never talk to them of our own necessities, but of their advantages. (ibid., Book I, Chapter II: 18)

In an economy where complete strangers produce for each other, there is nothing to offer someone else to produce for oneself other than what can be given in exchange. We do not go to those who sell to us and tell them how much we need their products. We only offer something of value to them (usually money) in exchange for what we want.

This is the world in which we live, and it was the world in which Smith lived, and probably all previous generations of the human race as well. Past the village and the world of tradition, economic activity was a process in which both parties saw themselves as gaining through exchange. But this commonsensical statement made an immense impact because things had never before been said just like that. It made the world of commerce and industry appear for the first time as a benevolent activity which would result in greater prosperity for an increasing number of people.

Attitude to Merchants

Not that it should be thought that Smith had a benign view of the merchant class. In one of the most famous passages from the *Wealth of Nations* he discusses the actual motivations that lie behind the ways in which businesspeople act: 'People of the same trade seldom meet together, even for merriment and diversion, but the conversation ends in a conspiracy against the public, or in some contrivance to raise prices.' (ibid., Book I, Chapter X: 144)

It has been pointed out that Smith, amongst the first true defenders of the market, at no point in the *Wealth of Nations* makes any statement that could be interpreted as partial to merchants and businesspeople as a class. He is highly cynical about their acquisitiveness. But he sees these characteristics as being nevertheless beneficial to society as a whole. Their single-minded pursuit of gain will ensure they are single-minded in their management of the businesses they run.

Attitude to Governments

Nor should it be thought that Smith had a kindlier view of governments, which he, in fact, thought of as even more wasteful, destructive and pernicious than business. And in this quote, where Smith talks about employing 'their capitals' he is referring to how private individuals manage their own wealth. This is a statement that has not lost its relevance since the day it was first penned:

> The statesman who should attempt to direct private people in what manner they ought to employ their capitals would . . . assume an authority which could safely be trusted, not only to no single person, but to no council or senate whatever, and which would nowhere be so dangerous as in the hands of a man

who had folly and presumption enough to fancy himself fit to exercise it. (ibid., Book IV, Chapter II: 478)

Smith wrote of the dangers of government spending with the kind of insight whose relevance the years since have done nothing to diminish. The propensities of governments to waste money were recognized by Smith in ways that every generation has had to learn over again for itself.

> It is the highest impertinence and presumption, therefore, in kings and ministers, to pretend to watch over the œconomy of private people. . . . They [governments] are themselves always, and without any exception, the greatest spendthrifts in the society. Let them look well after their own expence, and they may safely trust private people with theirs. If their own extravagance does not ruin the state, that of their subjects never will. (ibid., Book II, Chapter III: 367)

The consequence of the *Wealth of Nations* was to move the economy of England, and thereafter the economies of an increasing proportion of the world, in the direction of market forces. The effect of a greater reliance on markets in every economy where they have been introduced has been unmistakeable and positive. The growth in productivity and economic well-being has been a direct result of the introduction of private direction for economic activity.

In looking at Smith, it should be noted that most of what he had described was what would now be called a 'macroeconomic' view of the world. He did not particularly discuss individual markets. He talked literally about the wealth of entire nations, how increased levels of wealth for a country and improved standards of living for the individual inhabitants could be effected. The microeconomic side of Smith's approach was in the concept that leaving economic decision making to individual decision makers would set in motion processes that would lead to a vast improvement in value added per person employed.

The Importance of Saving

Amongst the most important messages provided by Smith was his insight into the crucial role of saving. It was saving that allowed investment to occur; saving being a decision to postpone current consumption and to allow one's income to be used by others to invest. For a society, saving means increasing expenditure on capital assets such as machinery and buildings. The more that is invested in capital, the faster an economy will grow.

> Wherever capital predominates, industry prevails. . . . Every increase or diminution of capital, therefore, naturally tends to increase or diminish the

real quantity of industry, the number of productive hands, and consequently
the exchangeable value of the annual produce of the land and labour of the
country, the real wealth and revenue of all its inhabitants. (ibid., Book II,
Chapter III: 358)

The basis for investment is saving, which Smith calls 'parsimony'.
Saving allows a community's resources to be employed productively,
that is, to be used in ways which increase the productive capacity of the
economy in general.

Whatever a person saves from his revenue he adds to his capital, and either
employs it himself in maintaining an additional number of productive hands,
or enables some other person to do so, by lending it to him for an interest, that
is, for a share of the profits. As the capital of an individual can be increased
only by what he saves from his annual revenue or his annual gains, so the
capital of a society, which is the same with that of all the individuals who
compose it, can be increased only in the same manner. (ibid., Book II, Chapter
III: 358–9)

Without saving there can be no investment and therefore no economic
growth. Saving is amongst the most crucial aspects of economic activity. It
is the absolutely necessary ingredient in increasing prosperity.

Parsimony, and not industry, is the immediate cause of the increase of capital.
Industry, indeed, provides the subject which parsimony accumulates. But whatever industry might acquire, if parsimony did not save and store up, the capital
would never be the greater. (ibid., Book II, Chapter III: 359)

This is a conclusion that has remained one of the major insights into
the operation of an economy. It is saving that finances investment. It is a
conclusion that tends not to be taught because rather than explaining the
importance of saving as essential for prosperity, saving is now often por-
trayed as a villain because saving in excess is seen as the most important
cause of recessions and unemployment.

Yet it is saving that is the absolute necessity as a foundation for economic growth. The modern attitude to saving as the cause of recession is a
dangerously misleading view of the true importance of saving in creating
growth and prosperity.

Specialization and the Division of Labour

Smith's major microeconomic insight was what he described as specialization and the division of labour. At the workplace, more output per person
could be achieved by breaking an entire production process into smaller

tasks in which individual workers could excel at the specific parts of the process they had been assigned: 'As it is the power of exchanging that gives occasion to the division of labour, so the extent of this division must always be limited by the extent of that power, or, in other words, by the extent of the market.' (ibid., Book I, Chapter III: 21)

The division of labour is limited by the extent of the market. And, while being a comment on the domestic economy, this was, in its way, also a comment on the advantages of international trade. The greater the size of the market, the more an economy could benefit from the productivity growth that would accompany division of labour at the enterprise and industry level. Small markets are less efficient. Being able to produce and trade either locally or across the world would improve the amounts of output available for sale.

Free Trade

On free trade itself, Smith wrote in its defence in ways that have appealed to economists ever since. It is difficult to get around the logic of what he wrote, and the growth in world trade and prosperity since his time has confirmed what was then more intuition and logic than an empirical reality upon whose evidence he could count. He starts with the observation that if an object is cheaper to buy than to make, then it should be bought and not made. From this he points out that what is true for an individual is true for an entire nation.

> It is the maxim of every prudent master of a family, never to attempt to make at home what it will cost him more to make than to buy. . . . What is prudence in the conduct of every private family, can scarce be folly in that of a great kingdom. If a foreign country can supply us with a commodity cheaper than we ourselves can make it, better buy it of them with some part of the produce of our own industry, employed in a way in which we have some advantage. (ibid., Book IV, Chapter II: 478–9)

This, along with much else in Smith, has become part of the central message of economic theory. There has been much elaboration along the way, and much has been qualified in comparison with Smith's views in 1776, but the *Wealth of Nations* remains a repository of economic ideas that provides a very good first approximation of the ideas that may be found in economic texts to this day.

DAVID RICARDO

It was not to be for another 41 years before a book as influential in its own time as the *Wealth of Nations* would be published. This was David Ricardo's *Principles of Political Economy and Taxation*, published in 1817.

What made this book so entirely different and yet revolutionary in its own way was that it was an economics treatise that was modern in its approach. Smith had been expansive and literary. Ricardo was narrow and deeply logical. His *Principles* began with a series of propositions about how economies worked and, from these axioms, he deduced the conclusions that would be translated directly into policy.

There are, however, a number of aspects of Ricardo that have had a major impact on economic developments up until this day. The first was the core issue of his writings which concerned itself with the distribution of income. Income was distributed with wages going to labourers, rents to property owners and the residual ending up with the owners of business in the form of profits.

Ricardo's discussion of profits, and especially their existence as a residual, was later taken up by Karl Marx, who used the same concepts to show, at least according to himself, that profits were nothing other than a surplus skimmed from the productivity of the workers. The workers produced while the profit owners earned large incomes although contributing nothing. Marx therefore argued that it was perfectly sensible to do away with those who took the profits since payments for their nil contribution to production had no justification.

Comparative Advantage

There was then the theory of comparative advantage which remains an integral part of economic discussion to this day. In explaining not just why trade occurred but why it could be of advantage to both parties (something not easily seen, as discussions of trade-related issues down to the present continually show), Ricardo developed a deeper understanding of the role of specialization and trade.

The central idea of comparative advantage is that it is not whether one country is *absolutely* more productive than another that allows trade to occur. What matters is whether one country is *relatively* better at producing something. And note there are two relativities involved: the relative cost of products within each economy, which is then compared with the relative cost in both countries taken together.

Take a simple example.

- Suppose in Country A, in *one* hour it can produce either one car or 1000 shirts.
- And suppose in Country B, in *two* hours it can produce either one car or 500 shirts.
- Country B is therefore not as good at producing either cars or shirts since in one hour it can only produce half a car and 250 shirts.
- But note this. In Country A the cost of one car is 1000 shirts, since every time a car is produced 1000 shirts could have bee produced instead. Meanwhile, using the same reasoning, in Country B the cost of one car is only 500 shirts. (That is, in A the opportunity cost of one car is 1000 shirts and in B the opportunity cost of one car is 500 shirts.)
- So although Country A is better at producing both products, it is relatively better at producing shirts. Country B is, however, not as good at producing either good, but is relatively better at producing cars.
- According to the theory of comparative advantage, Country A should produce only shirts which it should sell to Country B and use the money received to buy cars. Meanwhile, Country B should produce only cars and sell these to Country A and use the money it receives to buy shirts.
- The result is that both countries are better off because both will have more of both products, since each is concentrating on what it does comparatively better than the other.
- In A, since they are buying cars from an economy where the price is 500 shirts, it is better off if it gives anything less than the 1000 shirts it used to pay for each car. Meanwhile in B, it is better off if each time it sells a car to A it receives more than the 500 shirts in return it used to receive.

The Law of Comparative Advantage remains an important element in the explanation of why trade takes place. That is, it shows that countries trade with each other because it makes them better off. If trade did not make a country better off, you may be sure that trade would disappear.

JEAN-BAPTISTE SAY

Given his subsequent importance, the French economist Jean-Baptiste Say must be brought into the story. Say was for the most part a popularizer of the arguments that had been presented by Adam Smith. His *Treatise on Political Economy* was published in 1803 to acquaint the French public with Smith's ideas. However, it was not merely a restatement of Smith but had a number of innovations of its own.

The first of these was the introduction of a fourth factor of production beyond land, labour and capital. This was the additional input that was brought to the production process by the *entrepreneur*. Say explicitly recognized the crucial importance of the entrepreneur as the initiator and organizer of the production process. It was, as he wrote, through the entrepreneur that value-adding activity was able to take place.

For reasons unknown, independent discussion of the role of the entrepreneur remains relatively uncommon even to this day. Yet without the entrepreneur to identify value-adding possibilities and then to superintend the process all along the way, value-adding production would remain far less common, and prosperity would possibly have remained as elusive as it had been in all of the centuries prior to the arrival of the industrial revolution.

Say's Law

But Say's other innovation was the popularization of an economic principle which would be given the name 'Say's Law', but not until more than a century had gone by since its first discussion by Say in his *Treatise*.

Although there were a number of strands to the surrounding principle, in brief it may be stated as: demand is created by value adding production and by nothing else.

For goods to be bought, not only must goods be produced, but precisely those goods that others would be willing to buy must be the ones that need to be produced.

From this principle, there arose three conclusions that were accepted by the mainstream of the economics profession through until 1936:

1. 'Goods buy goods': to buy one first had to produce goods of one's own, sell these goods for money and then use the money received to buy the goods produced by others; thus it is the production of one's own goods that leads to the ability to purchase someone else's, even though money is used as the medium of exchange.
2. 'Demand is constituted by supply': in an exchange economy one cannot buy unless someone else has supplied, since unless someone supplies there can be no demand.
3. 'There is no such thing as a general glut': it is impossible for an economy to produce so much output that there would not be enough buyers for what had been produced, so long as what has been produced is what people want to buy; therefore demand deficiency across an entire economy can never be a realistic explanation for recession.

It was the rejection of this principle following the publication in 1936 of *The General Theory of Employment, Interest and Money* by the economist John Maynard Keynes – the most influential text on economics written during the whole of the twentieth century – that led to what became known as the Keynesian Revolution (Keynes, [1936] 1987). More about this in the chapter to come.

THOMAS ROBERT MALTHUS

Thomas Robert Malthus wrote one of the most sensational and influential books of all time. In 1798, he published his book *On Population* which argued that food production increased only 'arithmetically' while population grew 'geometrically' (Malthus, [1798] 1986).

He believed that natural rates of human reproduction, if unrestrained, would lead to geometric increases in population. The population would grow in a geometrical progression in a ratio of 2, 4, 8, 16, 32, 64. At the same time, however, food production would increase only in arithmetic progression: 2, 4, 6, 8, 10.

The consequence of these differential rates of growth was that population growth could be expected to outrun food production. Therefore availability of food for most people could be expected to be no better than just enough to prevent starvation, while for some, starvation was inevitable.

Population, Malthus argued, would expand right up to the limits set by food production. Moreover, even when productivity grew and economies were able to produce more food, the only result would be that population numbers would rise and keep rising until there was again only just enough food to go round.

The sole way out of this dilemma, Malthus argued, was through checks to population growth. There was 'moral restraint' that would be exercised so that numbers were kept down because marriage was delayed and the number of children diminished. And then there were the positive restraints, which would be imposed on populations by external factors, which he named as war, starvation, disease and plague.

Malthusian population theory meant that wages could never for long rise above the level that would just keep most members of the working class alive. This theory found its way into classical economic theories including those of Ricardo and Marx. Wages would always descend to subsistence levels in what was known as 'the iron law of wages'.

There is also an interesting sidelight to Malthus's population theory. Both Darwin and Wallace, the two originators of the theory of evolution by natural selection, reached their conclusions after reading *On*

Population. Since population would outrun the available food supplies, there would be a life and death struggle amongst all organisms for food to eat. Only the 'fittest' would win out in the struggle to survive because there was not enough to go around. Since only the fittest amongst living organisms would be expected to survive, only those best suited to enduring within existing conditions would win out over the rest, who would perish. The fittest would leave the most descendants and so it would be those characteristics that would predominate in the generations that followed.

It was because of his already established fame as the author of *On Population* that when Malthus came to write his own *Principles of Political Economy* which was published in 1820, his book would immediately attract attention (Malthus, [1820] 1986). And so it did. It commenced a debate that involved every major economist of the time and led within half a dozen years to the publication of a large number of books and pamphlets to rebut the arguments that Malthus had made.

What was at the core of this debate was Malthus's argument that the depressions which had followed the ending of the Napoleonic Wars in 1815 had been caused by a deficiency of demand. Too much was being saved and not enough was being spent to employ the entire working population of England. The result was a 'general glut' or overproduction: too much output relative to the willingness of those with incomes to buy.

Leading the opposition to Malthus's view was Ricardo. In one of the odder aspects in the history of economics, Ricardo and Malthus were the best of friends and frequent visitors to each other's homes. But on general gluts as well as much else, they were in complete disagreement and their differences were not only carried on in public but also in an ongoing correspondence which had been conducted for many years over many topics. And amongst the issues that they corresponded about was the question of overproduction. It was this correspondence that a century later would lead to a revolution in economic thought and the development of macroeconomic theory to demonstrate the possibility of demand deficiency.

JOHN STUART MILL

It was also in this debate that the contours of the classical theory of recession were developed. Indeed, the controversy continued for a generation after the publication of Malthus's *Principles* and was only ended with the publication of John Stuart Mill's *Principles of Political Economy* in 1848 (Mill, [1878] 1921). And the overwhelming view of the entire mainstream of the economics profession was that Say's Law was valid, so that demand deficiency or overproduction was never an actual cause of recession.

While there were many theories to account for recessions, and many more would be developed as time wore on, it was accepted with virtual unanimity that recessions were not caused by glutting of markets, but that the failure of everything produced to be sold was, whenever it occurred, due to some other set of circumstances.

Mill in his *Principles* spoke for the entire classical school, and his conclusion would be accepted right through to 1936 when Keynes would publish his *General Theory*. In concluding his argument, Mill wrote:

> I know not of any economical facts . . . which can have given occasion to the opinion that a general over-production of commodities ever presented itself in actual experience. I am convinced that there is no fact in commercial affairs which, in order to its explanation, stands in need of that chimerical supposition. (Mill, [1878] 1921)

Nor was this seen as a mere sidelight to other more consequential issues. There are two entirely different sets of assumptions and conclusions that one might reach, depending on whether or not one accepted the existence of demand deficiency as a realistic possibility. Because if one believes that demand deficiency is a realistic possibility, then not only is it necessary to devise policies to ensure that goods are produced and distributed, it is also necessary to devise policies to make sure everything produced gets bought. This is Mill again making this argument:

> The point is fundamental; any difference of opinion on it involves radically different conceptions of Political Economy, especially in its practical aspect. On the one view, we have only to consider how a sufficient production may be combined with the best possible distribution; but, on the other, there is a third thing to be considered – how a market can be created for produce. (Mill, [1878] 1921)

To Mill and the classical school, to believe in the possibility of demand deficiency so completely confused anyone trying to understand how an economy works that ultimately they would never get past the most basic aspects in trying to think through the mechanics of economic activity. As Mill wrote:

> A theory so essentially self-contradictory cannot intrude itself without carrying confusion into the very heart of the subject, and making it impossible even to conceive with any distinctness many of the more complicated economical workings of society. (Mill, [1878] 1921)

This is the judgement that classical economists made of the economic theories of Malthus. As we shall see, it was these same Malthusian views that would a century later be introduced into mainstream theory by

Keynes, who would be convinced that Malthus had been right all along. It was his own interpretation of Malthus's letters to Ricardo, which he read at the depths of the Great Depression in October 1932, that would lead to this complete reversal of what had been the hardest and fastest of classical conclusions.

THE LABOUR THEORY OF VALUE

From the earliest days of economics, the question of what created 'value' in the goods and services bought and sold was ongoing. With the influence of the *Wealth of Nations* came the acceptance of the notion that value of a good or service was in some way related to the amount of labour that was embodied in each item of production. Thus, Smith wrote:

> Labour was the first price, the original purchase-money that was paid for all things. It was not by gold or by silver, but by labour, that all the wealth of the world was originally purchased; and its value, to those who possess it, and who want to exchange it for some new productions, is precisely equal to the quantity of labour which it can enable them to purchase or command. (Smith, [1776] 1976, Book I, Chapter 5)

And then as the conclusion of an extended argument: 'Labour, therefore, it appears evidently, is the only universal, as well as the only accurate measure of value, or the only standard by which we can compare the values of different commodities at all times and at all places.'

Money, Smith argues, is the medium through which goods and services exchange, but relative monetary values represent the amount of labour found in the various products. It has been argued that in Smith's time, before the growth of the huge enterprises we now associate with the nineteenth century, labour may have been a reasonable proxy for the exchange value of goods and services. Be that as it may, it was at some level that labour was seen to embody the goods and services produced with their relative worth. It was this conclusion that was referred to as the Labour Theory of Value (LTV).

Ricardo took up the LTV although was somewhat troubled by the obvious inconsistencies that had arisen by the start of the nineteenth century. But he nevertheless endorsed some version of the LTV in his 1817 *Principles*. There he wrote: 'The value of a commodity, or the quantity of any other commodity for which it will exchange, depends on the relative quantity of labour which is necessary for its production, and not as the greater or less compensation which is paid for that labour' (Ricardo, [1817] 1951–73).

MARX AND THE LABOUR THEORY OF VALUE

But it was the extension of these concepts to the notion of the division of output amongst the three classes that would become the basis for socialist and Marxist agitation. There are land owners, workers and capitalists who earn profits, rents and wages. But the only source of value, according to Ricardo, was labour. Ricardo wrote: 'It is not by the absolute quantity of produce obtained by either class, that we can correctly judge of the rate of profit, rent, and wages, but by the quantity of labour required to obtain that produce.' (Ricardo, [1817] 1951–73)

It was from this that the socialist and then later the Marxist theory of the exploitation of the worker took much of its drive. If all value came from labour, that is from the efforts made by workers, then the profits earned by the capitalists in running their businesses are unjustifiable incomes taken from the worker who had created all of the value but did not receive all of the return. This became, in Marx's hands, the theory of surplus value. It is, in essence, a theory in which the entrepreneur creates no value and can therefore be discarded.

Marx's two main works were the *Communist Manifesto* which was published in 1848, and his *Capital*, the first volume of which was published in 1867. *Capital* was his major work of economics in which the issue of capitalist exploitation of the worker was laid out in what would eventually become three massive volumes of near-unreadable prose. The following is part of Marx's discussion of the theory of surplus value, which is presented only as an example of the way in which the book was written. It is to be looked at only for its interest as a specimen of Marx's style of writing – do not attempt to make sense of what it says.

> We have seen that the labourer, during one portion of the labour-process, produces only the value of his labour-power . . . The portion of his day's labour devoted to this purpose, will be greater or less, in proportion to the value of the necessaries that he daily requires on an average, or, equivalently, in proportion to the labour-time required on an average to produce them. During the second period of the labour-process, that in which his labour is no longer necessary labour, the workman, it is true, labours, expends labour-power; but his labour, being no longer necessary labour, he creates no value for himself. He creates surplus-value which, for the capitalist, has all the charms of a creation out of nothing. This portion of the working-day, for a definite period of time, I name surplus labour-time, and to the labour expended during that time, I give the name of surplus-labour. (Marx, [1867] 1918)

In the history of world politics, Marx's writings have been as influential as anything ever written. They created what became revolutionary movements in one country after another, and Marx's writings remain influential still both in practical politics and amongst social theories in every area aside from economics.

In terms of economics, however, so far as the mainstream economic theories found in market economies are concerned, Marx has had, and continues to have, almost no influence. Marx is seen as part of the classical tradition of Smith and Ricardo and is not associated with the developments in economic theories that have occurred since then. The Labour Theory of Value, which is embedded in Marx, was discarded during the next major development in economics, and as a result there has been little penetration of Marxist thinking into economic theory in general or in the market oriented economies of the West.

THE BREAKDOWN OF THE CLASSICAL SCHOOL

As the industrial revolution gained momentum, the economics of Smith–Ricardo–Mill, the classical school, were no longer capable of providing a sufficient basis for either understanding economic issues or in providing practical policy advice. At the centre of this break was the theory of value that had been at the core of the classical economists. The Labour Theory of Value simply could no longer even pretend to give an account of the relative prices of the goods and services sold on the market. The growth and prevalence of massive industrial businesses, whose most obvious characteristics were the immense amounts of physical capital that were built into the costs of production, rendered impossible any theory based on the assumption that relative values were based on relative labour content.

The development of massive industrial structures also destroyed the basis for *laissez-faire*, that is the notion that one could safely leave economic activity to the market without government involvement and regulation. When Smith and Ricardo wrote, industrial enterprises were small and generally non-intrusive. By the middle of the nineteenth century, the complex industrial societies which had arisen demanded the imposition of social controls to limit their impact. These issues have been very well described in the following passage:

> The 'market' model of Civil Society may be applicable to the very special conditions prevailing in eighteenth-century Britain, in the course of the first emergence of industrial society. Those conditions included the existence of, above all, a fairly feeble technology, one just about capable of improving significantly on traditional methods of production, and making sustained innovation appear attractive, but not capable of very much more. A feeble technology of such a kind can be given its head and it will not disrupt either the social order or the environment, or at any rate not too much. Compare this with the technology

available at present: any unrestricted use of it would – and quite possibly will
– lead to a total disruption of the environment and the social order. The indirect consequences of modern technology are terrifying. Moreover, technical
innovation is often on a very large scale and irreversible. In brief, both its scale
and its consequences are such that they cannot but concern society as a whole.'
(Gellner, 1994: 89)

Economic theory needed a means to think clearly about these questions but without also abandoning the desirability of organizng economic
activity around the actions of the entrepreneur. The growth of output per
person and the astonishing increases in per capita incomes demonstrated
the powerful forces that had been put into play by the capitalist modes
of production. What was needed was a theoretical structure that would
preserve the role of the entrepreneur while providing governments with a
technical apparatus that would guide the structuring of a sound regulatory
environment.

Also, under the pressure of socialist agitation, and especially because of
the Labour Theory of Value, there had been immense political pressures
that had developed over the distribution of incomes. If all value came from
labour, what justification could there be for earning profits? For the mass
of workers, although their real standard of living was rising, there was a
desire for an even larger slice of the income available. Economics therefore
needed to provide a theory which explained the role of the entrepreneur
and which showed that entrepreneurial incomes were not exploitation,but
a return for value-adding input.

Beyond this were the many conflicts of interest that became more and
more evident as industrial society became entrenched. In feudal aristocratic societies, most people had their place in society set at birth. But by
the time of the industrial revolution, this aristocratic division of political
power had almost completely broken down. How to resolve differences
between individuals and groups over economic questions became a more
and more important question.

Externalities

Many questions then arose surrounding the problems that would eventually
be described as '*externalities*'. In an industrial society, where the indirect
consequences of modern technologies are potentially devastating, a means
was required to assess more comprehensively not just the costs and benefits
of buyers and sellers, but the effects of those who are not even involved in
the transactions. A seller of a good or service whose production pollutes air
and water but at no costs to themselves is creating damage for those who
are harmed by the production process but receive no direct benefits.

The buyers of these goods and services are made better off by the product but the costs they are made to bear are only the direct costs of production – the resources, labour and capital used up. They are not asked to compensate those who have been harmed by the increased pollution as well as other forms of harm. There is thus a third party to the industrial process: those who are damaged by production but who are not considered during the normal operation of market processes since they are neither buyers of the product nor suppliers.

It thus became apparent that such externalities had to be taken into consideration by economists and embodied in economic theory. Without recognition of the effect of economic activity on third parties, economic activity would not accurately reflect the desires of the community for various goods and services, nor would prices properly reflect the actual costs of production.

MARGINAL REVOLUTION

It is frequently argued that what set this reconstruction of economic theory in motion was a passage found in the *Wealth of Nations*. Smith had written in 1776 about what has since been described as the diamond–water paradox:

> The things which have the greatest value in use have frequently little or no value in exchange; and on the contrary, those which have the greatest value in exchange have frequently little or no value in use. Nothing is more useful than water: but it will purchase scarce anything; scarce anything can be had in exchange for it. A diamond, on the contrary, has scarce any value in use; but a very great quantity of other goods may frequently be had in exchange of it. (Smith, [1776] 1976)

This was a return to the question of the sources of value. From where did value come? Why were diamonds expensive but almost useless, while water cost nothing but was necessary for life?

The answer was supplied during the first years of the 1870s with the almost simultaneous publication of three different works in three different languages, each of which supplied more or less the same answer. In England and in English, the answer was supplied by William Stanley Jevons in his *Theory of Political Economy*. In German, Carl Menger paved the way and in French, Léon Walras was the economist who began this revolutionary shift. All modern economics has descended through the concepts that were first put forward then by these three. Here we will concentrate on the approach taken by Jevons.

For Jevons, the value of a product was determined by how much one already had. Sale price was therefore determined by the price that could be charged for the *final* unit sold. Moreover, it was the personal estimation of the buyer that determined value, not some external source such as labour. It was utility, and in particular, the final or *marginal utility* that determined value. With diamonds, because they are so scarce, only those uses for which people would be willing to pay high prices can be satisfied. With water, on the other hand, because of its abundance in normal times, its use in keeping us alive is satisfied by the first amounts we use but, by the end, the value we receive in each time period from additional units of water is so low there is hardly any amount of money we are willing to pay for that last unit of water we use. Pricing was done 'at the margin'.

If, as Jevons wrote, value 'depends entirely upon utility' then all value is determined on the demand side of the economy. The classical economists had been production-oriented in their thinking about how economies evolved. By placing value onto the demand side, a very different perspective developed.

Marginal analysis then became the core of economic theory and was applied in more and more situations. In dealing with incomes, it was argued that each person receives as their income the value of their marginal product. That is, they receive the value of their own contribution to the production process. Therefore, because wage earners are not the sole producers of output, their return is only equal to the value of what they produced. Similarly, those who run business firms, the entrepreneurs, they too receive the value of their own contribution to total output.

This was the answer to Marx's Labour Theory of Value. Distribution of incomes was related to contribution to production. Labour received a fair return for its efforts which was related to the value of the output it had been responsible for creating. The goods produced have value only because those who buy them are willing to repay the costs of production. Wages, through supply and demand, would adjust to ensure that the return was equitable at least so far as the level of national productivity was concerned. Similarly, the owners of capital would receive their own return, which was justified by their having caused capital to come into existence and in the specific forms that would create the greatest amount of value. Those who built and owned the capital would receive their own fair return that was again related to the value of the final product on the market.

But the most important consequence of the marginal revolution was that the focus was concentrated more and more onto individual decision making rather than the theory of national wealth and prosperity. Although not described using the more modern term, microeconomics, the consequence of the marginal revolution was the development of that side of economic theory. At the core of the individual approach were the theories that related to marginal revenue and marginal cost.

THE THEORY OF THE BUSINESS CYCLE

Yet for all of the increased focus on individual decision making, the theory of the business cycle was being developed to build greater understanding of the causes of economic fluctuations and variations in the level of employment. In many ways, the cycle was seen as representing the not insubstantial cost of the tremendous net good achieved by market forces. A typical example put the argument this way:

> Believing as I do, in Competition, although fully aware, from personal experience, of its frequent hardship to the individual, I cannot see anything but a vast balance of good in a system which throws the weight of the competitive struggle on capital and organising brains – that is, on the factors most able to bear it – while it does so much for the consumer and the worker classes. (Smart, 1906: vii–viii)

The business cycle discussed what was straightforwardly obvious. Economies were cyclical in their level of activity. There were periods of prosperity, rapid growth and high employment which were followed by periods of recession, often deep recession, where economies slowed and employment fell. The pain that arose during the downturn in the cycle was offset by the good that came during periods of strong rates of growth.

A theory of the cycle had, however, developed with the intention of first explaining the causes of recessions and then with the growth of knowledge of the underlying dynamic, thereafter devising a programme to limit the depth and duration of the downward phase.

In Adam Smith there is already recognition that there are variations between periods in the level of activity and employment, and this was before there had even been anything like the full development of an industrial civilization in which a general downturn in activity would become a regular feature of economies. It was only during the first half of the nineteenth century that it became evident that economies were subject to regularly recurring downwards and upwards periods of recession and prosperity.

The theories of recession economists had developed were based on acceptance that the different phases of the cycle were interrelated. The downturn would contain the seeds of the future upturn just as periods of prosperity would lay the groundwork for the subsequent recession. The one aspect all agreed on was that, following Say's Law, whatever might be the cause of recession and unemployment, it would not be demand deficiency. Economies would never enter recession due to a lack of demand.

SAY'S LAW IN THE 1920S

Because these economic principles are associated with an economist whose books were written during the early years of the nineteenth century, there is a tendency to consider that these views were already musty and ancient when Keynes came to write his own economic analysis. In actual fact, the principles which underlay Say's Law remained an intrinsic part of economics throughout the nineteenth century and well into the twentieth.

The very phrase 'Say's Law' is itself twentieth century in origin. It was in a textbook written for his own students by the economist Fred Taylor and published in the 1920s that the term was first used. There he discussed the universally accepted principles associated with aggregate demand during the 1920s. In discussing these issues, Taylor wrote:

> Among the fallacious notions in popular thinking that have gained very wide currency are to be found a number which grew out of misconceptions as to the real source of the *general or total demand for goods*, and as to the methods by which that demand is increased or diminished. Several types of these fallacious notions may be cited. Thus, **governmental improvements of all kinds, including even those of questionable value, are often supported by business men and others on the ground that such improvements increase the total demand for goods**. (Taylor, 1925: 196, emphasis in bold added)

Taylor traced the refutation of this argument back to the early classical writers, and to J.B. Say in particular. He therefore explicitly states that this is why he has given the proper principle showing the identity of aggregate supply and aggregate demand the name 'Say's Law'. The first sentence of the passage, given that this is the precise reverse of modern economic theory, is especially ironic since Taylor emphasizes that at the time of writing the notions behind these principles were perfectly obvious to everyone:

> The points just brought out with respect to the relation between demand and the output of goods are so evident that some will consider it scarcely legitimate to give them the dignity derived from formal statement. On the other hand, the continued prevalence throughout the larger part of the community of the fallacious notions which these considerations are designed to correct seems to furnish ample ground for any procedure which gives these points adequate emphasis. I shall therefore put the proposition we have discussed in the form of a principle. This principle, I have taken the liberty to designate Say's Law;

because, though recognized by many earlier writers, it was particularly well brought out in the presentation of Say (1803). (ibid.: 201)

And what is this principle?

> **Principle** – Say's Law. The Ultimate Identity of Demand and Product.
> In the last analysis, the demand for goods produced for the market consists of goods produced for the market, i.e., the same goods are at once the demand for goods and the supply of goods; so that; if we can assume that producers have directed production in true accord with one another's wants, total demand must in the long run coincide with the total product or output of goods produced for the market. (ibid.: 201–202)

Taylor makes the qualification, 'if we can assume that producers have directed production in true accord with one another's wants', that is, if we can assume that producers have made no errors in what they choose to produce but have correctly anticipated what others will demand, then total demand must coincide with total production. They are then exactly the same. In aggregate, the demand for goods and services is funded by the supply of goods and services. That is all that can exchange because that is all there is.

Recessions are caused by a failure of producers to anticipate correctly what others will demand. The theory of the cycle, which explained the causes of recession, were based on explaining why businesses in general might fail to anticipate what consumers would demand.

KEYNESIAN REVOLUTION

The essence of the next major revolution in economics was the overturning of Say's Law by the English economist, John Maynard Keynes (which rhymes with brains, as he used to say). What made Keynes's arguments so formidable was that he, like Malthus, was at the time he wrote, the single most famous economist in the world.

Malthus's fame had come from his writing *On Population*. Keynes had become equally famous for having written *The Economic Consequences of the Peace* at the end of World War I (Keynes, 1920). The book had argued that Germany would be driven into national bankruptcy by the allied demand that it pay reparations to the French for the damage the German army had caused while camped on French soil and occupying the northern half of France from 1914 to 1918. *The Economic Consequences of the Peace* had been a worldwide best seller that had made Keynes famous over night. He remained the world's most famous and influential economist in 1936 when he would publish a book that would change the way in which recessions are understood and policies would thereafter be designed.

The Keynesian Revolution overturned the principles that underlay the actual set of beliefs that had been held by classical economists on the causes of the business cycle and the means for dealing with such downturns by substituting his own straw man version of Say's Law. It is these conclusions which are now embedded in macroeconomic theory and therefore also in macroeconomic policy right up to the present time.

11.   The Keynesian Revolution and Say's Law

The Keynesian Revolution, and therefore the origins of virtually all macroeconomic theory today, can only be understood in relation to Keynes's coming across Malthus's economic writings in 1932. In particular, it was his reading of the Malthus side of the Malthus–Ricardo correspondence, which had been unearthed in 1930 by his close associate Piero Sraffa, that turned Keynes's mind to the possibility of demand deficiency as a cause of recession. Until that time, economists had been near unanimous in arguing that insufficient demand as a cause of recession was fallacious.

There has been universal recognition amongst historians of thought that something does happen in late 1932 to turn Keynes in a new direction. Yet not one of the works devoted either to understanding the nature of the Keynesian revolution nor to examining the road between the *Treatise on Money* published in 1930 and the *General Theory* published in 1936, has suggested that the reason for this change in focus occurs specifically because Keynes was at that time updating his essay on Malthus for inclusion in a collection of his biographical writings. Indeed, there is no reason given of any kind why at that particular moment Keynes came to the conclusion that demand deficiency was the missing link in the theory of the cycle.

Yet it is as close to a certainty as one can have in such reconstructions that Keynes would never have written the *General Theory* as he did, focusing on demand deficiency, had he not become deeply interested at the end of 1932 in Malthus's economic writings. It was Malthus, of course, who had been the leading advocate in the nineteenth century of demand deficiency as a cause of recession and of increased levels of unproductive spending as the cure. Reading Malthus's letters to Ricardo, and then the text of Chapter VII of Malthus's *Principles*, ought to be recognized as the single most important reason why Keynes was to write what he wrote in the way he did.

Recognizing that this was the inspiration should make it easier to understand what the intent of the *General Theory* was and to understand the nature of the change in economic theory that occurs as a result. In the *General Theory* Keynes is very clear about what he has learned from reading Malthus.

The idea that we can safely neglect the aggregate demand function is fundamental to the Ricardian economics, which underlie what we have been taught for more than a century. Malthus, indeed, had vehemently opposed Ricardo's doctrine *that it was impossible for effective demand to be deficient*; but vainly. For, since Malthus was unable to explain clearly (apart from an appeal to the facts of common observation) *how and why effective demand could be deficient* or excessive, he failed to furnish an alternative construction; and Ricardo conquered England as completely as the Holy Inquisition conquered Spain. Not only was his theory accepted by the city, by statesmen and by the academic world. But controversy ceased; the other point of view completely disappeared; it ceased to be discussed. *The great puzzle of Effective Demand* with which Malthus had wrestled vanished from the economic literature. (Keynes [1936] 1987: 32, emphasis added.)

It was the 'great puzzle of Effective Demand' that Malthus had been wrestling with which had disappeared, and it was this that Keynes was intent on restoring to economic theory.

Nor was Keynes wrong on the implications of Say's Law to his contemporaries. It is precisely this issue that is the dividing line between pre-Keynesian economics and the economics that has dominated theory ever since. Mainstream economists before 1936 had actively denied any role for aggregate demand in understanding the business cycle. Although there had been some attempts to overturn the law of markets, demand deficiency as an explanation for recession was until then almost entirely the province of cranks. The two most important diagrammatic innovations of the 1930s were known as the 'IS–LM' curves published by Hicks in 1937, and the 'Keynesian-cross' diagram first published by Paul Samuelson in 1939. Both were developed in response to Keynes's *General Theory* and both feature in economics texts to this day.

The problem of recession as conceived in the *General Theory* was that an economy, once it has passed a certain level of production, will run out of demands for the goods and services it produces. This is not excess supply for individual goods and services, the 'particular glut' whose existence no one had ever denied, but an actual excess supply of all goods taken together, that is, a 'general glut'. Keynes made the possibility of demand failure the culminating point at the end of the introductory chapters of the *General Theory*.

The celebrated *optimism* of traditional economic theory, which has led to economists being looked upon as Candides, who, having left this world for the cultivation of their gardens, teach that all is for the best in the best of all possible worlds provided we will let well alone, is also to be traced, I think, to their having neglected to take account of **the drag on prosperity which can be exercised by an insufficiency of effective demand**. (ibid.: 33, emphasis in bold added)

The possibility of a failure of effective demand is the very point behind the theory taught to students to this day. It is taught to undergraduate economists worldwide, and is embedded almost universally in economic policies designed to pull economies out of recession. And while other possible explanations for recession are now usually discussed as well, demand failure remains the single most important concept most economists are taught in relation to the causes of recession and involuntary unemployment. It is the argument that recessions can best be understood as occurring because of a fall in aggregate demand that continues to mark economic theory to this day, along with the implication that stimulating demand through deficit spending is a valid and useful approach to take in dealing with recessions when and where they occur.

Aggregate demand is intrinsic to the modern understanding of the level of economic activity. The implication is that it is the level of aggregate demand that is responsible for the level of output, the rate of economic growth and the number of persons employed. An insufficient level of aggregate demand is held generally responsible for high levels of unemployment and it is almost universally accepted that deficit-financed public spending can permanently raise the level of output and thereby lower the rate of unemployment. There is an aggregate supply curve associated with aggregate demand, but its principal role is the determination of the rate of inflation. Production levels are not determined by supply capabilities but by the willingness of individuals to buy what has been produced with the incomes they have received.

Indeed, the issue went farther than this. Keynes argued that if Say's Law were valid, continuing and persistent unemployment simply could not occur, and this was unrecognized by classical economists whom he was about to correct. As he wrote:

> *Say's law*, that the aggregate demand price of output as a whole is equal to its aggregate supply price for all volumes of output, *is equivalent to the proposition that there is no obstacle to full employment*. If, however, this is not the true law relating the aggregate demand and supply functions, there is a vitally important chapter of economic theory which remains to be written and without which all discussions concerning the volume of aggregate employment are futile. (ibid.: 26, emphasis added.)

For the vast majority of the economics profession even now, this is the way in which Say's Law and its implications are understood.

UNDERSTANDING SAY'S LAW: MALTHUS AND THE 'GENERAL GLUT' DEBATE

What is relevant about Say's Law cannot be contained within a single statement. Say's Law, if it is to be understood in full, must be understood as a series of related propositions which, when taken together, constitute the basic ingredients of the classical theory of the cycle. The most extraordinary of the many ironies that have surrounded this issue since Keynes first pronounced on it in 1936 is that Say's Law was the foundation stone within classical theory for understanding why a cycle exists at all. Keynes's argument was that belief in Say's Law meant that classical economists assumed there was never at any stage an obstacle to full employment. The reality is that Say's Law was an integral part of the explanation why in fact unemployment actually occurred.

Keynes, in attacking 'Say's Law' in 1936 was not attacking some one-sentence statement of principle. In attacking Say's Law, he was attacking the entire classical theory of the cycle. Unless this is understood, it is impossible to understand in full exactly what Keynes was able to do. The propositions associated with Say's Law need to be seen as the constituent elements of the classical theory of the cycle and to understand why this was so, it is necessary to enter into some of the early history of economic theory itself.

What became the classical theory of the cycle was formed during what is now known as the 'General Glut' debate that lasted from the publication of Malthus's *Principles of Political Economy* in 1820 through until John Stuart Mill published his own *Principles of Political Economy* in 1848. What in particular distinguished Malthus's arguments from virtually all other writings on economic issues at the time was his belief that the recessions experienced by England at the end of the Napoleonic Wars had been caused by oversaving and demand deficiency. And so a debate was commenced across the whole of the economics community of the time, with a raft of books on economic theory published over whether there could be an excess supply of all goods and services taken together.

Importantly, it was not a debate over whether recessions and large-scale unemployment were possible. On this there was obviously unanimity. The only question was whether recessions, when they occurred, were the result of too much saving and too little effective demand. That this could never be a realistic explanation was ultimately accepted by the whole of the mainstream of the economics community.

Moreover, during classical times there was no economic principle known as 'Say's Law'. As discussed in the previous chapter, the term would not be coined until the twentieth century nor enter economic discourse until the 1920s. There was Jean-Baptiste Say's *théorie des débouchés*, known in English as the 'law of markets', which stated that demand was constituted by supply. It was the law of markets that was employed as part of the response to Malthus's views but as only one strand in a far more complex series of counter-arguments. It was a crucially important part of the argument, but it was only one of the arguments in a longer chain of reasoning. It was the entire set of counter-arguments that, when taken together, became the related propositions that formed the classical theory of the cycle. Leaving Say's Law in Keynes's vague and imprecise form of words – 'supply creates its own demand' – not only reverses the point that classical economists had tried to make – that demand in real terms can only be derived through the production of value-adding goods and services – but ignores every other related aspect that was central to an understanding of the classical theory of the cycle.

By discrediting the crucially central idea that demand is formed on the supply side of the economy, the related propositions that had emerged from the debate over Malthus lost their coherence. The publication of the *General Theory* caused the entire classical perspective on the business cycle to disappear. The propositions presented below are therefore intended to reassemble the arguments that were at the core of pre-Keynesian business cycle theory and need to be seen as the full meaning of Say's Law as it emerged during the General Glut debate. They are also put in a form so that the entire argument can be seen as a full and complete response not just to Keynes and the arguments of the *General Theory*, but also as a reply to modern macroeconomics to the extent that it continues to rely on demand deficiency to explain why recessions occur.

THE RELATED PROPOSITIONS OF SAY'S LAW

What follow are the related propositions which make up Say's Law. These were integral components of classical thought and must be appreciated to follow the classical theory of the cycle. They were accepted by the entire mainstream of the profession.

Proposition 1: Recessions are never due to demand deficiency

This is the starting point for any understanding of the pre-Keynesian theory of recession and Say's Law. Four examples of how this statement was an integral part of economic theory across the entire classical period, written by three of the greatest economists who have ever lived, will help put the law of markets into its proper context.

First Adam Smith. He specifically denies that there is any danger from oversaving and that a community has anything to fear from the saving of its more provident members. It was this argument that Keynes specifically set out to deny.

> What is annually saved is as regularly consumed as what is annually spent, and nearly in the same time too; but it is consumed by a different set of people. That portion of his revenue which a rich man annually spends, is in most cases consumed by idle guests, and menial servants, who leave nothing behind them in return for their consumption. That portion which he annually saves, as for the sake of the profit it is immediately employed as a capital, is consumed in the same manner, and nearly in the same time too, but by a different set of people, by labourers, manufacturers, and artificers, who reproduce with a profit the value of their annual consumption. His revenue we shall suppose, is paid him in money. Had he spent the whole, the food, clothing, and lodging, which the whole could have purchased, would have been distributed among the former set of people. By saving a part of it, as that part is for the sake of profit immediately employed as capital either by himself or by some other person, the food, clothing and lodging, which may be purchased with it, are necessarily reserved for the latter. The consumption is the same, but the consumers are different. (Smith [1776] 1976: 359)

A second example is Alfred Marshall, writing in a publication co-authored with his wife, Mary Paley Marshall, in 1879. Here it is made abundantly clear that deficient aggregate demand is not the proper explanation for depression.

> After every crisis, in every period of commercial depression, it is said that supply is in excess of demand. Of course there may easily be an excessive supply of some particular commodities; so much cloth and furniture and cutlery may have been made that they cannot be sold at a remunerative price. But something more than this is meant. For after a crisis the warehouses are overstocked with goods in almost every important trade; scarcely any trade can continue undiminished production so as to afford a good rate of profits to capital and a good rate of wages to labour. And it is thought that this state of things is one of general over-production. We shall however find that it really is nothing but a state of commercial disorganisation. (Marshall and Marshall [1879] 1881: 154)

And lest it be thought that this is the early Alfred Marshall which was later subsumed by a different point of view, in a section introduced into the fifth edition of the *Principles* in 1907 he emphatically made the point again. Note that problems on the demand side are seen only to exacerbate a problem that has been due to other causes.

> It is true that in times of depression the disorganization of consumption is a contributory cause to the continuance of the disorganization of credit and of

production. But a remedy is not to be got by a study of consumption, as has been alleged by some hasty writers. (Marshall, [1920] 1947: 711n)

Finally, Friedrich Hayek. His 1931 article, 'The "paradox" of saving', is a full-scale discussion, more than 40 pages in length, on the arguments of two economists who had argued during the 1920s and 1930s that over-saving was the cause of recessions. Hayek's opening paragraph is not only an attack on the belief that excess saving is a cause of recession, but he also specifically refers to the *théorie des débouchés* as providing the appropriate position. It is nothing other than a straightforward statement of the classical position. Hayek wrote:

> The assertion that saving renders the purchasing power of the consumer insufficient to take up the volume of current production although made more often by members of the lay public than by professional economists, is almost as old as the science of political economy itself. The question of the utility of 'unproductive' expenditure was first raised by the Mercantilists, who were thinking chiefly of luxury expenditure. The idea recurs in those writings of Lauderdale and Malthus *which gave rise to the celebrated* Théorie des Débouchés *of James Mill and J. B. Say,* and in spite of many attempts to refute it, permeates the main doctrines of socialist economics. . . . But while in this way the idea has found a greater popularity in quasi-scientific and propagandist literature than perhaps any other economic doctrine hitherto, fortunately it has not succeeded as yet in depriving saving of its general respectability. (Hayek, 1931, emphasis added)

It is highly noteworthy that it was only five years later that the *General Theory* would in fact do what Hayek had feared, and 'deprive saving of its general respectability'.

Proposition 2: Demand is created by supply and by nothing else

This proposition is a restatement of Jean-Baptiste Say's original *théorie des débouchés*, wrongly characterized by Keynes as 'supply creates its own demand'. Moreover, the statement that demand is created by supply may be the most important concept in coming to grips with the classical theory of the cycle, but because it is so foreign to modern macroeconomic thought, it may also be the most difficult. Yet it was fully accepted by pre-Keynesian economists.

Here is James Mill, in the first presentation during the early years of the nineteenth century of what would become the classical theory of cycle, explaining the significance of this principle. He could not be more emphatic nor does he leave any doubt about just how crucial he believes this principle to be.

No proposition however in political economy seems to be more certain than this which I am going to announce, how paradoxical soever it may at first sight appear; and if it is true, none undoubtedly can be deemed of more importance. The production of commodities creates, and is the one universal cause which creates a market for the commodities produced. (Mill, [1808] 1966: 135)

Moving forward a century, the same concept is found in the following passage from one of the most widely used economic texts ever published, in which this principle is stated in very clear terms:

It is only because our exchanges are made through money that we have any difficulty in perceiving that an increase in supply is (not 'causes') an increase in demand. . . . An increase in the supply of cloth is an increase in the demand for other things; and *vice versa*, an increase in the supply of anything else may constitute a demand for cloth. What is divided among the members of society is the goods and services produced to satisfy its wants; and the same goods and services are both Supply and Demand. (Clay, [1916] 1924: 242)

The notion of aggregate demand separate from aggregate supply was foreign to pre-Keynesian economic thought. Aggregate demand grows at the same rate and by the same amount as aggregate supply, and will not grow unless supply has grown. It is not, however, just any production that will lead to an increase in aggregate demand. What creates demand is the production of forms of output for which enough buyers can be found to cover in aggregate the entire costs of production. Only if the goods and services produced can be sold for more than was paid for the inputs that went into their production can it be said with certainty that value has been added during the production process. Conversely, if the goods and services produced do not create more value than is used up in the production process, there can be no increase in aggregate demand because there has been no increase in aggregate supply in any relevant sense.

Proposition 3: The process involved in purchase and sale is the conversion of one's own goods or services into money and then the re-conversion of the money one has received back into other goods and services. There is no implication of a barter economy. Money is intrinsic to the processes involved.

At the very core of the classical propositions surrounding Say's Law is an appreciation that money is infused with value only by being received in exchange for value-adding production. The process is one that may be characterized in the formula $C–M–C'$ where the set of goods or services in one's own possession (C) is converted into a different set of goods or services (C') by the sale of what one owns for money (M) and then the reconversion of the money received into what one wishes to buy. Keynes had accused classical economists of confusing a barter economy with the operation of a money economy, but from the first statements on Say's Law by Say himself, that had never been the case. Here is J.B. Say, in the fourth edition of his *Treatise*, trying to explain the obvious.

> Should a tradesman say, 'I do not want other products for my woollens, I want money', there could be little difficulty in convincing him that his customers could not pay him in money, without having first procured it by the sale of some other commodities of their own. . . . You say, you only want money; I say, you want other commodities, and not money. . . . To say that sales are dull, owing to the scarcity of money, is to mistake the means for the cause; an error that proceeds from the circumstance, that almost all produce is in the first instance exchanged for money, before it is ultimately converted into other produce. (Say, 1821)

But more importantly, the process lay in ensuring that those who produced made sure that they created value in the process. Demand was only constituted by the value added that arose from the sale of goods or services to others. If output could not be sold at prices which repaid the costs of production, then no value added had occurred. That this frequently did take place provided the core insight into the classical theory of the cycle. That demand was built on productive activities was also pointed out by the economist Ludwig von Mises, who was explicitly following Say in making this point:

> Commodities, says Say, are ultimately paid for not by money, but by other commodities. Money is merely the commonly used medium of exchange; it plays only an intermediary role. What the seller wants ultimately to receive in exchange for the commodities sold is other commodities. (Mises, [1950] 1980)

To understand demand being constituted by supply, it is necessary to recognize that in a properly functioning economy, purchases are effected by the revenue from the previous sale of goods and services or with money borrowed from others who have earned incomes by producing. For those who earned their incomes from the sale of goods and services, the process is direct. The creation of value and the sale of what had been produced provided the income for the purchase of other goods and services. For businesses investing borrowed funds, the purchases are effected through the transfer of funds through a saving–investment process. For governments, purchases are effected through revenues raised through taxation of the incomes of those who had sold goods or services to the market.

Proposition 4: Recessions are common and result in high levels of involuntary unemployment

It really ought to be unnecessary to point out that this proposition ought to be completely non-controversial. It really ought to have been inconceivable to have suggested, as Keynes did in 1936, that economists until then had had no explicit theory of involuntary unemployment and recession. Yet one of the consequences of the publication of the *General Theory* was the belief that classical economists had no theories to account for recessions and involuntary unemployment. It is therefore necessary to make the explicit statement that classical economists did indeed have such theories of recession and they most assuredly did understand that involuntary unemployment was a frequent feature of economic life. The theory of the business cycle had been developing for over a century by that stage, so that for Keynes to have stated of his fellow economists that they had no theory of involuntary unemployment was absurd.

A compendium of all of the theories of the cycle is found in a League of Nations publication by Gottfried Haberler, titled *Prosperity and Depression* whose first edition was published in 1937, the year following the publication of the *General Theory*. The first words of the Preface ought to make it absolutely plain that recession and unemployment were amongst the most important questions under examination by the economics community of the world during the 1930s, and had been for generations:

> This book has its origin in a resolution adopted by the Assembly of the League of Nations in September 1930 by which it was decided that an attempt should be made to co-ordinate the analytical work then being done on the problem of the recurrence of periods of economic depression.
>
> The literature concerning economic depressions and what is currently and somewhat loosely described as the trade cycle is abundant. . . . It is apparent from the persistence with which depressions occur, from the gravity of their economic and social effects, and from the growing consciousness of that gravity, that – however abundant the literature on the subject, however elaborate and specious the theories – our knowledge of the causes of depressions has not yet reached a stage at which measures can be designed to avert them. (Haberler, 1937)

That what ought to have been seen as absurdly improbable was nevertheless accepted from the moment it was first published is an issue that demands the attention of historians of ideas. Here it should merely be noted that Keynes's statement, that economists before him had no theories to explain recessions and unemployment, is false as a moment's reflection ought to have led anyone to recognize at the time, just as it ought to be recognized today.

Proposition 5: Recessions are due to structural problems of one kind or another. In particular, recessions occur where the structure of supply does not match the structure of demand.

For anyone basing their understanding of these issues on Keynes's writings, it is something of a surprise to discover that the law of markets was at the very centre of the classical theory of the recession and, in fact, provided the foundation for the theory of the cycle as understood by classical economists. Because demand was constituted by supply, cyclical activity was understood to be the result of individuals and businesses producing what could not be sold at prices which covered costs. Why this might happen was the underlying issue, but that it frequently did happen, of this no one had the slightest doubt. The more than one hundred-year classical literature on the nature and causes of the business cycle written before the *General Theory* was published, is a testament to the recognition that pre-Keynesian economists gave to unemployment and recession.

Torrens, writing in 1821 in a direct response to the arguments presented by Malthus, makes the point as explicitly as it is possible to make it. The classical theory of the cycle was built on these very concepts. Demand is constituted by supply but only so long as supply consists of what those with incomes to spend want to buy. Keeping demand and supply properly proportioned was the imperative, but once that had been achieved, all went well. It was when the proportions were not maintained that recessions would occur. Torrens, in making this point, first notes that there is no possibility that supply will ever outrun demand if producers make the right production decisions.

> So long as the proportion is preserved, every article which the industrious classes have the will and power to produce, will find a ready and profitable vend. No conceivable increase of production can lead to an overstocking of the market. . . . *Increased production will create a proportionally increased demand.* . . . (Torrens, [1821] 1965, emphasis added)

What is particularly notable is that Torrens uses almost the very words Keynes would use to summarize Say's Law. 'Increased production will create a proportionately increased demand' is the lineal ancestor of 'supply creates its own demand'. Torrens is invoking Say's law of markets to show that demand deficiency is never a problem. But he does not conclude from this that economies cannot therefore go into recession or that there are no obstacles to full employment. He instead uses this very principle to explain why recessions occur. Following on from the above passage, Torrens immediately sets out the consequences if something should happen to disturb the balance between the structure of production and the structure of demand.

> This happy and prosperous state of things is immediately interrupted when the proportions in which commodities are produced are such as to disturb the equality between effectual demand and supply. . . . Then gluts and regorgements are experienced.

Even in 1821 Torrens was not the first to make this point, but he made it very well. A lack of proportion between supply and demand is the cause for a descent into recession. The problems of recession are due to structural problems in an economy, not because of a failure of demand. It required an understanding of the law of markets to understand that recessions occur when what has been produced does not coincide with what those with incomes want to buy.

In these passages, Torrens captured the theory that during the following century became the common ground amongst the economics community in discussing the business cycle. Recessions and depressions were due to structural problems. Haberler, in his *Prosperity and Depression*, provided a synopsis of the theory of the cycle as it had been understood until then. In summarizing the views of the economic profession of his time, he wrote:

> An expansion or contraction may be interrupted on the one hand by an accident . . . or it may on the other hand itself give rise to maladjustments in the economic system. . . . Most cycle theorists have tried to prove that the second type of restraining force is all-important. (Haberler, 1937)

This is Torrens once again. It is this maladjustment in the structure of production, where demand and supply are out of proportion with each other, that was the fundamental explanation for recession. Demand deficiency played no part in the process within orthodox theory.[1]

Where demand was crucial was in relation to the structure of demand relative to supply, that is, in situations where what buyers would have been willing to pay the full costs of production for, did not match what suppliers had actually put on the market. Starting from the proposition that demand is constituted by properly proportioned supply, recessions are caused by events that mislead producers into producing goods and services that cannot be sold at cost-covering prices.

Proposition 6: Overproduction of individual goods and services occurs continuously within economies and can lead to a general downturn in an economy

Walter Bagehot, as editor of *The Economist* during the middle years of the nineteenth century, wrote one of the most influential works on the operation of the money market. As part of this work, he included a chapter on the nature of the business cycle, in which he described the evolution of a general downturn built out of a downturn in one part of the economy. Given Keynes's accusation that classical economists had ignored monetary factors and their effects on economic activity, it should not go unnoticed that the following is from Bagehot's *Lombard Street* which had as its subtitle, *A Description of the Money Market*. What Bagehot wrote was this:

> No single large industry can be depressed without injury to other industries; still less can any great group of industries. Each industry when prosperous buys and consumes the produce probably of most (certainly of very many) other industries, and if industry A fail and is in difficulty, industries B, and C, and D, which used to sell to it, will not be able to sell that which they had produced in reliance on A's demand, and in future they will stand idle till industry A recovers, because in default of A there will be no one to buy the commodities which they create. (Bagehot, 1873: 121–2)

The essence of this process is the creation of an economic downturn built upon the systematic failure of producers to sell what they have produced in their own markets. It accepts that when the recovery comes, there may be different firms and industries in different proportions. But the conception that lies behind it is that the pieces in the economy must interlock as firms provide a market for each other with the entire structure ultimately aimed at producing goods and services for final home consumption.

Proposition 7: Monetary factors, most notably structural imbalances in the market for credit, can also be and often are an important cause of recession. Even where monetary instability has not been the originating cause of recession, monetary factors will often deepen a recession brought on for other reasons

It is because Keynes argued that classical economists thought only in terms of real variables that such an obvious statement even needs to be made. It was, in fact, the specific conclusion reached by Becker and Baumol in a landmark 1952 paper that ought to have put this issue to rest for all time, and also to have raised some questions about the foundations of the Keynesian economic theory that had been built on the rejection of so flimsy a straw man. Becker and Baumol could not have been more explicit in dealing with this caricature of classical theory which they labelled 'Say's Identity'. In discussing what they term 'the clearest statement on the point' – in a famous essay published by John Stuart Mill in 1844 – they wrote: 'It is all there and explicitly . . . In reading [Mill's essay] one is led to wonder why so much of the subsequent literature (this paper included) had to be written at all.' (Becker and Baumol, 1952)

Monetary factors can and do cause recession. It is only stating what should be obvious, that classical economists were fully aware that monetary factors were often part of the process even when not the initiating factor in causing recessions to occur.

Proposition 8: Because recessions are not due to a failure of demand, practical solutions to recession do not encompass large increases in the level of public spending

The policy consequences of Keynesian theory have over the years provided ample evidence that on this matter classical economists were correct. There has been no instance of a peacetime increase in public spending during recession that has led to recovery. Reductions in taxation have a different effect on economic outcomes, and can be consistent with classical principles in generating economic growth. Increases in public spending, however, are not. John Stuart Mill's statement is about as clear-cut as one could find.

> The utility of a large government expenditure, for the purpose of encouraging industry, is no longer maintained. . . . It is no longer supposed that you benefit the producer by taking his money, provided you give it to him again in exchange for his goods. (Mill, [1874] 1974)

Since the publication of the *General Theory*, all this has changed round again. The utility of a large government expenditure, for the purpose of encouraging industry, is precisely what is maintained.

UNDERSTANDING THE CLASSICAL THEORY OF THE CYCLE

It was Keynes himself who made it clear that the economics of the *General Theory* was to be seen as a refutation of Say's Law. Recessions, he wrote, were caused by a deficiency of aggregate demand. This was contrary to mainstream classical thought. Classical economists argued that economies are not driven by demand but by value-adding production which is what they referred to as 'supply'. They were virtually unanimous in arguing that raising demand without an increase in the level of value-adding output cannot be an answer to recession and unemployment.

This was summarized by classical economists in various ways: demand is constituted by supply; there is no such thing as a general glut; overproduction is an impossibility. However, the most remarkable short statement, not just on the nature of aggregate demand but also on the related issue of how recessions occur, can be found in Ricardo's reply to Malthus in a personal letter written on 9 October 1820. Ricardo was writing a few months after Malthus's *Principles* had been published:

> 'Men err in their productions, there is no deficiency of demand.' (Ricardo, 1951–73, vol. VIII)

This is, to begin with, a statement on the causes of recession: 'men err in their productions', that is, there is some kind of market disequilibrium which has occurred across the economy. And beyond that, it is a statement of what does not cause recessions: 'there is no deficiency of demand'. Whatever might have caused the recession, it is not due to a lack of demand. What is found in Ricardo's short statement is in summary form the classical theory of recession with its explicit rejection of demand factors as their cause.

Within Ricardo's short and to-the-point statement there is no ambiguity of meaning, none of the uncertainty that currently exists over what 'supply creates its own demand' does or does not mean. Ricardo's brief statement of classical principle means that when recessions occur, they cannot be understood as a consequence of too little demand, but should be understood as some sort of derangement within the market process.

Macroeconomics replaced the classical theory of the cycle in the 1930s and has been Keynesian ever since. No metaphorical statement on the death of Keynes or of Keynesian economics can be true so long as aggregate demand maintains its presence at the core of macroeconomic theory and policy. Because of the near universal acceptance of Keynesian theory within the mainstream, economists have repeatedly formulated policies around the need to stimulate demand during periods of high unemployment. The pervasive presence of the theory of aggregate demand has caused a blackout curtain to fall across the whole of macroeconomic theory, making it all but impossible to understand the underlying workings of an economy or to provide useful advice when recessions occur, as they inevitably must.

NOTE

1. There was, however, an under-consumptionist literature which argued that too little demand from consumers was the systematic cause of economic recession. It was a theory shunned by the mainstream.

12. The basic Keynesian macroeconomic model

The basic macroeconomic model taught across the world is a direct descendant of the economic theory proposed by Keynes in his *General Theory* published in 1936. This is how the original Keynesian explanation for recession worked.

- As income rises the level of consumption rises, but not at the same rate.
- Therefore, the higher the level of income, the greater will be the level of saving, not just in absolute terms but as a proportion of income.
- If the level of output is going to soak up all of the additional savings being generated, investment must also rise at the same rate as savings are rising.
- Business confidence, called 'animal spirits' by Keynes, is the key to business being willing to invest.
- However, the rate of interest will not fall enough to encourage businesses to spend a sufficient amount on investment goods to soak up all of the savings generated. Because of what is termed a 'liquidity trap', not all savings generated at a full employment level of output will be used.
- Therefore, the level of savings will be greater than investment at the level of GDP required to create full employment.
- Therefore, the economy will reach an equilibrium level of GDP even though there are high levels of unemployment.
- The problem is too much saving relative to the willingness of businesses to invest.
- Therefore, the only adequate solution is for governments to increase their own level of spending to soak up the savings that private sector firms have refused to borrow and invest.

Keynes described this as the 'fate of Midas' – that is, a community can become so rich that it ends up being poor. As he wrote:

Of two equal communities, having the same technique but different stocks of capital, the community with the smaller stock of capital may be able for the time being to enjoy a higher standard of life than the community with the larger stock; though when the poorer community has caught up the rich – as, presumably, it eventually will – then both alike will suffer the fate of Midas. (Keynes, [1936] 1987: 219)

Why should a poorer community with less capital enjoy a higher standard of living than a richer one with more capital? Because a rich community will save so much that mass unemployment is the result.

And was this some prospect far down the track when the world had become far richer than it was then? Why no, not at all. It was the very condition of the UK and the US right then, in the period immediately after the end of World War I. Again, this is Keynes in 1936 writing in his *General Theory*:

> The post-war experiences of Great Britain and the United States are, indeed, actual examples of how an accumulation of wealth . . . can interfere, in conditions mainly of *laissez-faire*, with a reasonable level of employment and with the standard of life which the technical conditions of production are capable of furnishing. (Keynes, [1936] 1987: 219)

These countries have become so wealthy that they have become poor. This is the Keynesian message, and the fault lies in the saving that takes place in richer communities.

MAKING SENSE OF THE KEYNESIAN MODEL

Central to macroeconomics is the study of what causes the level of output to deviate from its highest potential level. It therefore attempts to explain why unemployment exists and, almost as an afterthought, it attempts to explain changes in the rate of inflation. Finally, macroeconomics makes a stab at explaining economic growth.

Following Keynes, the single most important element in macroeconomic analysis is *aggregate demand*. In macroeconomics, the driving force behind the level of activity, and therefore the rate of unemployment, is the level of demand in an economy for everything that the economy produces.

Whatever might be the productive potential of an economy, it is the total amount that buyers wish to buy that will determine how close to full employment an economy is.

These buyers are typically divided into a series of classes, the same as those used to calculate the level of GDP using the expenditure approach:

- C: consumers – the purchasers of the end products of the production process;
- I: investors – private sector purchases of assets to be used in the production process;
- G: governments – purchases made by the public sector either as final consumption (as for example the public service) or as investment (such as roads and schools);
- X: exports – purchases made by buyers living in other countries.

This is domestic demand, the total of everything bought in an economy during some period of time. But what is bought includes not just those goods and services produced within the economy but also includes goods and services imported from overseas.

Therefore, just as with the national accounts, to calculate the level of production, from the total level of domestic demand the level of imports must be taken away.

- M: imports – local purchases of goods and services produced in other countries.

The total level of domestically produced goods and services is therefore represented by the following equation. The letter Y stands for GDP or production or national income or output, all of which are seen as equivalent in meaning so far as aggregate economic activity is concerned:

$$Y = C + I + G + X + M$$

That is, total *production* (Y) is equal to everything bought inside the domestic economy ($C + I + G + X$) minus everything imported from other countries ($-M$). Net exports (NX) are defined as exports minus imports ($X - M$). The equation therefore becomes:

$$Y = C + I + G + NX$$

It is this concept and this equation that is at the core of modern macroeconomic theory. The level of production (Y) is dependent on the aggregate level of demand. The higher are the various components, the higher is the level of production with this conclusion: the higher the level of production, the higher will be the level of employment (all other things being, of course, equal).

CIRCULAR FLOW

The busy little diagram in Figure 12.1 provides an approach to understanding the direction of expenditure in a very simplified model. It is not
perfect as a model, but it moves you closer to what needs to be understood.

(1) Start with the 'owners' of the factors of production. These are the
     individuals who supply the market with the various inputs needed to
     produce. There is an arrow that points north, which shows that there
     is a real movement of such inputs from their owners to those who use
     these factors.
(2) These factors of production are land, labour, capital and the activi-
     ties of entrepreneurs. The first three factors – land, labour and capital
     – exist in an extraordinarily large number of forms and are shaped
     into various types of output under the direction and control of entre-
     preneurs who own and run business firms. These businesses produce
     goods and services, some of which are in fact themselves used as
     factors of production by other firms. The remainder are consumption
     goods that are bought by consumers in the current period and then so
     far as economic activity is concerned, disappear from the production
     and spending stream.
(3) Now we must follow the money. In return for the use of the various
     factors, payments are made to their owners. These come in the form
     of, for example, profits, rent, wages and interest. They are a money
     return to their owners. The money in this way comes into the hands

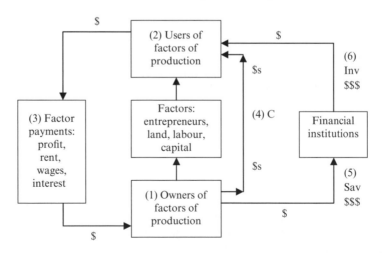

Figure 12.1   Circular flow of income: the basic Keynesian model

of the owners of the factors of production; that is, the factors having originated in Box (1) means that the money payments return to Box (1).

(4) Those who have received this money for their productive efforts must now do something with the money they now have. Some of the money received is spent on consumption goods and goes straight back into the revenue stream of businesses.

(5) Some of the money received, however, is saved and goes to financial institutions of one sort or another.[1] These can be banks, finance houses or whatever. But wherever these funds go, they are presumed not to go straight back into the revenue stream of business. They must first flow through a financial institution where the saving occurs.

(6) If the economy is to retain its current level of output and employment, the money borrowed from financial institutions must be borrowed by others and used for investment purposes. The level of investment spending leaving such financial institutions must be at least as large as the savings that have come in. Otherwise, the level of business receipts, consumption plus investment, will be smaller than the level of incomes paid out at (3).

The circular flow diagram, represents what Keynes was getting at when he wrote the *General Theory*, as simple as the diagram may appear to be.

SAVING IN KEYNESIAN AND CLASSICAL MODELS

The circular flow diagram also presents a simplified means of comparing the Keynesian and the classical models. The Keynesian version is that there are serious impediments caused by the different saving and investment decisions that prevent the circle from being closed. In the classical model, this is never the problem when recessions occur.

The obstacle for Keynes occurs in that box marked 'Financial institutions'. It is into these that savings are directed. The question for Keynes was whether the level of investment going out would be equal to the level of savings going in.

Keynes made the point that those who invest and those who save are different people who make decisions for entirely different reasons. There is therefore no reason to believe that the amount that is saved at a full employment level of output would be anywhere near the amount that investors intended to invest.

Indeed, as far as Keynes was concerned, the likelihood was that the level of saving on the one hand and the intention to invest on the other would diverge at the full employment level of output, with the level of saving normally far exceeding the level of investment.

In the classical model, however, saving and investment would be equilibrated by adjustments to the rate of interest. Interest rate determination was based on the supply and demand for savings. Interest rates would rise or fall to ensure that all savings that became available would be mopped up by the market.

The underlying logic amongst classical economists was that anyone who had income in excess of spending requirements would put those funds into a savings institution of some sort for which they would receive an interest rate return. No such institution could or would pay a positive interest rate return without lending those funds to others at an even higher rate of return. There was therefore a certainty that all savings would be put to work and none would remain uninvested.

It was Keynes's argument that the rate of interest would not fall to its equilibrium level but would remain too high. The result would be an excess supply of saving at the full employment level of output. The result would be that the economy would contract, and as the economy contracted, the level of saving would fall. The economy would eventually contract until the level of saving was equal to the intended level of investment. This was Keynes's 'paradox of thrift'. Higher saving, rather than leading to faster growth, would cause the level of ouput to fall.

Thus, in the classical model, interest rates would adjust until $S = I$. In the Keynesian model, the entire economy would adjust until $S = I$.

In the classical model there would therefore be no unemployment *due to demand deficiency* while in the Keynesian model there often was. In the classical model there were a large number of reasons that an economy might go into unemployment, but demand deficiency was never one of them. In the Keynesian model, all other reasons for recession were ignored, with only demand deficiency being admitted as a cause.

LEAKAGES AND INJECTIONS

To the previous circular flow diagram is now added the government sector, which involves taxes (T) which lower business revenues, and government spending (G) which raises them (see Figure 12.2).

With the introduction of the government, incomes received by the owners of the factors of production are either spent on consumption goods (C), used as savings (S) or paid to governments as taxes (T). These subtractions from the spending stream are given the name *leakages* or *withdrawals*, indicating that they represent a diversion of purchasing power away from buying.

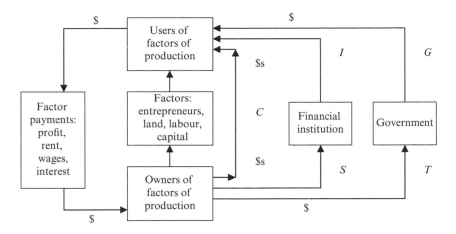

Figure 12.2   Circular flow with government

For businesses, their revenues can now come as spending by consumers on consumer goods and services (*C*), spending by businesses on investment goods (*I*) or as some form of spending by governments on the goods and services sought by the public sector (*G*). These additions to the spending flow are referred to as *injections*.

The equilibrium level of aggregate demand, now made up of *C* + *I* + *G*, is equal to the level of outlays by those earning incomes, which is made up of *C* + *S* + *T*. In equilibrium, the level of consumption drops out on both sides and we are left with equilibrium where *I* + *G* = *S* + *T*.

In the Keynesian framework, however, saving at the full employment level of output can frequently be expected to exceed investment. An important part of the response when such oversaving-induced demand deficiency occurs is to increase the level of public spending to make up the difference. Thus, although savings might be greater than investment, this could be counterbalanced if government spending were greater than taxation.

BRINGING IN THE FOREIGN SECTOR

The final addition required to complete the model is the introduction of the international sector. Not all of the income earned necessarily flows back into domestic firms. Some is spent on goods and services produced in other countries. Such imports (*M*) are another form of leakage as the expenditure of domestically earned incomes disappears from the domestic spending stream.

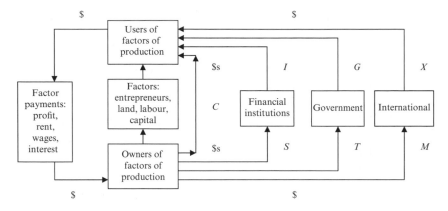

Figure 12.3   Circular flow with international sector

The total use of the funds received can then be listed as consumption (*C*), saving (*S*), taxes paid (*T*) and imports (*M*). That is, *C* + *S* + *T* + *M*.

At the same time, some of the demand for domestic production comes from the international sector. These are a nation's exports (*X*), which are another form of injection. They add to domestic aggregate demand which now totals consumption (*C*) plus saving (*S*) plus investment (*I*) plus exports (*X*). That is, *C* + *I* + *G* + *X*.

Total spending in equilibrium, *C* + *I* + *G* + *X*, is equal to total leakages from the spending stream, made up of *C* + *S* + *T* + *M*. If one again drops *C* from both sides, it can be seen that the equilibrium condition is where:

$$I + G + X = S + T + M$$

The expenditure side of this equation, *I* + *G* + *X*, is the sum total of possible injections. The side of this equation showing the categories taken from the spending stream, *S* + *T* + *M*, are total leakages. In equilibrium, injections must equal leakages and the entire economy will adjust its level of output to ensure that this equality finally occurs. And as can be seen in Figure 12.3, the top half of the flow is equal to the bottom half when the economy reaches its equilibrium point.

INVENTORY ADJUSTMENTS

There is one final matter to understand in the Keynesian model, and that is what happens when the two sides of the leakages–injections equation are not equal. Well, in fact, they are always equal. But what allows that to happen is that the level of investment is divided into *intended* investment and *unintended* investment.

If part of the production for a period remains unsold, then these goods remain as part of inventories. Since they are part of the inventories of businesses that were not intended to remain, they are classified as unintended inventory accumulation, which is taken to be a form of investment spending.

If, on the other hand, the level of expenditure is higher than the level that had been expected, then stocks of goods disappear more rapidly than had been intended, and the fall in the level of inventories held is described as unintended inventory decumulation and is shown as an unexpectedly large level of investment spending.

Equilibrium only occurs when the level of investment at the end of a period is equal to the investment that had been intended when the period began. In each time period, the level of injections will equal the level of leakages. Where the disequilibrium shows up is in the actual level of sales relative to the level of sales that had been expected before the period began.

If they are higher than had been expected, business inventories fall relative to expectations, leading to more production and investment. If sales are lower than had been expected, then inventories end up higher than had been expected and businesses reduce production.

But it is the level of demand that makes all the difference. It is aggregate demand that drives this basic Keynesian model either upwards or down.

THE BASIC KEYNESIAN EQUATION

The graphical version of the Keynesian model will be built in the same way as the circular flow diagram, adding in additional sectors until the full model is on display. It should also be noted that there will be three different versions of the Keynesian model discussed, each one of which has been part of the traditional approach. These are:

- 'leakages' and 'injections';
- summing up the various forms of spending;
- and finally, what is known as aggregate demand and aggregate supply.

We start with the traditional way Keynesian economics has been taught. There are many other presentations that have been developed, but this is the one that gets closest to Keynes's original concept.

And here we begin with a cut-down version of an economy where there are only consumers and investors, C and I. There is no public sector. Aggregate demand for GDP (Y) is thus the total demand for consumption goods by consumers plus the total demand for investment goods by business. Thus:

$$Y = C + I$$

It was then noted that GDP can either be consumed (C) or saved (S). So we have another basic equation:

$$Y = C + S$$

Therefore, in equilibrium:

$$I = S$$

That is, the economy comes to its resting point when the level of investment is equal to the level of saving. What is important about this model is that the labour market has no influence on the level of economic activity. Saving and investment come to an equilibrium and the unemployment rate is whatever it is.

The Basic Leakages–Injections Framework

The basic diagram showing the equilibrium between investment and saving, begins with the assumption that investment is a particular amount while the level of saving rises with the level of income. This is shown in Figure 12.4

The level of income is shown on the horizontal axis and the level of saving and investment are shown on the vertical axis. The diagram is to be read from the bottom up. You should begin from the horizontal axis and look at each level of national income, Y.

- The investment line I states that **if** the level of income is at some level, **then** the level of investment will be whatever it happens to be, which can be read from the vertical axis.
- In just the same way the saving line S states that **if** the level of income is at some level, **then** the level of saving will be whatever it happens to be, which can also be read from the vertical axis.

On the diagram, the level of investment is assumed constant at all levels of income. Investment (I) and saving (S) are on the vertical axis; income

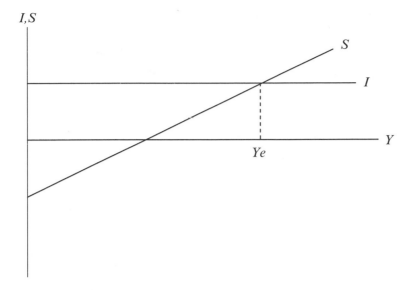

Figure 12.4   Equilibrium where saving and investment are equal

(Y) on the horizontal. Since, by assumption, the level of investment is decided independently of the level of saving, and is determined at the start of the period before anything has occurred, the level of investment remains unchanged whatever the actual level of GDP eventually happens to be.

Meanwhile, as the diagram shows, saving increases as income increases. The higher the level of national income, the higher the level of savings. Equilibrium occurs where investment and saving are equal.

If Y is below Ye, so that investment is greater than saving, then the economy will expand up to Ye where $I = S$. If, on the other hand, saving is greater than investment, so that not everything produced gets bought, the economy contracts until it reaches Ye, again shifting until $I = S$. Once at Ye, nothing shifts.

The Basic $C + I + G + X - M$ Framework

The same sort of equilibrium can be shown from the expenditure side, although it is slightly more complicated to understand.

The basis of the diagram is the 45-degree line which comes half-way between the vertical and horizontal axis (see Figure 12.5). What is notable about the 45-degree line is that everywhere along the 45-degree line everything on the vertical axis is equal to whatever is on the horizontal axis. If one takes any point on the 45-degree line, then if the amount shown

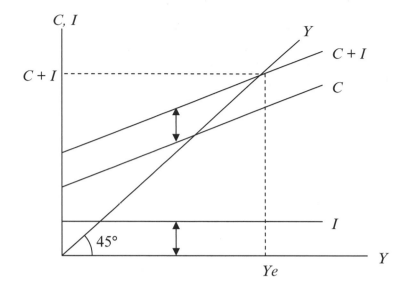

*Figure 12.5   Equilibrium where consumption and investment equal
        production*

on the horizontal axis is $10 000 000, then the same $10 000 000 is found on
the vertical axis.

On the horizontal axis in the diagram is the level of output. On the vertical axis is the level of aggregate demand, made up in this simple example
by Consumption and Investment, *C+I*.

Along the 45-degree line, therefore, the level of aggregate demand,
shown on the vertical axis, is equal to the level of output, shown on the
horizontal axis. It can be useful to think of this line as the level of GDP
(*Y*), since the core issue will be the vertical distance between the level
of demand at full employment and the level of production required to
achieve that level of employment.

Since equilibrium occurs where aggregate demand is equal to the level of
production, equilibrium therefore occurs somewhere on the 45-degree line.

The *C* line shows the level of Consumption as income rises. Its upwards
slope shows that as income goes up, the level of consumer demand goes
up. The *I* line shows the level of investment at each level of income. The
perfectly horizontal slope indicates that, as before, the level of investment
does not change as the level of income goes up.

Neither the *C* nor the *I* line ever appear again and are rarely needed for
the rest of the analysis. They are there to show the ingredients of the *C+I*
line discussed next. Indeed, until we get to the final total level of aggregate

demand, $C + I + G + X - M$, we will not have reached the full specifications for the economy. Until then, the additional bits added on should be seen as staging posts on the way to the final theory.

C + I

The level of I is then added to the level of C to find the total level of aggregate demand in this very simple economy. This is shown by the $C + I$ line. Where $C + I$ crosses the 45-degree line the level of aggregate demand is equal to the level of production.

If the actual level of Y is greater than the equilibrium level, Ye, the level of production is therefore greater than the level of aggregate demand. Inventories are therefore increasing faster than intended and businesses will reduce production. The economy will slow. GDP will fall and move towards the equilibrium level of output.

If, on the other hand, the actual level of production is less than the equilibrium level, more is being bought than businesses are producing. Inventories will be falling. The economy will therefore expand as entrepreneurs try to meet the increase in sales. The economy will grow until production and demand are the same.

Production Function

And while the level of employment is not shown on the diagram, it is the very purpose of this analysis. The assumption that lies behind both of these diagrams and all Keynesian models is that the higher the level of demand, the higher will be the level of production, and therefore the higher will be employment.

A 'Keynesian' policy, therefore, is to increase the level of production by increasing the level of demand. The assumption behind a Keynesian model is that as the level of spending goes up, the level of production goes up, and therefore so, too, does the number of jobs.

The diagram in Figure 12.6 shows what is known as the *production function*. It may seem an odd term although there are reasons for it. But what is important is what it shows, which is the relationship between the level of output and the level of employment.

As the level of GDP increases, more employees are required. Thus at an income level Y_1 there is employment level N_1. As the level of production rises, here to Y_2, the level of employment required is higher, in this case N_2. More production requires more people to have jobs.

If this were a strictly private sector relationship, where individuals are hired only where they are expected to create more value than they cost to

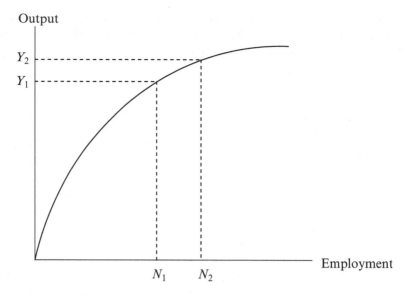

Figure 12.6   Production function

employ, there is no question that in normal times, as the level of output increased, all other things being equal the number of persons employed would go up as well.

The question, though, remains as to whether Keynesian type spending on goods and services whose costs are greater than the value being created, has the same effect on employment, especially in the longer run.

Bringing $C+I$ and $I=S$ Together

The two graphical forms of equilibrium determination are shown in Figure 12.7. The equilibrium in the top diagram occurs where $Y = C+I$. In the bottom diagram equilibrium occurs where $S=I$. The two diagrams show exactly the same set of relationships, but in a different way.

Here we find only the basic market case where there is no government sector. In the upper diagram we have consumption and investment, C and I.

There is first the level of consumption at all levels of GDP. It is read vertically and in the form of a typical 'if–then' statement as all such curves in economics are. Any point on the C-curve, the consumption line, states that **if** the level of output is at some particular level, **then** the level of consumption will be whatever is shown on the vertical axis.

The same is shown by the investment curve. It states that **if** the level of

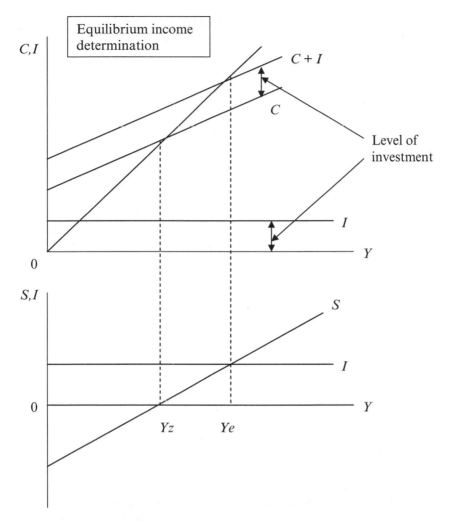

Figure 12.7   Equilibrium income expenditure and saving analysis

GDP is at some particular level, **then** the level of output is at the amount shown on the vertical axis.

The figure for aggregate demand in this model is shown by the $C+I$ line. It is found by vertically summing the level of consumption and investment at each level of output.

The $C+I$ line shows that **if** the level of output is at some level, **then** the total level of aggregate demand will be whatever is shown on the vertical axis. And while the level of investment is the same at all levels of production, because consumption rises as income rises, so too does the $C + I$ line. Aggregate demand goes up as the level of national income goes up.

EQUILIBRIUM

In the upper half of the diagram, equilibrium occurs where the $C + I$ line meets the 45-degree line. Here the level of total demand represented by consumption and investment on the vertical axis is exactly equal to the level of production on the horizontal axis. This occurs at a production level of Ye. Everything produced finds a market.

The equilibrium in the investment/saving approach occurs where $I = S$. This takes place at the same level of output, Ye. It is towards this level of production, and its associated level of employment, that the economy will move.

It should be seen that the information shown on both halves of the diagram is based on the same sets of underlying economic conditions. In the top half equilibrium occurs where $Y = C + I$, and in the bottom half where investment equals the level of saving generated at that level of national income.

INTERLUDE ON SAVING IN MODERN ECONOMIC ANALYSIS

The potential villain of the piece in Keynesian economic theory is saving. Excess saving causes an economy to stagnate. Classical economists had argued that saving is what drives an economy forward. Since it is saving that finances investment and therefore growth, an economy could not, according to classical economists, have too much saving. The greater the level of saving, all other things being equal, the faster the economy would expand.

In contrast, in modern macroeconomic theory, where demand rather than production is seen as the single most important impetus for economic activity, saving, rather than being the feedstock for capital investment is instead a withdrawal from the spending stream. It lowers growth rather than increases it.

A prime example of this way of thinking is outlined in the following passage:

> The classical economists argued that saving was a national virtue. More saving would lead via lower interest rates to more investment and faster growth.

Keynes was at pains to show the opposite. Saving, far from being a national virtue, could be a national vice. . . .

As people save more, they will spend less. Firms will thus produce less. There will thus be a multiplied *fall* in income. . . .

But this is not all. Far from the extra saving encouraging more investment, the lower consumption will *discourage* firms from investing. If investment falls, the aggregate expenditure line will shift downwards. There will then be a further multiplied fall in national income. . . .

[This phenomenon] had been recognised before Keynes. . . . But despite these early recognitions of the dangers of underconsumption, the belief that saving would increase the prosperity of the nation was central to classical economic thought. (Sloman and Norris, 2002: 417)

Much of the policy development that has occurred since Keynesian economics became the basis for macroeconomics has centred around the need to maintain the level of aggregate demand in an economy to ensure that all savings are soaked up. Saving in a Keynesian model remains a problem.

BRINGING IN GOVERNMENT

In a closed economy with only the private sector, equilibrium occurs where $C + I$ equals Y. Domestic private demand is all there is. But in every economy there is more than just the private sector. There is always a government undertaking various activities. The government, or public sector, must therefore also be brought into the story.

Using only the 45-degree analysis to begin with, the government can be brought in by adding a constant amount of spending to the level of spending shown by $C + I$. If government purchases of goods and services (designated by the letter G) are added in, then the total level of spending becomes $C + I + G$.

In Figure 12.8 we now find that the level of aggregate demand is made up of the total expenditure by consumers, private investors and the government. Government is a catch-all for everything that government buys. So far as public spending goes, government may spend on its own consumption items (salaries paid to public servants, for example) or it may represent forms of government investment (such as expenditure on roads or public housing). It all comes to the same thing.

The level of aggregate demand is made up of $C + I + G$, while the equilibrium level of output is at Ye. Here total demand is equal to the total level of production. Everything produced finds a buyer.

But note that even here there is no necessity that the equilibrium level of production will employ everyone who wants a job. Yf is the full employment level of production. It is the level of production that would require

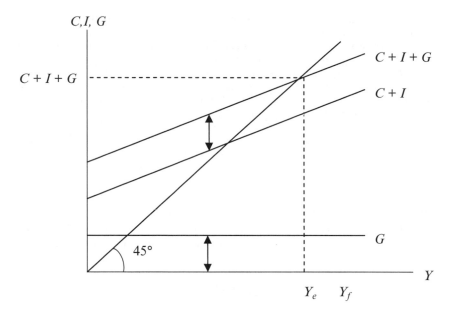

Figure 12.8   Consumption, investment and government spending

the efforts of the entire workforce to produce. Unless the economy is at that level of output, unemployment continues to exist.

EXPORTS AND IMPORTS

$C+I+G$ only represents the domestic economy. What must still be included is the international sector. Part of domestic demand are exports sold in other countries. Part of what is bought in the domestic economy is purchased from other countries. The level of aggregate demand for the production of domestic producers must therefore take into account foreign trade.

Adding in expenditure on exports by foreign buyers, which increases demand for domestic production, and taking away the value of imports from foreign producers, which reduces demand for domestic production, provides the final components of aggregate demand.

These net exports (NX in Figure 12.9) are made up of exports minus imports ($X-M$). The full equilibrium in an open economy is made up of production, Ye, equal to all the components of aggregate demand $C+I+G+(X-M)$. It is here in a Keynesian model that the entire economy comes to rest.

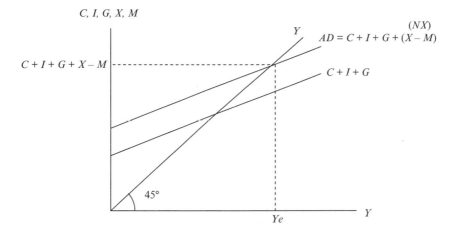

Figure 12.9 Introduction of foreign trade

It is demand, and demand alone in this model that determines the level of economic activity.

INJECTIONS AND LEAKAGES

The saving and investment model was also expanded to take into account all of the various forms of spending, such as investment, as well as all of the various forms of withdrawals from the spending stream, such as saving.

Just as with the circular flow diagram, to investment (I) on the expenditure side was added government spending (G) and exports (X). All of these were seen to add to aggregate demand, and the higher they were, the higher the level of economic activity would be.

These were the *injections*, and they were, in total, $I + G + X$.

On the other side of the ledger as shown by the circular flow diagram, as a subtraction from the spending stream to go along with saving were added taxation (T) and imports (M). The higher any of these might be, the lower the level of aggregate demand and therefore the lower the level that economic activity might be.

These subtractions from the spending stream were the *leakages* or *withdrawals*, and they were totalled as $S + T + M$.

Figure 12.10 shows that equilibrium occurs where $I + G + X = S + T + M$. All of the expenditure going into the economy is balanced by all of the leakages. Consumption (C), as was shown in the circular flow diagram, is

I, S, G, T, X, M

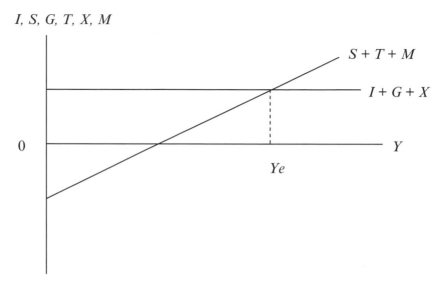

Figure 12.10   Leakages and injections

netted out as consumption spending goes straight to business without any intermediary, as is the case with the other forms of spending.

Again saving is a problem. Saving too much slows an economy. Higher saving will raise the $S + T + M$ line and therefore lower the level of equilibrium output. You might therefore think that taxation would also be seen as a problem, but since taxes are used to finance government spending, there is not necessarily a problem involved.

Finally, net exports are seen as a potential stimulus to activity, but we have in a sense conceptually returned to the world before Adam Smith, because here it is exports which are good for an economy, while imports are bad.

From this simplified model can be seen the public policy advice that is given to governments during recessions. Increase spending and lower taxes. Higher spending pushes the $I + G + M$ upwards, with Y rising as a result. Lower taxes causes the $S + T + M$ line to move down, again raising the level of output.

KEYNESIAN POLICY

Keynes's aim was to show how government spending could lift an economy and push it into higher levels of national output, and therefore

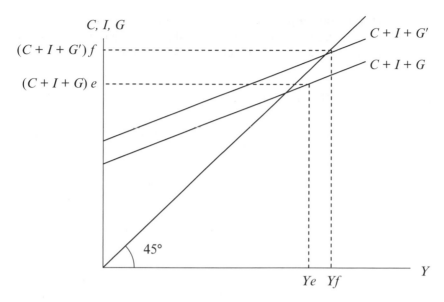

Figure 12.11   Creating full employment through higher public spending

into higher levels of employment. It was this that has since been named a 'Keynesian' policy.

In the standard Keynesian model where we have left out the international sector, we start with the $C+I+G$ line. If aggregate demand cuts the 45-degree line at a level of economic activity below the full employment level, the economy will remain just there until something happens to change it. Because the economy is in equilibrium, something outside the system must change for this to change.

The Keynesian notion is that governments can rescue the economy from its recessionary level of activity. By increasing government spending (G), the total level of aggregate demand will increase, and therefore economic output will increase, and therefore employment will rise and unemployment fall.

Figure 12.11 shows two aggregate demand curves. The first, showing total aggregate demand of $C+I+G$, reaches an equilibrium at Ye, which is below the full employment level of output at Yf. The Keynesian answer is to increase the level of aggregate demand through higher levels of public spending.

The level of public spending rises from G to G'. As a result, the level of aggregate demand rises from $C+I+G$ to $C+I+G'$.

The level of national output therefore rises from Ye to Yf, and the level of employment moves to the full employment level.

Since *Yf* is the full employment level of output, the actions of the government have brought the economy into full employment, which would not have occurred had the government not acted as it did.

DEALING WITH RECESSION

Government spending, of course, exists in every economy, so $C+I+G$ can represent an economy in full employment or in recession.

Suppose an economy that had been at a full employment level of output goes into recession and, for whatever reason, the level of investment falls, so the level of output is below the full employment level of output.

In Figure 12.12, the level of investment has fallen from I, when there had been full employment, to Ir which is a lower level of investment (r representing recession). Because the entire level of demand has fallen because of the fall in investment, the aggregate demand curve falls from $C+I+G$ (not shown on this diagram) to $C+Ir+G$. Output falls from *Yf* to *Yu*, and high rates of unemployment occur. This new lower level of aggregate demand is shown by the aggregate demand line marked (1).

The Keynesian answer is for government spending (G) to rise to take up the fall in aggregate demand. G rises to *Gs* (*s* for stimulus) which is comprised of the previous level of government spending plus the additional expenditure on the stimulus.

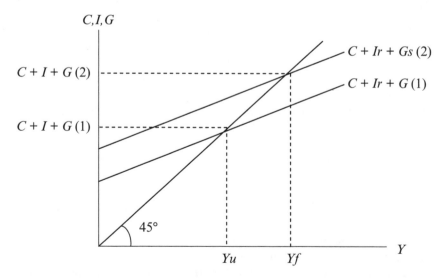

Figure 12.12   Government spending to restore aggregate demand

The level of aggregate demand therefore rises to $C + Ir + Gs$. To the extent that spending itself is the driver of economic activity, the level of aggregate demand has returned to the full employment level.

But not all is as it was. Compared with the previous $C + I + G$, there is now less private investment since Ir is lower than the previous I, and there is more government spending, which has gone up from G to Gs. Since public spending is less productive than private spending, the economy is not as productive as it had previously been, even if employment does return to its previous level, which is by no means certain.

THE MULTIPLIER

There is one last piece of Keynesian theory that needs to be included, and that is the theory of the multiplier. The theory states that an initial increase in public spending, say $100 million, will lead to an eventual increase in the level of output of some multiple of that initial spending.

If the multiplier is 2, then $100 million in initial spending will lead to an increase of $200 million in total output. If the multiplier is 4, then an initial increase of whatever amount will lead to spending rising four times as much.

The reasoning is that each person receiving the first round of expenditure will spend some themselves and save the rest. This first round of expenditure has second round effects, since the persons who receive this initial spending, spend some of it in turn while also saving the rest. Ultimately, an increase in public spending spreads farther and wider, and the benefits of increased activity are amplified.

This story is told in all macroeconomic texts and has been almost since 1936 itself, along with methods of calculation that provide a precise estimate of what the numerical value of the multiplier might be. But as these multiplier effects have never been observed in practice, the concept is not of much use other than to understand what Keynesian economists are saying about the effects of an increase in public spending on the level of GDP in general.

SOME FINAL THOUGHTS ON PUBLIC SPENDING

Amongst the major deficiencies of the Keynesian model is its assumption that all expenditure, in terms of economic activity, comes to the same thing. This is obviously untrue, and it often translates into policy decisions in which productive private sector spending is replaced by far less productive, and often unproductive public sector spending. They are not equivalent.

First, public spending directs the economy in a completely different direction than private sector expenditures. This point does not just relate to final goods and services but to the entire structure of production that provide inputs into such public sector projects. An entire network of inter-related businesses are supported through the subsidized projects. Call it charity and welfare if you must; just do not confuse it with an increase in value-adding production.

Secondly, the things that governments produce are not sold on the market, so there are no additional consumer goods available to buy with the incomes earned by producing what the government has decided to subsidize. The effect on purchasing power is dubious at best.

Thirdly, because the different direction such additional public spending flows into sets up an entirely different structure of production for the economy as a whole, existing economic relationships are disrupted when there are already major disruptions taking place because the economy has entered recession.

Fourthly, it is a further reminder that when the economy begins to recover, there will need to be a further contrary set of disruptions as resources are redirected to the economic structures that are supported by private sector activity. One has to assume that these emergency forms of public spending, brought on to limit the impact of recession, will be reversed.

Rather than this being a simple shift from one set of final demands to another, it will require a major restructuring of all of the industries involved in producing whatever the additional public sector spending had been devoted to producing. Not only will businesses producing the additional public goods experience a fall in demand, but so too will producers of every one of the inputs. They will also be affected with major disruptions to demand for their products.

NOTE

1. To be strictly accurate, according to Keynes it was also possible to 'hoard' money, meaning that individuals would keep their purchasing power literally in the form of cash. With interest rates low, there would be a 'liquidity preference' where individuals kept cash on hand because they feared a capital loss on their savings if their money was tied up in the bond market as interest rates rose. The money thus held was an even more relentless reason to explain why money earned in production would not re-enter the spending stream. (See *The General Theory*, [1936] 1987 pp. 166–70 if you think no one would be so absurd as to suggest any such thing.)

13. Aggregate demand and aggregate supply

This chapter is about the application of Keynesian theory to dealing with both unemployment and inflation.

This chapter also contains quite a few diagrams. None of them are difficult but all are necessary to get a sense of the policies that are used to keep unemployment and inflation down to 'acceptable' levels.

But the central point of this Keynesian analysis is this: an economy has only so much capacity and if you try to push an economy beyond its productive capabilities, it will 'overheat'. This overheating will create an inflationary environment which comes with a series of very harmful economic consequences of their own.

On the other hand, if there is not enough demand, then the economy will slow and unemployment will rise. So policy makers, even while they are worried about the inflationary effects of too much demand, are also worried about the employment effects of too little.

HISTORICAL INTERLUDE

The 45-degree line model with its 'Keynesian cross diagram' was the core of macroeconomic teaching from the 1940s through to the early 1970s. It was near enough all aggregate demand and not much else. But as there were no major recessions during the period, although a few minor downturns did occur, the model continued to be taught in this way because events in the real world had not yet shown it to be dangerously incomplete.

It was in the late 1960s and early 1970s that the first major post-World War II economic downturn took place and the causes were very far from anything happening on the demand side. If anything, it demonstrated that a demand-side understanding of economic events provided no insight into many of the most important problems an economy might face.

The Vietnam War had pushed public spending in the United States upwards since the cost of the war had to be added to the normal activities of government. In the United States, as well as in similar economies, there was also a push for much greater spending on social welfare programmes.

Yet rather than these economies flowering under the increase in demand, they began to wilt. What made matters worse was the continuing upwards pressure on the price level as inflation began to accelerate across the world. But what caused inflationary pressures to rocket was the almost simultaneous 'oil shock' and wage explosions of the early 1970s.

The oil shock, as it was called, quadrupled the price of a barrel of oil virtually over night. It caused a massive and almost immediate rise in prices at the pump. It slowed economic activity while at the same time pushing inflation well up.

Coincident with, but also in many ways caused by the rise in oil prices, were the worldwide wage explosions which affected one economy after another. Annual wage increases well beyond 10 per cent became common. Again this led to a slowdown in economic activity and an even larger rise in the price level.

It therefore became immediately evident that the simple Keynesian-cross 45-degree line diagram could not explain what was taking place. The Keynesian-cross was therefore replaced with another model almost completely patterned after supply and demand curves found in microeconomics. These were the *aggregate* demand and *aggregate* supply curves which are now staples within macroeconomic theory.

What *AS–AD* brought to attention was first the fact that the supply side of the economy had something to do with the level of activity. Second, the aspects it focused attention on were the forces causing inflation. Keynesian-cross diagrams had no inflationary dimension, while *AS–AD* curves did.

Eventually, even the *AS–AD* apparatus was modified to return economic theory towards classical pre-Keynesian thought by the introduction of the Long Run Aggregate Supply Curve (LRAS). It was an attempt to show that in the long run, fluctuations in aggregate demand have no effect on the level of economic activity – almost in its own way a reintroduction of Say's Law. But that is in the long run. In anything shorter, aggregate demand was still seen to have large effects, which is why, from a Keynesian perspective, an economist's work is never done.

AGGREGATE DEMAND AND AGGREGATE SUPPLY

Most importantly in understanding the short-run version of *AS–AD* is that there are no changes in the underlying conditions of aggregate demand or supply. The aggregate demand and aggregate supply curves are schedules of different possible combinations of the price level and aggregate output over a period of time, say a month or a quarter. Nothing

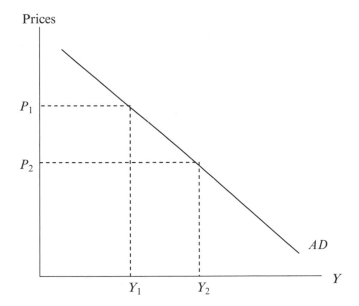

Figure 13.1 Aggregate demand

much changes to the underlying structure of an economy in a month or in most quarters.

The most important assumption is this: the level of nominal (money) wages are kept constant. Although along both the *AD* and *AS* curves the price level is rising, nominal wages do not change. Therefore, higher prices have a negative effect on aggregate demand while those same higher prices have a positive effect on aggregate supply.

Or to put it another way, as the price level goes up, buyers, whose incomes do not change, become more reluctant to buy, while sellers, whose labour costs do not change, become more willing to sell.

If, for example, wages are some fixed amount, say $6000 a month, and the price level (represented here by the CPI) is at 100.0, then the real wage is $6000. If, however, the wage is $6000 and the price level is higher, at say 120.0, then the real wage will have fallen, in this case to $5000 a month. The higher the price level, the lower will be aggregate demand. This relationship is found in Figure 13.1.

The aggregate demand curve shows different combinations of the price level and the level of aggregate demand. At higher prices less is demanded while at lower prices more is demanded.

The diagram is again in the form of an **if–then** statement. It states that **if** prices are at some level, say P_1, **then** the level of aggregate demand is Y_1.

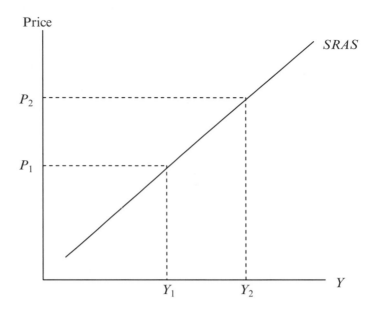

Figure 13.2   Aggregate supply

If, however, the level of prices is lower, at P_2, then with the same nominal incomes in combination with a lower price level means that real incomes are higher. You can buy more with prices lower. Therefore aggregate demand will be higher, in this case at Y_2.

The idea is similar for Aggregate Supply. Shown in Figure 13.2 is the short-run aggregate supply curve (SRAS). This shows, like the *AD* curve, combinations of the price level and level of output that sellers would be willing to sell at different prices. Since business costs remain constant along this curve, the higher the price level, the more that sellers would be willing to sell at those higher prices.

Here, too, is an **if–then** relationship that is read from the price level axis. Since we are dealing with the short run, everything is assumed constant, and especially the cost of labour.

The higher the price level, that is the more that can be received for each unit of output, the more businesses will be willing to produce. Since labour costs in particular are assumed not to change during the period, if prices are higher more will be produced.

Thus, **if** the price level is at P_1, **then** businesses in aggregate would be willing to produce a level of output represented by Y_1. **If**, however, prices were higher at P_2, with all production costs constant, businesses would be willing to produce an even greater amount of output, here represented by Y_2. Hence the upwards slope of the short-run aggregate supply curve. With higher prices come higher profits and therefore higher levels of production.

EQUILIBRIUM

Equilibrium, as with the microeconomic supply and demand, occurs where Aggregate Demand equals Aggregate Supply. This is shown in Figure 13.3.

Where the two curves meet is found a simultaneous determination of the price level and the level of production. Output is at *Ye* and the price level is *Pe*.

There is again nothing in this equilibrium position that would ensure that the economy is at full employment. It is a Keynesian model. Therefore the equilibrium in the demand and supply of goods and services places a limit on the overall level of production.

Behind the *AD* curve are all of the usual elements of aggregate demand, *C, I, G, X* and *M*. Whatever pushes the components of aggregate demand upwards will push the *AD* curve to the right. If these underlying factors reduce the collective willingness to buy, then *AD* moves to the left.

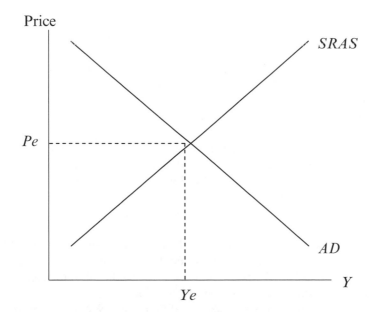

Figure 13.3   Macroeconomic equilibrium

So far as the *SRAS* curve is concerned, its position is dependent on production costs. Anything that reduces production costs per unit of output will move the curve to the right. Anything that raises production costs per unit of output, will move the curve to the left.

Although the curve is short-run, and most of the underlying elements are supposedly frozen, if wage or other production costs move up or down, there is a shift in the curve. Higher costs move the curve to the left. Lower costs move the curve to the right.

But note this. In the short run, there is almost nothing that policy makers can do that would cause the *SRAS* curve to move to the right. Moving the *SRAS* curve to the right requires long, patient efforts to raise the productiveness of the economy. Technological change, improving skill levels, and innovation are the kinds of changes that will lead to the slow drift of the *SRAS* curve to the right.

But there are many changes that can move the *SRAS* curve to the left, and these are generally changes that raise the costs of production. Thinking back to the 1970s, the combination of the rise in the cost of oil and coincident wage explosion would have moved the *SRAS* curve to the left. The result would have been the rise in the price level and a large fall in output. With the large fall in output would have come the fall in employment.

TYPES OF UNEMPLOYMENT AND THE NATURAL RATE

Modern macroeconomic policy cannot, however, be understood without first understanding the modern classification of unemployment. There are, broadly speaking, three types. Although each has the same immediate consequence – someone is without a job – they are very different for policy purposes.

There is, first, *frictional unemployment*. Frictional unemployment is the naturally occurring unemployment that cannot be escaped in even the best managed economies. It is the unemployment that exists because economies are dynamic. Some businesses are shutting down while others are opening up. Jobs are being lost in one enterprise while other jobs become available somewhere else.

People therefore lose their jobs as the economy adjusts and, until they find their next job, they are unemployed. Some people just quit their jobs and look for another. Others are new entrants to the labour force who are unemployed while they look for their first jobs.

This kind of unemployment is actually healthy. Workers look for the jobs in which they can make their highest valued contribution to output.

This can take time, so even their period of unemployment can be seen as productive.

The second form of unemployment is what is referred to as *structural unemployment*. This is a very difficult form of unemployment to overcome. It comes about because not only do people lose their jobs, but the very skills they have are no longer sought by the labour market.

Logging as an industry slows and people whose job it has been to fell trees lose their jobs. Their sole commercial skills, however, may only be related to their forestry work. They are unemployed and willing to work but no jobs available in the economy match the kinds of things they can do.

The final category of unemployment is described as *cyclical unemployment*. This is the kind of unemployment associated with downturns in the economy. The most notable characteristic of an economy in recession is the large and often rapid rise in unemployment.

Related as such unemployment is to the business cycle, it would be expected to go down as soon as economic recovery began. When the economy has returned to its full employment level, all cyclical forms of unemployment will have disappeared.

This is, in fact, the very definition of *full employment*. There will always be frictional and structural unemployment in even the best of economies, but cyclical unemployment occurs only when the economy is performing below its potential.

The level of economic growth when economic activity is at its equilibrium level is described as *potential GDP*. The unemployment rate when GDP has reached its potential is described as the *natural rate of unemployment*.

The natural rate of unemployment, whatever it is, is the full employment rate. And what is that particular rate? It is different in every economy and is only determined by those responsible for economic management.

INFLATION AND ITS PROBLEMS

But unemployment is not the only problem an economy must deal with. Inflation creates massive problems on its own, and therefore must also be avoided. The dilemma here is that many of the actions that lower unemployment also tend to raise inflation, while many of the actions taken to lower inflation raise unemployment.

Inflation is a continuous ongoing reduction in the value of money. When inflation occurs, the purchasing power of a unit of currency continues to fall so that as time passes, each unit of currency buys less than it did in the time period before. It is an insidious process that creates many problems in the management of an economy.

The most obvious manifestation is a rising price level. Inflation comes in many forms, from the creeping 2–3 per cent growth in prices that most economies now tolerate as an acceptable price to pay, to the many thousands of per cent annual growth rates that are found during hyperinflations.

But because during inflation there are so many who gain from its existence, especially governments, and because the cures are almost always extremely painful, once inflation sets in it is difficult to root out.

The problems, however, need to be understood:

1.   Money no longer maintains its secure role as a store of value. The purchasing power of a unit of currency continues to fall so that other means of holding wealth are sought. Since all other forms of wealth holding are more costly and less fluid, the effect of inflation is to make it more difficult to conduct one's daily life.
2.   Savings are eroded and can be entirely lost. Money kept as cash loses value. But even money kept in interest-bearing deposits may be subject to loss if interest rates do not rise as rapidly as the price level.
3.   This problem is worsened to the extent that interest earnings are taxed. Even if money is earning a nominal return as rapid as the growth in the inflation rate, once taxes are paid, the real value of the sum of money saved will diminish. Unless interest covers not only the inflation rate but also the tax rate on savings, the purchasing power of savings will fall.
4.   Forward planning within business becomes more difficult. A large part of the planning process involves estimates of future costs and revenues. In an inflationary environment such projections become much more uncertain.
5.   Businesses become much more tentative in terms of investment. The more clouded future state of the economy adds to entrepreneurial risk and reduces confidence. Businesses seek a higher than normal return on their investments before they become willing to commit their funds.
6.   Wage increases accelerate. Workers act to protect their earnings by pressing for higher incomes as prices rise. Various techniques, such as cost of living adjustments, are included in contracts entrenching the inflationary process. Industrial disputes increase as wage earners intensify their attempts to maintain their real incomes.
7.   Lenders are robbed while borrowers receive an unearned return. Money lent out on the expectation that the payment of interest and eventually the repayment of the principal will actually provide a positive return find out instead that the money returned to them is less in real value than the money paid out.

8. In contrast, debtors receive a windfall return which allows them to pay their contracted debts in a debased currency.
9. Interest rates rise to quite high levels as an inflation premium is added to the other factors that will induce lenders to lend. High interest rates become a major deterrent to investment.
10. Additional unemployment is created as the economy fails to adjust fully to the movement in relative prices. The lower level of real investment and the slower growth in sales as prices rise and businesses find it more difficult to cover costs, lessens the willingness of firms to employ.
11. Inflation does not affect all prices to the same extent nor do its effect descend on all members of a community at the same time. Those selling products whose prices rise last, or in occupations where incomes are the last to rise, find they are losing out to those whose product prices or nominal incomes rise sooner than theirs. Others are able to buy before prices adjust to their new, higher level.

Inflation lowers living standards, reduces growth and adds to uncertainty. It makes individuals waste time and effort on finding means to protect themselves from inflation rather than adding to the aggregate level of goods and services. They try to hedge against inflation rather than adding to the sum total of products available on the market.

Yet once the process begins, no one knows how to make it stop. No one wants to become the first to choose not to demand an inflationary increase in payments that compensates them for the rise in the price level. Whether it is income earners of some sort thinking about the wages they receive, or business owners and the prices they charge, or government concerned with taxes and other imposts they impose, by being the first to restrict one's income for the national good, means that they have chosen to reduce their own command over goods and services while leaving others to move ahead.

So rather than anyone being willing to step back, each group, and most individuals within each group, continue to work in their own interests, seeking higher nominal returns for the goods and services they provide. It is a problem almost impossible to end without a major economic downturn and a huge dislocation in activity.

NATURAL RATE OF UNEMPLOYMENT AND LONG-RUN AGGREGATE SUPPLY

This brings us back to the natural rate of unemployment, which has a very important additional characteristic. The natural rate of unemployment is the rate of unemployment at which the rate of inflation will remain unchanged.

According to the theory, if the actual unemployment rate falls below the natural rate, the rate of inflation will begin to rise. If, for example, the natural unemployment rate is 6 per cent and the actual unemployment rate is lower, at 5 per cent, then the assumption is that inflationary pressures will increase and the price level will rise.

If, however, the actual unemployment rate is above the natural rate, then the inflation rate will diminish. Therefore, if the natural rate is 6 per cent but the actual rate of unemployment is 7 per cent, the rate of inflation will begin to fall.

Only where the actual rate of unemployment coincides with the natural rate will the inflation rate stabilize. If inflation is at 3 per cent per annum, then it will stay at 3 per cent per annum. If it is at 5 per cent, then it stays at 5 per cent. Therefore, if the aim is to lower the rate of inflation, the only way this can be done, according to the theory, is to raise the actual level of unemployment above the natural rate and maintain that higher rate of unemployment until the inflation rate falls to the desired level. At that point, the unemployment rate can be lowered to its natural rate and kept there.

It is the manipulation of the actual rate of unemployment relative to the estimated natural rate which is at the centre of anti-inflationary policy.

INFLATIONARY POLICY AND THE SRAS

In understanding this policy, it must first be seen that a rise in inflation will set off a series of responses throughout the economy by which various groups will attempt to defend their real levels of income. Since inflation lowers the purchasing power of incomes earned, an acceleration of inflation will create increased pressures for higher money incomes and especially wage rates because of the higher prices being paid for goods and services.

Higher incomes will push the *SRAS* curve to the left so that the economy cannot for very long break past the barrier imposed by the natural rate of unemployment. It is the upwards limit imposed by technology, existing capital and labour force skills.

In Figure 13.4 there has been an increase in aggregate demand, with the *AD* curve moving from AD_1 to AD_2. It might have been caused by an increase in consumer confidence or in investment expectations or public spending.

The reasons do not much matter but the consequences do. There are many things that might push aggregate demand outwards but if the

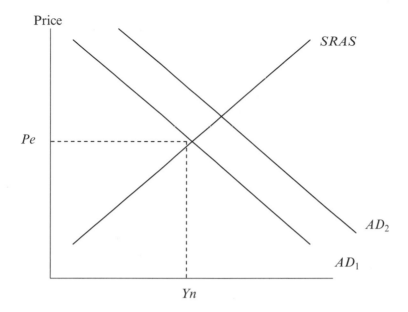

Figure 13.4   An inflationary increase in aggregate demand

economy is already at its natural rate of unemployment, the concerns about an acceleration of inflation begin to mount in the minds of those responsible for managing the economy.

In the diagram in Figure 13.4, the new equilibrium occurs at a level of GDP higher than *Yn*, *Yn* being the level of output at which the unemployment rate is at its natural rate. Because the economy is trying to produce beyond its potential – it is outside of its production possibility curve – there are shortages of all kinds of inputs, and particularly of labour. Prices begin to rise, and it is at this point that wage earners become concerned about their loss of purchasing power.

The result is a far more intense effort by working people to increase their wages to compensate for their loss of purchasing power. And it is through these kinds of circumstance that an inflationary spiral begins to gather momentum.

The increase in aggregate demand beyond the economy's potential level of GDP, which occurs where the unemployment rate is at its natural rate, has a number of consequences:

- Aggregate demand having gone up for whatever reason, the *AD* curve moves to the right.
- This sets off inflationary pressures since demand pressures begin to

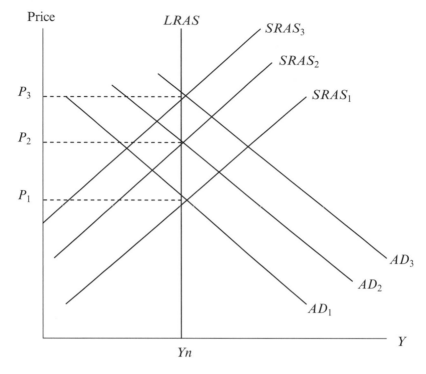

Figure 13.5   Tracing out long-run aggregate supply

exceed the ability of the economy to produce. Of particular importance is the effect on wage rates which begin to increase, which in
turn pushes the *SRAS* curve to the left.

- The increases in money wages received lead to an increase in the
  demand for goods and services which therefore pushes the *AD* curve
  even further to the right.
- The continuous shifting of *SRAS* to the left as costs increase and
  the almost simultaneous shift of the *AD* curve to the right as more
  money is being earned traces out a series of points.
- The points traced out become what is known as the Long-Run
  Aggregate Supply curve (*LRAS*).

As shown in Figure 13.5, the long-run aggregate supply curve is in practice
the equivalent of the production possibility curve. It is the maximum an
economy can produce. If demand is greater than potential supply, whatever may happen in the short run, ultimately forces are set to work that
bring the level of production back down to *Yn*.

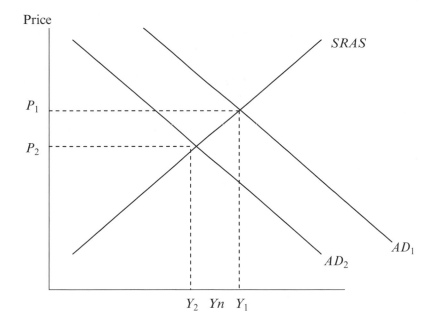

Figure 13.6 An anti-inflationary policy on aggregate demand

Yn is the level of output that represents the economy's potential level of GDP. It is the level of output in which cyclical unemployment just reaches zero. There is still frictional and structural unemployment but the unemployment rate is at its irreducible minimum rate given all of the circumstances that exist in that economy at that time.

In fact, once inflationary pressures intrude, the level of output may fall below *Yn* for an extended period as the inflation rate is brought down. If inflation only increased prices but had no effect on output, there would be little need for concern about prices. That, however, is not how things work.

To get inflation down requires a prolonged period of high unemployment to beat inflationary expectations out of the system. Only when people no longer expect prices to keep on rising at inflationary rates will they settle for moderate increases in incomes that are consistent with low and stable rates of inflation.

It is the role of policy makers to do their utmost to convince those who set prices and pay wages that inflation has finally disappeared. Only then will wages be set at rates of growth that keep the inflation rate down within some kind of either notional or explicit target range.

Thus, as shown in Figure 13.6, an anti-inflationary policy may need to pull the *AD* curve so far to the left that the equilibrium occurs at Y_2, which occurs below *Yn*. Below *Yn*, the actual level of unemployment is below its natural rate and the economy is growing below its potential growth rate.

Such reductions in aggregate demand could occur through cuts to government spending but almost never do. The technique used is to raise interest rates to reduce private sector expenditure, especially private sector investment.

Keeping the level of economic activity below the economy's potential will eventually squeeze inflation out of the economy. Eventually the economy can once again be allowed to grow at its potential where the unemployment rate is at its natural rate. It's a long process and in the meantime the economy must experience higher rates of unemployment and lower levels of production than it is capable of producing. It is immensely costly, but then so too is inflation. Curing inflation never comes cheap.

PHILLIPS CURVE

The last piece in the conceptual matrix within the Keynesian macroeconomic framework is the Phillips curve. According to the Phillips curve relationship, the lower the level of unemployment, the higher the level of inflation becomes. As aggregate demand increases, the greater is the pressure on resources and especially on labour costs. Therefore, inflationary pressures rise with higher employment, which itself is derived from increasingly rapid economic growth.

Similarly, as growth slows there is less pressure on resources, fewer wage demands and a lower rate of inflation. This relationship is shown in Figure 13.7; the Phillips curve is named after the economist Bill Phillips. Phillips curve analysis remains at the heart of the inflationary control policies of central banks.

As Figure 13.7 shows, there is a choice, a trade-off, between higher inflation but with lower unemployment on the one hand, and lower inflation but with higher unemployment on the other.

The theory suggests that the lower the unemployment rate, the greater are the inflationary pressures. Lower unemployment creates pressure for wage increases and price movements in general. Higher unemployment reduces the pressure on wages and prices.

Anti-inflationary policy has been designed to limit the growth in prices through adjustments to the rate of unemployment.

In every economy those in charge of economic management estimate the natural rate of unemployment in their own economy. This is the rate of unemployment at which the 'optimum' rate of inflation will occur.

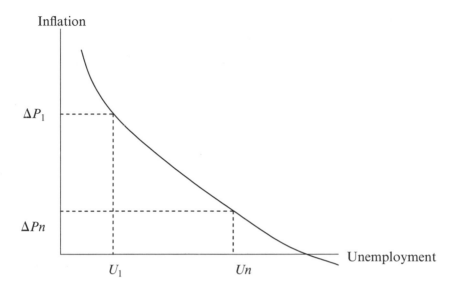

Figure 13.7   Phillips curve

What is this 'optimum'? It is the rate of inflation that those in charge of managing an economy are prepared to live with over the longer term.

In the Phillips curve diagram in Figure 13.7, the natural rate of unemployment is shown at *Un*. At this rate of unemployment, the inflation rate will be at ΔPn, which is low enough to satisfy those who manage the economy.

If unemployment falls below this rate, say to U_1, the inflation rate rises to ΔP_1, well above the optimal rate. Those who manage the economy then take steps to raise the unemployment rate, which essentially consists of raising unemployment. According to the Phillips curve, the higher unemployment rate will lead to a lower rate of inflation. As crude as this mechanism is, this is the way inflation is kept low.

The natural rate of unemployment will, however, rise and fall over time depending on various factors that affect how prone an economy is to inflation. If, for example, unions become less militant, the Phillips curve will move inwards towards the origin. The unemployment rate associated with the optimal inflation rate will therefore fall.

This is shown in Figure 13.8. The outermost Phillips curve indicates that the desired inflation rate, ΔPn, to begin with requires an unemployment rate of *Un*. But if unions become less militant, and the economy is less strike-prone, or indeed if there is structural change of any kind that reduces pressures on the price level, the Phillips curve moves inwards towards the origin.

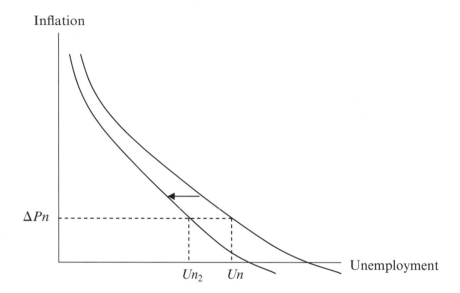

Figure 13.8   Inwards shift of the Phillips curve

With the Phillips curve having shifted to the left, it is now possible to achieve the same desired inflation rate, but with a lower rate of unemployment at Un_2. But such changes take time and require institutional changes, often of the most profound kind.

TECHNOLOGICAL IMPROVEMENT AND LRAS

Over time, as technology improves, the quantum of capital is increased and labour force skills improve, the *LRAS* curve will move to the right and higher output occurs, but with no additional inflationary pressures. Until such improvements occur, movements of aggregate demand will only cause the price level to rise without increasing the level of employment or economic activity.

Figure 13.9 shows how non-inflationary economic growth is supposed to occur in a perfect world. Here we have economic growth but without price movements. Technological improvement and higher investment cause the short-run aggregate supply curve (*SRAS*) to move outwards as does the long-run aggregate supply curve (*LRAS*). Income earners at the same time receive higher payments and this pushes the aggregate demand curve (*AD*) to the right as well. But since aggregate supply has also increased, there is no effect on the price level. The price level stays at

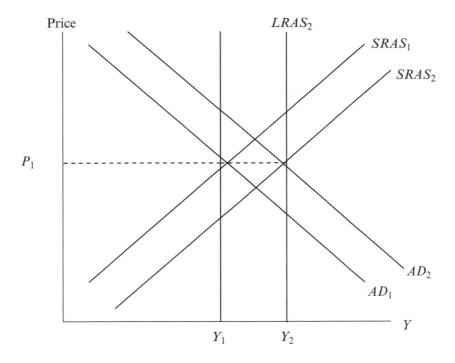

Figure 13.9   Non-inflationary growth

P_1 the whole time. There is no inflation even while the economy continues to expand.

It is this which is the aim of economic policy, and it is this diagram which explains what policy makers using a Keynesian framework are trying to achieve.

14. The classical theory of the business cycle

To understand the theory of recession as it was understood before Keynes's *General Theory* was published, one must begin with Say's Law. As discussed in Chapter 10, Say's Law is the name popularized by Keynes to describe what he said were the core macroeconomic principles of classical economic theory. It was defined by him as 'supply creates its own demand' by which he meant that classical economic theory had argued that all incomes earned would with certainty be immediately spent on buying everything that had been produced. Therefore, according to Keynes, classical economists had argued that an economy would always be at full employment, since everything produced would be bought.

To put this in another way, according to Keynes's interpretation of Say's Law, the incomes received in supplying goods and services to the market would always be spent on demanding the goods and services whose production had allowed those incomes to be earned in the first place. Everything would therefore be bought and no one would become unemployed because aggregate demand could always be expected to keep up with aggregate supply.

In terms of the circular flow diagram, the flow of demand into business would always match the flow of payments, leaving business at the full employment level of income. In that original Keynesian model, saving would always equal investment at a level of production at which everyone who wanted a job had a job. In relation to the expanded leakages–injections approach, $S + T + M$ would always be equal to $I + G + X$, again at the full employment level of output. Whatever else might happen in an economy, recessions would never occur because demand could never be deficient.

IMPORTANCE OF SAY'S LAW IN CLASSICAL BUSINESS CYCLE THEORY

Classical economists did not, of course, believe they had no explanation for recessions and unemployment. Keynes merely argued that this was the implication of having accepted the validity of Say's Law.

Say himself had pointed out that in an exchange economy, one set of goods exchanged for other sets of goods, with money merely acting as an intermediary that allowed such trade to take place. I work and contribute to the production of some good or service. I am paid money for what I have produced. Others do the same and we each buy from each other using the money we have received for having created something of exchangeable value. Money makes the exchange more efficient but, beneath it all, the actual purchase is made with each person's own productions as represented by the money received as income.

Demand, once the mediating role of money was removed, was made up of the supply of other goods brought to market. Demand is created by supply.

What none of this suggested was that the purchasing power that was in the hands of those who had earned incomes would always be spent immediately if economic conditions became uncertain. Nor did this suggest that there would never be occasions when economic conditions became even more uncertain than usual. Nor did the theory suggest businesses would never make mistakes about what buyers wanted to buy. Nor were there any doubts that innovation and change might well upset previously made expectations about what could and could not be produced at a profit. Nor did it suggest that governments would never make major errors in their economic management. Nor did it suggest that the financial system would never create more credit or less credit than the underlying level of savings in an economy.

There were many different sets of problems that were well understood by classical economists as potential sources of instability and recession. What was more often remarked upon by classical economists was how well a market economy worked. It was the fact that the economy operated as well as it did that was recognized as remarkable. That it would from time to time break down and recessions would occur, was just seen as being in the nature of things.

THE CLASSICAL THEORY OF RECESSION

Given Say's Law, that demand is created by value-adding supply, the explanation for recessions was invariably found on the supply side of the economy. If production was properly proportioned, so that everything produced met the specific demands of others, everything would find a market.

The classical theory of recession hinged on explaining why production decisions would at different times not match the specific demands of buyers. Moreover, it went beyond the question of why some particular business might have produced the wrong goods or services. There are always firms making bad production decisions. It went beyond that to asking why producers in large numbers would have ended up producing what could not be sold. The central question was why a large number of firms would end up making these wrong economic decisions at one and the same time.

It is thus one of the strange ironies in the history of economics that Say's Law, the very theory that was once seen as a part of the explanation for recessions and large-scale unemployment, is now said to have been the reason why classical economists could not explain why recessions took place at all.

CO-ORDINATION AND TIME

There are a number of dimensions of an economy's production process that are of major relevance in understanding recession. The first is the broad division of productive activities across an economy which are only coordinated through the price system and market mechanism.

Economies are built on specialization and the division of labour. Activity takes place in the myriad of business enterprises scattered across an economy who must somehow coordinate their activities with each other. Most such enterprises produce inputs for sale to other enterprises. Shifts in demand patterns are the rule rather than the exception.

Because no such body can exist, no central planning agency can ensure producers produce exactly what buyers want to buy. To believe some central agency can plan ahead for an entire economy is one of the major fallacies often associated with economic cranks. No single person, no central body, no government agency can ever know anything remotely like what needs to be known if an economy is to adjust to new circumstances.

It is only through decentralized decision making of entrepreneurially managed firms, where incomes of the owners and managers of the enterprise are directly dependent on the profitability of the business, that it is possible to have an immediate and concentrated response to changes in the circumstances in which a business finds itself.

Leaving the decisions that affect incomes and wealth creation in the hands of governments is a certain recipe for poverty and economic decay.

Uncertainty, indeed radical uncertainty, pervades the business environment. Producers have only a general idea of how much of any product will be sought during the period ahead, normally based on their experience of the past to which are added various considerations about the nature of the market as a whole as they look forward into the future.

Steel producers, for example, make production estimates based on demand over the recent past, to which are added their own best guesses about what other circumstances might apply. Users of steel must depend on the relative accuracy of such forecasts when they are themselves trying to work out their own needs and likely cost structures. And so on across the economy as each and every business independently works out what inputs they will need while others are deciding the level of production of those very inputs.

To say it again, there is no centralized coordination because there never can be, since each of those decisions is based on a vast array of circumstances, many of which will be unknown until the very last moment. Just how much steel will be needed by the construction industry is unlikely to be known with any accuracy at the start of the year, but will depend on how many buildings are commissioned once the year has begun.

In the meantime, that same steel might be demanded by the car industry which may turn out to have either a very good year or a very bad year, which will affect, either upwards or downwards, the demand for that steel. And so on with every other industry that uses steel. And so on with every other product that is used as an input.

The need to adjust production in every single industry as the year unfolds is a straightforward certainty. What others will demand will be different, sometimes extremely different, from what had been predicted when the decisions were made to produce the various forms of output.

Coordination of the many hundreds and thousands of businesses across even a medium-sized economy is a gigantic operation that can only be determined in real time by businesses that individually react to their own orders and the prices charged by those from whom they themselves buy.

That this coordination process sometimes breaks down should be seen as a fact of economic life. But understanding the nature of the process of economic activity should make it clear not only why such breakdowns occur from time to time but also why, even though recessions are inevitable every so often, there is no other way that an economy can be managed if higher real incomes and greater personal wealth for a larger and larger proportion of the population are the aims.

And beyond the economic benefits, personal freedom – not being dependent on governments for anything beyond national defence, the police, the law courts, the administration of justice, sound regulations of economic activities and the provision of welfare for those who may need such assistance from time to time – becomes the additional benefit of managing an economy in this way.

PRODUCTION IS IN ANTICIPATION OF DEMAND

The second issue beyond the difficulty of coordination is the recognition that every product that is on the market and available today is the product of decisions that were made in the past, often the distant past.

All production is in anticipation of demand. Every product produced for sale has been in preparation for a period of time before it has actually reached the market. And because every production decision comes well before the product is finally put up for sale, it cannot be known in advance with any kind of certainty what economic circumstances will be like when the product finally reaches the market.

A decision to produce at a profit means that costs must be taken on before revenues can be earned. There is therefore every possibility that when the product is finally brought to market, there may not be enough demand to ensure the good or service will cover all of its costs.

This may be because the producer had made a mistake in the decision to sink capital into that particular product. This is an extremely common outcome. There just isn't the market that had originally been anticipated. Such businesses lose money and either change their ways or stop production.

In an economy that is performing well, business mistakes are just part of the landscape. There are an endless series of attempts to earn profits through production and, while some fail, others succeed. This is how economies move forward through time.

But so far as the business cycle is concerned, this needs to be understood: the normal coming and going of individual firms is not the cause of recession. Where recessions originate is where systematic problems in the structure of the economy lead businesses into making production errors across a broad front. It is not just the coming and going of single firms in a competitive economy.

Recessions are caused by wholesale distortions in the structure of the economy with origins somewhere inside the operation of the economic system. It was to analyse and understand these structural problems that was at the core of the classical theory of the cycle.

RECESSIONS AND THE SUBSEQUENT UPTURN ARE ALMOST ALWAYS UNEXPECTED

Although the business cycle is a regular occurrence, with bad times following good, it is never predictable. Most typically, the downturn comes as a surprise as a period of prosperity suddenly turns into a period of recession.

As much as cyclical activity can be predicted to occur at some stage, when the downturn comes it is often greeted as if such events had never previously taken place. And the longer the time between such downturns – that is the more probable the next downturn becomes – the more astonished people seem to be when the inevitable finally shows up.

There appears to be a narrowness and concentration of focus within economies that assume that present conditions, whatever they are, will persist into the future. The assumption is that either the good times will go on forever or, when recessions strike, that the downturn will never end.

In many ways, it is precisely because the downturn is unexpected that it is able to occur at all. If it were generally understood that some particular feature of contemporary economic conditions were about to change and with major consequences across the economy, then actions to forestall and to take in stride such imminent changes would be factored into decisions being made.

That the unexpected can be expected nevertheless remains outside the perception of most of those engaged in economic activity, since the unexpected can occur in so many different ways. At any moment in time, there are many possibilities that may or may not come to dominate reality.

Business and other economic decisions very seldom can or do take these global issues into account. Businesses just get on with doing business, just as workers and consumers continue to act based on what they know. What they know is seldom related to the economic factors that are bearing down on an economy at some particular moment, specially when their effects are uncertain and may not appear until quite some time into the future.

RECESSIONS TYPICALLY SPREAD FROM AN INITIAL LOCALIZED DOWNTURN

Recessions do not begin as a full-scale downturn across all industries at one and the same time. A downturn will typically begin in one or two strategic industries and then spread out from there.

But beneath the specific industries first affected is a web of purchase and sale that penetrates deeply into the entire structure of the economy. A downturn in one industry leads to a fall in demand for the productions of the industries providing its inputs. These industries in turn begin to contract, with effects on other industries. This continues deeper into the economy until virtually every industry is affected.

The effect on the economy overall is a general recession in which, by the time it is in full swing, the industries in which the downturn began may no longer be identifiably more at risk. Enterprises generally feel the effects and, in a major downturn, no industry is certain to remain safe.

The most visible part of the downturn is the high level of unemployment. From a national economic point of view, the loss of production is regrettable but can be accommodated without much difficulty. Where the major problems occur, however, is in relation to unemployment. The large number of jobs lost has a massive human dimension.

In retrospect, and looked at from above, a one or two-year period of recession is embodied in the nature of the modern economy. For the individual experiencing this prolonged period of unemployment can be a personal and financial catastrophe.

As businesses contract and either refuse to hire new employees or lay off existing employees, there is a gloom that descends that is transmitted into the area of consumer demand. The effects are experienced throughout the retail sector as lower employment leads to lower incomes and makes the jobs of those still working more tentative.

Such tentativeness also spreads to investment decisions. The future becomes more clouded. Some decisions to invest are cancelled; others are postponed. There is a general fall in activity in every branch of the economy, irrespective of where the problems have begun.

The same occurs in reverse as the upturn starts. Industries begin to pick up one by one. There is always an economic logic that can be identified afterwards on why one area began to grow again, but in the midst of recession, determining in advance where the upturn will begin is not possible.

But for all that, the upturn does begin, and with the first shoots of economic improvement come the secondary effects as businesses increase their orders with each other. As some industries begin to pick up, so too do others. The momentum begins to build and eventually a full-scale recovery begins.

Recovery brings with it higher employment. The gloom which had descended begins to lift. New jobs open and those who had been unemployed return to work, often in industries completely different from the industries where their last jobs had been.

RECESSIONS AND ECONOMIC GROWTH

When the recession has run its course, the very structure of the economy may be quite different from the structure which had existed when the downturn began. The reason for the recession in the first place was that a significant proportion of firms across the economy were incapable of generating profits. They were using the community's resources in ways which were not value-adding given all of the other aspects of the economy.

The new firms, or those which are expanding, are typically different from those that had existed before. That is, in fact, the very purpose of recession: to ensure that the structure of production is properly related to the structure of demand.

An organic private-sector-driven recovery such as this is self-sustaining into the future. The economic momentum will continue to build and conditions will improve until the next downturn occurs, once again surprising everyone with its appearance.

THE CONTOURS OF THE BUSINESS CYCLE

That economies regularly go through periodic fluctuations in their level of activity has been well understood amongst economists since the early nineteenth century. Whether the measure is the level of production or the level of employment or some other measure of economic strength, the expectation is that in some periods these will be at a much higher level than in other periods. What models of the cycle do is provide an explanation as to why these fluctuations occur.

The basic structure of the cycle is shown in Figure 14.1. There are four distinct phases, each one following on the other, and most importantly,

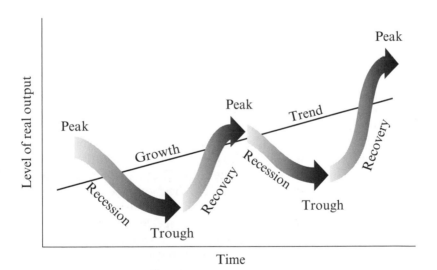

Source: Alan Ellman, 'The blue collar investor blog', available at http://www.bluecollar investor.com.

Figure 14.1   Business cycle

each phase leading to its successor because of the ways that businesses, consumers, governments, the employed and the unemployed behave.

In looking at the diagram it is important to bear in mind that, although typically drawn in this way, it contains one very important misrepresentation: both the length of time for each phase of the cycle and the amplitude in the level of activity during the phases of the cycle are shown as unchanging. The time between one trough and the next is shown as more or less unchanging, as is the depth of the recession or the height of the recovery reached.

In actual fact the length of each phase, and both the height and the depth to which activity may reach, will differ in each and every cycle. No two are alike, either in their amplitude or in the length of time that each phase may last.

The down phase of the Great Depression, for example, was the deepest that has ever occurred, and it lasted far longer than any previous depression. No other recession has shown so large a downturn, although there have been many others since the 1930s.

All that one can know with any certitude is that wherever one happens to be, it will be succeeded, at some moment in time, by the next phase. Every downturn, sooner or later is followed by an upturn, and vice versa. Every period of growth, no matter how sustained it may be, eventually turns into a recession.

THE PHASES OF THE CYCLE

The diagram thus shows the stylized structure of the cycle. Begin, first, with the trough, the lowest point in the cyclical movements of the economy. It is here that the rate of growth of GDP will be at its lowest, and where it will in fact typically be negative, while the unemployment rate will have reached its highest level. Here the old proverb, that it's always darkest before the dawn, shows its meaning. There is general despondency in the community, workers are fearful for their jobs and depressed profits and high levels of bankruptcy are common in the business world.

Yet economic conditions are about to change, and the next phase of the cycle is about to begin. This is the recovery phase, the phase of economic upturn. It often occurs only slowly at first, but once the corner has been turned, economic conditions improve, and improve on a broadening front. This is, overwhelmingly, the result of various spontaneous actions by businesses to find their way out of difficult economic conditions. But once commenced, the upturn then continues, usually for a number of years, until the next phase of the cycle is reached.

This next phase is normally referred to as the peak of the cycle and is usually experienced as an economic 'crisis' of some sort. It is the top of the roller coaster from which point economic conditions start to unravel. It usually occurs without much prior notice but when it does there is a sudden realization that conditions are about to turn down. It is that bleak moment, lasting for a few months, that heralds the arrival of the next downwards phase.

This final phase is the downturn or recessionary phase, characterized by a slowdown in economic growth – frequently an actual contraction in national output – and a sharp rise in unemployment along with a fall in employment. It is a phase of the cycle that can come with varying degrees of severity and will be accompanied by high levels of personal distress. In the classical theory of the cycle, the downturn is an inevitable part of the rhythm of economic activity. Its eventual arrival is a certainty; only its length and depth will vary between cycles.

It should also be noted that during classical times right through to the Great Depression in the 1930s, with the downward movement of economic activity there was also a parallel downwards movement in the level of prices. As the economy went into recession, there was typically a fall in the price level which was reflected in the use of the term 'deflation'. Similarly, with the recovery in the level of activity, there was typically a recovery in the level of prices as well.

Finally, what the diagram in Figure 14.1 also makes clear is that although there are periods of prosperity followed by periods of recession, the general trend is upwards. Over time our economies become more wealthy and the average standard of living continues to grow. To the extent that history can be a guide to the future, there is no reason that this pattern should not continue for as long as economies remain open and markets are allowed to allocate resources to where they will receive their highest return.

CONTRAST WITH MACROECONOMICS

Study of the theory of the cycle all but disappeared with the advent of Keynesian economics and macroeconomic theory in the 1930s. What did not disappear, however, was the cycle itself.

The certainty is this. Cyclical economic activity can be expected irrespective of the kind of economic system put in place.

Even an entirely agriculturally based economy will experience cycles as a result of changes in weather patterns between one year and another. But the theory of the cycle was designed to explain their occurrence in market-based industrialized economies, that is, in modern economies where prices and output are determined by the forces of supply and demand.

Yet even while cyclical activity remained a certainty, with an upturn inevitably following each downturn, Keynesian economics was sold on the basis that an upturn could not be expected without government expenditure since an underemployment equilibrium would hold an economy rigidly in place. In the original Keynesian model, there was no guaranteed up-phase of the cycle, even though every recession both before and after the publication of the *General Theory* has ended with an upturn.

High levels of public spending during recessions were looked upon by classical economists as likely to cause a recession to deepen rather than to turn up sooner than it otherwise would have done. Given that GDP statistics record public spending as value adding by definition, GDP has typically been a misleading indicator. But the data on employment and unemployment have been stubbornly difficult to budge with higher levels of public spending.

To a classical economist, the only spending that can contribute to faster growth and higher employment is growth associated with increased value added, that is, with the production of goods and services that are self-financing through the sale of the products themselves. Since most forms of government spending are unlikely to lead to increases in value-adding production, not only is there no actual momentum offered by such increases in government outlays, the effect is actually negative, slowing real growth rather than adding to it, irrespective of what the national accounting data may say.

Yet even with the virtual dominance of Keynesian economics, theories of cyclical activity are accepted by many while other such theories are being devised based on recognition that systematic errors in production decisions are inevitable. To understand the nature of recession, their inevitability, and the steps that need to be taken when recessions occur, it is essential to understand the theories of the cycle that had once dominated economics. In spite of its long dominance, if one's aim is to understand the causes of recession and the kinds of policies needed to create the conditions for recovery and a return to full employment, Keynesian economic theory is a dead end.

PROSPERITY AND DEPRESSION

The most useful compendium of classical models of the cycle may be found in a book published in 1937, the year following Keynes's *General Theory*.

Gottfried Haberler's *Prosperity and Depression: a Theoretical Analysis of Cyclical Movements* was commissioned by the League of Nations at the start of the Great Depression in 1930, but was not published until the Great Depression was well and truly over.

Its aim was to 'examine existing theories with a view to ascertaining what they had in common, the points at which differences of opinion arose, and, in so far as possible, the causes of those differences'. The various models of the cycle discussed below will follow Haberler's (1937) analysis.

The Basic Framework

One observation should, however, be made first. All classical theories of the recession were based on explaining why a large proportion of those who had produced had, for one reason or another, produced what did not end up being bought.

Theories of the cycle were *structural* in nature. They explained why those who bought were unwilling to buy the products of those who had produced. The economic system was understood to depend on reasonably accurate sales forecasts by businesses who would design their production processes in conformity with their expectations of which products would find a market – and in this we are referring not just to consumer goods but to the production of inputs as well.

It was to explain why such forecasts might have turned out to be wrong that the theory of the cycle was designed. Wrong, not for an individual business, since that would occur on a daily basis everywhere across an economy, but wrong on a system-wide basis so that the economy would find a large proportion of its productive efforts had been channelled into producing what could not be sold at prices that covered their costs.

Purely Monetary Theories

Purely monetary theories of the cycle are related solely to the flow of credit, with downturns seen to originate in the banking sector. To quote Haberler: 'Changes in "the flow of money" are the sole and sufficient cause of changes in economic activity, or the alternation of prosperity and depression, of good and bad trade.'

As the flow of money turns up, the economy picks up. When the flow of money slows, the economy contracts. In explaining the occurrence of recession, it is necessary to understand the sources of the money supply itself which, for the most part, consists of bank credit:

> Bank credit is the principal means of payment. . . . It is the banking system which creates credit and regulates its quantity. . . . A single bank cannot go very far in expanding credit on its own account; but the banking system as a whole can, and there is a tendency to make the whole system move along step by step in the same direction. If one bank or group of banks expands credit, other banks will find their reserves strengthened and will be induced, sometimes almost forced, to expand too.

The upswing in the cycle occurs through an expansion of credit and lasts as long as the credit expansion goes on. An increase in the supply of money, that is credit, will have an expansionary effect on economic activity. Start with an economy in recession and follow the effects of an expansion in credit: 'Demand exceeds anticipations, stocks decrease, dealers give large orders to producers, and prices rise. Production increases and unemployed factors of production are gradually absorbed.'

The principal means of such expansions is a decline in the discount rate and other factors which lead to a decline in the cost of credit; that is, interest rates are made to fall through increases in the supply of credit.

But at some stage capacity constraints are reached and are possibly exceeded if credit growth is not restrained early enough and hard enough. These are the classic symptoms of what is now commonly referred to as a 'credit bubble': prices of particular assets rise at rates well beyond the underlying productivity of the economy.

Eventually, as concerns with inflation increase and banks become concerned about the viability of their loans, credit growth is diminished as interest rates are pushed up. The economy then reaches a crisis point and the down phase of the cycle begins.

> If the quantity of money diminishes, demand falls off, and producers who have produced in anticipation of the usual demand will find that they cannot sell the usual output as the anticipated prices. Stocks will accumulate; losses will be incurred; production will fall; unemployment will be rife; and a painful process in which wages and other incomes are reduced will be necessary before equilibrium can be restored.

This is the very common face of recession which has occurred through a contraction in credit. With the flow of credit diminished, and the related rise in rates of interest, some investment projects become non-viable. The result is a slowdown in investment, a fall in economic activity and a rise in unemployment. The downturn continues until there is a revival in credit markets, at which point the fall in economic activity is reversed and the recovery begins anew.

What is important to recognize in such theories is that the real economy plays no part in either the upturn or the downturn. It is purely credit-driven. Savings and availability of resources do not affect the cycle, which is entirely a monetary phenomenon. In theory the economy could expand forever were it not for the contractions in credit that are brought about by the banking system.

But, as Haberler notes, 'that prosperity could be prolonged and depression staved off indefinitely, if the money supply were inexhaustible, would certainly be challenged by most economists' (1937: 28). Other theories of the cycle certainly accepted a good deal from the pure monetary approach, but added real considerations about the nature of the economy itself.

Over-Investment Theories

Over-investment theories explained the cycle in terms of disharmonies between, on the one hand, production of consumption goods and, on the other hand, production of investment goods. These were the most common theories of the cycle. Such theories were based on the occurrence of serious maladjustments which developed during the up-phase of the cycle. These were often related to monetary factors, but were not exclusively caused by such monetary factors.

Equilibrium across the economy was seen to depend on:

i.   the decisions of the population on how much to spend and how much to save;
ii.   the decisions by consumers on how to allocate their expenditures between different kinds of consumer goods;
iii.   the decisions by producers on how to allocate their own expenditures between different forms of inputs and capital goods.

In this analysis, the economy is represented by the always-present series of decisions that are constantly being changed. Both consumers and businesses are continuously shifting their patterns of expenditure and continually revising their plans.

If the decisions do not mesh, so that there is an inconsistency amongst all of the independent decisions being made across the economy, there is an eventual breaking down of the economy into recession. Production decisions are revealed to have been incompatible with concurrently made decisions either to save or to buy.

Why might such incompatible decisions be made? There were three broad categories of theory. Each of these will be discussed in turn below.

a) Money and the structure of production

There are, first, theories which were broadly similar to the purely monetary theories. These theories argue that the interaction of the monetary and real economies causes the breakdown. The economy simply does not generate enough savings to finance all of the investment decisions that have been made during the upturn. More investment projects are commenced than can be completed given the level of savings available. There is, therefore, a breakdown in the financing of activity that causes a series of production decisions to fail.

The process may be made all the worse through the ability of the banking system to create credit beyond the community's willingness to save. The resulting distortions in the structure of production, along with increases in inflation, cause the economy to become even more misshapen.

Once the downturn has begun, irrespective of in which corner of the economy the downturn had commenced, the effect on activity is cumulative. The falling away of activity, as investment projects are abandoned through lack of finance, causes the rollback in production in each of the firms and industries affected in the initial stage. The effect on the banking system, in which more and more loans become 'non-performing', only adds to the depth of the subsequent downturn. The downturn continues until at last the trough is reached, savings are restored and an upturn can commence.

b) Non-monetary over-investment theories

Here, too, the problem originates in the production of capital goods, but money plays virtually no part in the process. The concept is based on a shortage of the physical resources needed to complete investment projects. The problem is based on there being too little saving.

Moreover, the various inputs are seen as *complementary goods*, that is, they are used in conjunction with each other, often in more or less fixed proportions. As the economy expands, there are differential rates of growth in various industries until a situation is reached where some industries find they cannot find a market because the complementary goods, which are used in conjunction with the first good, are unavailable. Haberler describes these circumstances in this way:

> The result is a situation in which there is shortage and plenty at the same time. As these categories of goods are complementary, a shortage of one category means *ipso facto* over-production of the others. It is as if one glove of a pair were lost. The one that remains constitutes a useless and unsaleable surplus stock; the missing one represents an actual deficiency.

At this point, the downwards turn in the economy is accelerated by both psychological and monetary effects as confidence disappears and credit dries up. Both consumers and investors become more reluctant to spend. Meanwhile various rigidities become more apparent, such as a reluctance on the part of some businesses to adjust their prices to take account of the fall in demand and a similar reluctance on the part of wage earners to allow their wages to fall, even as unemployment goes up.

c) Over-investment due to changes in the demand for consumer goods
The basic concept is usually referred to as the *acceleration principle* and has been grafted onto Keynesian theory.

The theory builds on the notion that a change in the demand for goods and services bought by consumers leads to a proportionately much larger change in demand in the same direction for the inputs needed for their production. As soon as the growth in the demand for consumer goods slows, there is an exaggerated fall in the demand for inputs. Such inputs are referred to as 'higher order' goods, and the further from a consumer in the production chain an input is, the 'higher' that input is seen to be. (A shirt, for example, is a consumer good, cloth production is of a higher order, and the growing of cotton is of a higher order still.) Haberler describes the theory in this way:

> Slight changes in the demand for consumers' goods may thus be converted into violent changes in goods of a higher order; and, as this intensification tends to work through all stages of production, it is quite natural that fluctuations should be most violent in those stages of production which are farthest removed from the sphere of consumption. In certain circumstances, it may even happen that a slackening in the rate of growth of demand in one stage is converted into an actual decline in the demand for the product of the preceding stage.

Thus, according to this theory, the cycle is driven by large changes upwards or downwards in the market for inputs which occur even when there are small changes in the demand for consumer goods. In Keynesian models, the accelerator is often paired with the multiplier to generate cyclical movements in activity.

Entrepreneurial Error and Creative Destruction

Theories based on systematic errors in the decision making process were put forward by some as the basis for understanding the cycle. They are based on an understanding that the entire downwards movement in an economy can be started by mistaken decisions in some particular sector, which then spread outwards from that initial fall.

According to such theories, businesses might, for example, be misled about the likelihood of generating a positive return on investment. This makes little difference at the trough of the cycle, but becomes more apparent as the economy gathers strength.

Take as an example two businesses which identify an increase in the demand for steel so that each begins to build a plant that will fill 60 per cent of the expanded market. In the end, adding 120 per cent of needed capacity to the economy means that when such businesses are finally in a position to produce, the size of the market is too small to repay both sets of investment. The problems involved were well described by Haberler:

> Error theories stress the great complexity of our economic system, the lack of knowledge, the difficulties in foreseeing correctly the future demand for various products. One producer does not know what the other is doing. A given demand cannot be satisfied by producer A; producers B, C, D, etc., are accordingly called upon to satisfy it, and this creates an exaggerated impression of its volume and urgency. This leads to competitive duplication of plant and equipment, involving errors in the estimation of future wants. (1937: 104)

At the top of the cycle there can be a wide variety of redundant investments. These are not due to an insufficiency of saving to complete the various projects, but occur because the decentralized decision making of the economy causes over-investment in particular forms of production to occur.

To compound the problem, business decision making is often by its nature secretive. Business-in-confidence is a norm in the commercial world. One must therefore expect such errors in the commercial world, with the result that there may often be more capital sunk in some areas of production than is warranted by the eventual level of demand.

The subsequent recession has the role of rationalizing the economy's capital structure. Resources are redeployed into areas where a greater return on investment can be earned. Misreading the future and maladjustments in production are inevitable when the future is unknowable. (Allowing for government planning would be infinitely worse, since governments know far less than any market participant and there are literally tens of thousands of markets in a modern economy.) Moreover, many such investments must be made many years before they are required to earn the revenues which justified their construction in the first place.

Beyond this, mistaken investments occur because of innovation and technological advance. No one can be expected to know in advance what will be invented at some stage in the future or which inventions will lead to a commercial application. But they will occur, and regularly do, causing adjustment problems for existing firms employing old technologies or producing goods or services that are no longer sought after.

New products, industrial techniques and forms of capital equipment are introduced with increasing frequency. Such innovation and technical change make previous forms of output or production processes less competitive and often totally uncompetitive. *Creative destruction* is the phrase often used in describing this process, as the new pushes out the old.

Everything about an existing business may in such circumstances be perfectly fine, except that demand for the goods or services it produces has fallen away because some new form of output or some improved form of production technique have been discovered which have consequently either lowered the costs of production or caused the demand for the older product to disappear.

Out and out error or innovation and creative destruction, so far as a business is concerned, amount to the same thing. They lead to firms finding that they cannot earn the profits they originally believed they would because the level of sales does not reach their original expectations. The result is a downturn in activity as the economy goes through its processes of adjustment.

The economy may end up stronger, and living standards may end up higher, but the transition is experienced as a downwards turn in the level of economic activity in which recessionary conditions may occur.

Under-Consumption Theories

There were many varieties of under-consumption theory going back almost to the beginning of economics. Malthus's theories were one example but all were based on some flaw in the economic system which meant that, for one reason or another, not everything produced would be bought.

These, rather than being theories of the cycle as such, were more in the way of being explanations for recession. Such theories, in fact, had no means to explain an economic upturn since the circumstances that had caused the downturn would operate even when the economy was going well.

Under-consumption theories argued that the downturn was due either to the failure of consumers to spend all of their incomes or was because purchasing power had for some reason not been distributed at the same time as production had taken place. The basic assumption in all such theories of recession was that production would increase more rapidly than the ability or willingness of consumers to spend.

Theories of under-consumption had the least credibility amongst mainstream classical economists. They were seen as unable to shed light on most aspects of the cycle. Nevertheless, such theories existed in great number and had a great appeal amongst those without formal education in economics.

The form of the theory which was rejected for its incoherence by the vast majority of economists argued that purchasing power was lost to wage earners because of the ways in which incomes were transferred between businesses and their employees. There was some flaw in the economic system that prevented producers from receiving the incomes that would allow them to purchase what they had produced.

In this version, purchasing power is somehow lost. Incomes do not rise by a sufficient amount to permit everything produced to find a market. In regard to such theories, the conclusion that was reached at that time remains the conclusion amongst economists to this day. Whatever else might be the cause of recession, it would not be because purchasing power is insufficient. Those with the purchasing power might not use the incomes they have received, but that purchasing power had been distributed, that is, that there is enough purchasing power in the hands of all buyers taken together was and is accepted universally.

Logically possible but also universally rejected by the mainstream was the possibility that purchasing power received might not be spent, which was the most common form of explanation for under-consumption, typically based on theories of over-saving. It was the voluntary decisions to save, resulting in a failure to buy everything produced, that led to a disequilibrium between production and sales. If money saved is not invested, then a process of slowdown and contraction takes place.

Haberler found this a very unconvincing explanation for cyclical activity. Savings may rise relative to investment once the recession has commenced and business confidence has fallen. But as he makes clear, it cannot be seen as a cause of the downturn; only as a consequence:

> During the depression, when the spirit of enterprise runs low and pessimism prevails, it is probably true to a large extent that saving engenders deflation [a fall in demand and lower prices] rather than new investments, and that the slump is to that extent prolonged and intensified. But the breakdown of the boom can hardly be explained in this way. There is no evidence that an absorption of savings occurs during the boom or before the crisis; on the contrary, there invariably exists a brisk demand for new capital, signalised by high interest rates. There is an excess of investment over saving and not the contrary. The situation changes, of course, completely after the turning point, when the depression has set in. Then there is an excess of savings over investment.

In addition, Haberler points out the important role that saving plays as the feedstock for investment. Nevertheless, he notes that 'if the money saved is not invested, a cumulative process of deflation will start and saving may thus defeat its own end'. He points out that there is no evidence of a rise in saving taking place at the end of a boom, but as pure theory it is possible. It just never happens to take place in practice.

Psychological Theories

The fundamental concept that surrounded psychological theories of the cycle was related to the level of business confidence and expectations. Haberler discusses the crucial significance of the inability to see the future other than as a form of conjecture:

> With the introduction of the element of expectation, uncertainty enters the field. Future events cannot be forecast with absolute precision; and the farther they are distant in the future, the greater the uncertainty, and the greater the possibility of unforeseen and unforeseeable disturbances. Every economic decision is part of an economic plan which extends into the more or less distant future. In principle, there is therefore always an element of uncertainty in every activity. There are, however, certain cases where the element of uncertainty is especially great and conspicuous, such as the case of investment of resources in long processes and durable plant and the provision of funds for these purposes. The longer the processes in which capital is to be sunk, and the more durable the instruments and equipment to be constructed, the greater the element of uncertainty and risk of loss.

Because all economic decisions, aside from the most trivial, are associated with a degree of uncertainty, economic outcomes are affected by swings of optimism and pessimism. During periods when confidence is high, economic conditions are self-reinforcing as expansion in one industry promotes the expansion of others. When, however, pessimism begins to rule, the process is reversed and the downturn becomes cumulative.

Whether such psychological theories can stand on their own as an explanation for the cycle, there was no question that the level of confidence would add momentum to whichever direction an economy was heading at any particular moment in time. In combination with other factors driving an economy upwards or down, business confidence plays a significant role in exaggerating whichever direction an economy happens to be moving at the time.

SUMMING UP

The business cycle is built into the structure of a market economy. Economic downturns can never be avoided. Careful economic management can perhaps reduce the frequency and most certainly can minimize the depth to which economies descend, but they will never prevent recessions from occurring.

The problem lies in the belief that the natural state for an economy is for it to be growing, with unemployment low, when the reality is that the natural state for an economy is that it is adjusting to new circumstances during every moment of every day. Those new circumstances often come from outside the economy itself but more often than not are generated by the way the economy is evolving.

Businesses do things. They change what and how they produce. Every change in products and productive technique leads to shifts of some sort in the rest of the economy to accommodate each change made. The result is that each and every business is under constant pressure to be the one producing what buyers want, at the lowest price.

The classical theory of the cycle recognized that there were problems in the nature of economic activity that cause businesses to mistake what others will want to buy or to make decisions to do particular things that turn out not to have been profitable. Sometimes they are the actions of other businesses that cause those calculations to turn out wrong, and sometimes problems occur because the decisions that have been made are inconsistent with economic realities that could not be divined when the decisions were made.

In the end, an economy can avoid recession only when all of the following conditions are present:

- every decision made by every business is consistent with every decision made by every other business;
- producers produce exactly what buyers want to buy, and this includes not only producers of final consumer goods and services but also producers of every input used in the production processes of all other firms;
- savers save enough to finance all of the investment decisions being made;
- new innovations are always expected and never disrupt markets;
- the future provides no surprises so that everything turns out just as everyone thought it would – no one involved in economic activity is ever disappointed.

It need hardly be said that these conditions can never exist. And when these conditions are not met, recession and high rates of unemployment are frequently the result.

Their absence causes production and sale to become dislocated. There is a maladjustment in the structure of production. There is a failure of coordination within the economy as a whole.

The classical theory of the cycle typically examined reasons why an economy might fall into recession because of factors internal to its own operation. They thus failed to analyse what was even then a major cause of such dislocation but one which, since classical times, has become ever more common and widespread. And this is the disruption that takes place because of the actions taken by governments. It is the ways in which governments foster recessions and create unemployment that will be looked at next.

15. Cyclical activity and governments

The classical theory of the cycle explained the periodic upwards and downwards movement in the level of economic activity with reference to changes brought about by circumstances prevailing during each phase. The seeds of the subsequent recession are sown during the upturn. The factors that will lead to revival come into play as the economy moves into deeper recession.

At the centre of the response to existing circumstance are entrepreneurial decisions made in one business after another. The owners and managers of every business are intensely interested in the state of the economy, the level of demand for the products they sell and the cost of buying in the inputs they use. They are mindful of the actions of their competitors. They are aware that no competitor will inform its competition ahead of time of any changes that it plans to make. The unexpected happens all the time. And all the while, each business continuously seeks new and better products and new and better (and not just cheaper) ways to produce.

Beyond all of this there is the unknown future about which all economic decisions are made, but about which no facts can be known. There are therefore tremendous risks experienced by every business as it decides what to do.

But then, behind the natural ebb and flow of the market, are the actions taken by governments and government agencies. Governments do four things. They spend, they tax, they regulate and they make adjustments to the market for credit. Each of these government actions can and do have major effects on economic outcomes but whose effects no one can predict. And certainly no business can be expected to forecast with perfect accuracy the effect of some government action on its own business, given how large and extensive an economy is.

But what is most apparent from the history of economies is that the actions taken by governments will frequently do great harm to the economies being managed. Unless one brings in the role of government and its effects on production and employment, understanding the causes of the cycle will remain incomplete.

It is governments that are now, and may always have been, the single most important cause of recession. It is their actions, rather than the market itself, that are far more likely to cause instability, recession and unemployment.

Yet what is notable from examining Haberler, which was published in 1937, the year after Keynes published his *General Theory*, is that none of the discussions of the causes of the cycle examine the possibility that the actions of government may themselves be a major factor in causing economies to enter recession. All of the theories discussed are theories of how economies enter recession and then recover without the involvement of governments, either as a cause or as a cure.

How realistic this was even during the 1930s is questionable. The Great Depression may have been initiated by decisions of the Federal Reserve in the US and the Bank of England in London to raise interest rates in 1928 and 1929 to slow what were seen as economies which had expanded beyond their potential.

These effects on activity were then heightened by the American decision to implement the highest tariff levels in US history, a decision which then led to similar actions being taken across the world. The subsequent fall in activity created a depression that would become the deepest ever experienced and one which would take a world war to finally bring to its end.

If one, in fact, looks at what made the recessionary phase of the Great Depression last as long as it did and reach the depths that were reached, it is quite clear that whatever may have started the downwards process in the first place, it was government action, particularly in the United States, which accelerated and deepened the process. These were some of the actions taken in the US:

● central bank actions to raise interest rates in 1928 and 1929 to contain inflationary pressures (when the recorded growth in the price level showed no economy-wide price increases at all);
● largest tariff increase in US history in 1930 to protect domestic industry from foreign competition;
● deliberate policy to maintain real wages as recession deepened in order to maintain the level of demand;
● large increases in unproductive forms of public spending to reduce unemployment;
● intensification of efforts to limit production to allow producer prices to rise;
● massive new government regulations to prevent businesses following their most productive paths to growth aimed at limiting the effects of competitive forces.

Each of these, other than the increases in public spending, would be seen today as inappropriate if the aim was to create growth and employment. Indeed, all would be recognized by economists as likely to worsen employment and slow activity.

No discussion of the cycle can therefore be complete unless it is also understood that governments themselves are now a major contributor to economic instability, and may well have themselves become the major cause.

HOW ECONOMIC THEORY IS USUALLY TAUGHT

The approach taken to teaching economics has become one in which the market mechanism is in many ways taught only so that there is a basis for explaining why markets might in some circumstances not operate properly. The market mechanism is seldom explained as what it is: the sole means to achieve prosperity and the basis for a continuing improvement in living standards for an entire population.

And even where the role of the entrepreneurial-driven market is taught, it is a minor issue. It is not the take home message, but often merely background.

Microeconomics

In a standard introductory text, somewhere at the very start is the theory of supply and demand. An explanation is given of how the economic system will generate a price for each item sold through the anonymous forces of the market. There is then a discussion of how such prices change through changes in various *ceteris paribus* conditions.

Little will be said about the price system in its entirety. Little if anything will be said about the market system generally, nor about individual decentralized decision making and the role of the entrepreneur. There will merely be a discussion of how supply curves and demand curves intersect at a particular price and volume with no sense of the dynamics of a world in which everyone is a demander and most adults below the retirement age are producers. No sense of a world unfolding as individuals lead their lives, in the midst of which are actions taken to produce and to buy.

From there on, the rest of a typical text will discuss how things are apt to go wrong. There is a microeconomic model described as 'perfect' competition. It is a model that describes how in some markets each individual firm is so small relative to the entire level of sales that it faces a perfectly elastic demand curve at the price determined by the overall supply and demand for the product.

This is a market that, at most, represents a handful of situations, mostly in the agricultural sector, and where the specific conditions for such 'perfection' are properly described (as, for example, the need for complete knowledge about the future), it is made absolutely clear that such a market cannot exist.

Beyond perfect competition, every other market type is understood as representing some form of 'imperfect' competition. That is the word that is used. Thus, whether or not by intent, given the meaning associated with the term 'imperfect', what is conveyed by the use of the term is that every other market type should be seen as flawed in some way. If only perfect competition could prevail in every market, it is generally implied and sometimes said, the economy would be operating as efficiently as possible. Given that this is not the case, inefficiency must abound.

And the worst of all possibilities is monopoly. Where monopolies exist, the effect, as shown in text after text, is to restrict output and raise prices above the levels that would have occurred had a perfect market existed. If the point is made that it is only through the various forms of imperfect market that innovation and novelty occur, it is hardly emphasized, and generally downplayed.

There is then the use of the phrase 'price discrimination' to describe the completely legitimate practice of businesses selling the same product to different people at different prices as a means of increasing their own profitability. Since discrimination is a word loaded with negative connotations, the implication is that there is something not quite right about it. But really, is there something wrong with selling arena tickets to children at a lower price than to adults?

Having shown that markets are likely to lead to excessive prices and lower levels of production, the stage is set for a discussion of 'market failure' and 'externalities'.

Market failure is an important theme in introductory economics as normally taught, and in its original form meant an inefficient allocation of resources. The economy did not produce as much value added as it might have done, leaving us inside the production possibility curve. The notion has expanded in its general usage amongst non-economists to encompass any outcome that is different from the outcome that policy makers would prefer.

But the major difficulty is that we now embed the notion of market failure in how we teach before we have made sure that there is an understanding of what market success actually means. And what is certainly almost never taught is government failure, which is the departure from an efficient allocation of resources caused by governments.

Amongst the most important examples of market failure is what are referred to as externalities. An externality is a cost imposed on some third party not associated with the purchase and sale of the particular product. The typical example is some form of pollution, where the market will produce more pollution than is socially optimal.

If some resource has no owner – the air, say, or some body of water – then businesses will be more likely to dump waste products without regard to the effects on others. Business is thus associated with negative outcomes for the environment.

And while it is perfectly sensible to point such problems out, attention is then given to conceptual solutions so useless in practice that it is a wonder that they are ever introduced at this level. The core concept is something called 'marginal social costs', which are the additional costs to society as a whole caused by some change in activity.

Seldom is there a presentation that points out that as wealth has increased across a community, a reduction in polluting forms of activity has arisen naturally in the political response to such problems. Certainly problems abound, but it is not the normal practice to stress that the benefits of a market economy are massive in comparison with the problems that it generates.

Nor is it common practice to stress that it is only because there is private ownership and a price mechanism that realistic solutions to such problems not only can be but have been developed. Given production techniques in the modern world – where the nature of the production process is driven by technological specifications – every economy faces the same problems in dealing with such externalities. But given the origins of such problems, how often is it pointed out that no genuine solution is possible without economies organized around entrepreneurial decision making and the pursuit of a profitable return unless we are prepared to sacrifice massive amounts of our productive potential?

Macroeconomics and the Theory of the Cycle

Then with the introduction of macroeconomics, the entire economy is seen as continually teetering on the brink of recession, inflation and high rates of unemployment. These are economies that, so far as these theories are concerned, could not possibly be left to themselves, as entrepreneurs go about their business producing for others within the regulatory environment set by governments.

This is in an economy which, if left to its own devices, will spin out of control into high rates of inflation or instead fall into an underemployment equilibrium in which high levels of involuntary unemployment abound.

Macroeconomics as now taught is the direct descendant of Keynes. It is sometimes urged that Keynes is a relic of the past whose views have now been transcended. The reality is that Keynesian theory and concepts are embedded as solid as rock into modern theory. Deficiency of demand is a constant concern in just the same way that excess demand beyond an economy's potential is itself a major concern.

The result is that few are any longer taught that economies have major propertics for self-adjustment and are able to recuperate on their own without major government involvement in the process. The notion that the cycle is cyclical and can be counted on to provide most of the momentum towards recovery is now unknown and untaught. It is a notion foreign to the ways in which economics is now presented.

NOT TAUGHT ABOUT MARKETS

By the time students have emerged from an introductory course, they know next to nothing about the market process itself but have been presented with massive evidence that an economy left on its own (which no economy ever is) will create major problems at every turn.

They will not come away with an understanding that the market economy is one of the most beneficial social inventions ever developed by human societies. They will have no concept that an economy in which entrepreneurial decision making is the basis for economic activity cannot be improved upon by any other set of social arrangements. They will not be instructed that a heavy-handed government response aimed at reversing the down phase of the cycle is possibly unnecessary, and there will certainly be little inkling given that such policies may be positively harmful.

The market does need regulation, but it needs regulation that allows market processes to work. What are not needed are government actions that take the place of the market by determining by directive what can and ought to be the outcome of entrepreneurial actions by businesses trying to find a market.

To believe there is any other set of arrangements outside the market that will lead to personal prosperity across a society is to be left in complete ignorance about how living standards and the good life can be created in our world of scarcity, shortages and radical uncertainties about the future.

And over and above all, it will not be pointed out, let alone stressed, that the market economy is the only set of economic arrangements consistent with personal freedom and individual liberty. The political benefits of a market economy may themselves be the greatest benefits that such arrangements bestow.

None of this is generally taught, and most students of introductory economics typically know next to nothing at all of these matters.

THE CONSTANT INVOLVEMENT OF GOVERNMENTS

What the typical approach to economic theory now does is underscore the belief that an economy must have government involvement at virtually every turn to rectify and adjust the outcomes the market would itself produce.

Rather than understanding that a functioning market economy for the most part needs government involvement to provide a regulatory framework, the message now being given, whether overt or tacit, is that governments are a constant necessity to correct at every turn the major failings of an entrepreneurially managed market economy. And these are not just minor adjustments here or there. The way that economics is presented is that governments must become a constant presence, time and again altering the circumstances in the field to head off major instability or rectify high levels of social injustice.

Economic texts at the introductory level are designed as users' manuals for government action to remedy all manner of problems. Such texts typically and almost exclusively deal with what may go wrong so that it can be understood how governments can be used to put matters right.

GOVERNMENT POLICY AND RECESSION

Until the Great Depression, governments were largely 'hands-off'. The approach taken by governments was generally straightforward: regulations were introduced where problems were recognized and protection for workers and consumers were needed. But for the most part there was a recognition that the private sector could be expected to manage itself. The following were amongst the more important limitations that governments placed on their own involvement in economic matters:

- there were strict limits on protectionist measures designed to impede trade;
- the gold standard was maintained as the means to determine the value of each currency in relation to all other currencies;
- budgets were balanced;
- taxation was kept low;
- public spending was kept at a small proportion of total national production.

This is not to suggest that social legislation played no part. The regulation of industry – the introduction of child labour laws, the restrictions on the working week, mandated safety legislation – grew out of the recognition that there had to be standards imposed to ensure the health, safety and welfare of the community and of its working population.

But the assumption was that that economic activity was largely the realm of entrepreneurial activity and private ownership. Whatever a government might be capable of, running a business was not one of its skills.

Since the start of the twentieth century the approach has been increasingly different. This has in many ways been brought on by the two world wars, where government activity became more and more entrenched. Adding to the pressures for more government direction involvement was the Russian Revolution in 1917, which made central planning appear to some to be the wave of the future.

Keynesian economics was, in effect, a watered down version of central planning mixed with private ownership. But what had become clear long before World War II was that governments were taking on more and more of the role of economic managers. It did not require Keynes to write the *General Theory* for governments to feel themselves adequate to the task of direct management of the economies they oversaw.

It is now quite possible that the classical theory of the cycle has been superseded by the actions of governments. It is even possible that the cycles, even as they were experienced during classical times, were driven by the actions of governments.

But since the early years of the twentieth century, as governments have taken on a greater and greater role as managers of our economic affairs so they have increased their intrusions in economic affairs with the specific intent of changing macroeconomic outcomes. This is a role that governments more and more see themselves as capable of assuming for themselves, however little evidence there may actually be in practice that they are capable of achieving the outcomes they seek.

RECESSIONS AND POLITICAL DECISIONS

Today there is no aspect of an economy's structure towards which governments do not believe themselves capable of making positive contributions. Governments believe themselves able to make adjustments in the widest array of economic circumstances with little concern about potential collateral damage.

Such actions are not undertaken with a sense of dread at the possible unintended consequences. They are undertaken with a confidence that is simply unwarranted by our level of knowledge about the effects that government-induced changes will cause. It is economic expertise that is often the single most important promise that those in governments offer, and there is an enormous self-belief in political leaders that they can change things for the better.

A partial list of the various areas where governments and the bureaucracy are actively involved in crafting outcomes and dictating policy include all of the following:

- monetary and banking policy;
- interest rates adjustment;
- taxation – involving both tax rates and the structure of the taxation system;
- spending – dealing with both the level of spending and its direction;
- regulation – combining both overall rules of conduct as well as specific directives to take particular actions at particular times;
- exchange rate adjustments – with even a floating exchange rate subject to actions from time to time to shift the value of the currency;
- tariffs and other protectionist measures;
- income redistribution as a conscious policy aim;
- higher and higher welfare payments to an increasing proportion of the population;
- wages and industrial relations.

The fact that so many policies are also driven by the public's demand for greater public services and increased protection from the vicissitudes of life means that governments find themselves offering more because there is a political market for what they do. The demand by the public for governments to take greater command over the resources of the community may bring some kind of explanation for the actions that follow, but shows little appreciation of how poorly done these tasks are or how costly they have become.

APPLYING THE THEORY OF THE CYCLE TO POLITICAL DECISIONS

The theory of the cycle was built around an appreciation that production takes place in anticipation of demand. And the reason that things do not always work out is often because of decisions taken by governments to change the contours of the economies, which invalidate the previous decisions made by business.

An entrepreneur thinks about production and sale in an economy which can be imagined in many different ways. But large-scale actions by governments in any single one of the above list of areas can create major shifts in the economic circumstances in which a business trades.

Decisions to pump increased levels of liquidity (that is, money) into the economy or then, later on, to remove this added liquidity can have major effects in both instances. Higher inflation or slower growth make the present significantly different from how it was imagined when it was only the future.

In classical times the pushing up of demand through the creation of credit by the central government was the very meaning of the term inflation. (The term that has come into fashion has been the discussion of a 'bubble'.) There is liquidity poured into the economy which has a massive impact on some specific area of activity which grows well beyond its relative contribution to the economy because of the effect on prices. The bursting of the bubble thereafter has an effect on the overall level of activity, not just in that sector but elsewhere.

And to the extent that such bubbles affect the banking industry and the availability of finance, so much the worse for the economy overall.

Changes in tax rates or in the level of public spending can have major effects on the level of economic activity and its direction. Much will depend on how such changes affect after-tax revenues or where sales had been directed. Higher taxation can slow activity and increased public spending can come at the expense of private sector activity and especially productive investment

Poorly designed regulations can have devastating effects on the activities of many firms at one and the same time. And as emphasized by business cycle theory, it is not where a downturn starts that matters, but where it finishes.

In the end, it is the pulling the rug out from under business that can often be the cause of recession. Businesses have imagined a future, based on what they then knew, that did not eventuate because of the actions that were taken by governments.

Were governments to make their decisions based on an understanding that it is entrepreneurially managed firms that must carry the weight of economic activity, decisions made would be more consistent with economic growth. Were such decisions made with greater sensitivity to the needs of business, there might be fewer fluctuations in economic activity.

Instead, the attitude too often taken by government is that they are able to stabilize economies, create growth and promote lower unemployment through their own actions and decisions.

POLICIES IN RECESSION

A counter-cyclical policy should be based on harnessing entrepreneurial activities and market forces to achieve restoration of strong rates of growth. There are things that can be done, most of which are related to ensuring that business costs are brought down as quickly as possible so that the impact of the recession is minimized and recovery occurs as quickly as possible.

A priority would be lower taxes, especially taxes on business. Increases in after-tax cash flows in healthy firms will provide the momentum for an upturn. Lowering tax levels will assist in the expansion of profitable sectors of the economy.

The containment of real wages should also be a priority, with efforts made to ensure that as few employees as possible price themselves out of a job and as many others as possible are priced into jobs. Whatever might have been the real level of wages that could be supported by an economy before recessionary conditions set in, as conditions begin to contract, real wages should come down to allow as many jobs as possible to be preserved. This, too, will contribute to putting industry on a more profitable foundation.

Rolling back some of the restrictions placed by governments on business and business development would also assist in the recovery process. A more market-oriented perspective on regulation and business incentives would foster expansion where it might not otherwise take place.

There should also be containment in the level of unproductive forms of public spending. As the private sector contracts, there is even less ability for the economy to support the size of the public sector. Limiting the growth in *non-value-adding* forms of public spending, and if possible, lowering such spending will reduce the pressure on private industry.

There should, however, be increases in public sector infrastructure programmes that genuinely create value. The problem is always to get the timing right since the various lags between actually recognizing that such programmes are needed and actually putting such programmes into motion may well be too long to do much good. The danger is that the spending will occur after the trough has been reached and recovery is in place. Then, rather than softening the downturn, such outlays will diminish the private sector's ability to grow.

There may also be opportunities for temporary work programmes, with employees paid at or near the minimum wage. Such work programmes should not be seen, either by those who run them or by those who are employed, as anything more than a stopgap between genuinely productive jobs.

But as an absolute rudder to help governments to determine what actions they should or should not take, there should be a commitment to a return to fiscal balance at the earliest possible date. Recessions come with lower tax revenue and higher welfare payments. A budget surplus can be expected to fall into deficit, and where there is already a deficit, the likelihood is that its size will increase. Living with such deficits is the only alternative.

As the economy recovers, the deficits will diminish. Keeping in mind that recessions will pass but the debts accumulated to finance recovery will be very long-lasting ought to be an important antidote to the rush to higher expenditure as the economy slows down.

Tax increases in the midst of recession to lower the deficit are especially counterproductive to the needs of the moment. If the deficit is to be deliberately increased, cutting taxes, particularly taxes on business, will at least have the practical value of raising cash flow just when it is needed most and will put funds into the hands of those who are most likely to use the community's resources productively. This is the most direct way to preserve jobs.

Interest rate reductions should be part of the process. An economy in recession may generate fewer savings than an economy experiencing strong growth but there will also be far less demand for those savings. Such reductions in rates should be achieved by taking as much extraneous pressure from domestic rates as possible. Reductions in production costs, wages, taxes and public sector demand for resources will themselves induce a fall in rates, as would the existence in the first instance of a recessionary fall in economic activity.

An economic environment in which businesses find reduced production costs, lower real wages, a reduction in taxes, less regulation and falling rates of interest would be one in which the downturn would be arrested and an upturn would be expected to occur.

ACTIONS THAT SHOULD NOT BE TAKEN

For many, leaving things to the market would not appear direct enough nor would there be a general willingness to generate recovery by raising the profitability of business. These are political issues, and where such attitudes prevail, recovery will be slower and more uncertain. Yet there are popular solutions that are themselves part of the problem. Three are discussed below.

1. Public spending to restore growth causes output to be built on a false platform. Public sector construction projects, without an increase in value relative to their costs, is a loss-making enterprise, just as it would be in the private sector.

Keynesian-based macroeconomic theory tells you that there are multiplier effects. Even if the original outlay loses money, it is said, all of the secondary expenditures on various goods and services do their part to keep the economy growing. But if the initial expenditure loses money, then all of the secondary expenditures that hang off it are contributions to an overall loss-making project.

If every one of the related expenditures had been part of a single enterprise, this would be easier to understand. The fact that this spending is divided into individual payments to individual enterprises disguises the fact that whatever is being produced is not leading to the creation of enough value to repay all of the costs.

The economy is not creating enough additional value to validate the increase in the total level of spending. In the end, there will either be inflation, or cuts in other forms of public spending to finance repayment of the debts incurred when the deficits were run up, or there will be large increases in taxation to fund the expenditure. Nothing in an economy comes free.

To believe that deliberate increases in deficits through higher levels of public spending lead to recovery is the Keynesian fallacy and should be avoided at all costs. Some public works are useful. But the belief that the single most important requirement to pull an economy from recession is high levels of public spending and a vastly increased deficit is a danger.

2. Trade protection is a cure infinitely worse than the disease. Protecting local jobs against imports is a common response to recession. The question that is asked is why should domestic sales go to producers in foreign lands when there is already a high rate of unemployment at home?

Yet it should be obvious that raising domestic production costs during a downturn, which is what taxing imports amounts to, is the reverse of the policy needed to regenerate growth. It is also counterproductive to long-term growth to be depriving domestic industry of the often superior products that can be sourced in other countries, which is part of the reason that such imports have been sought out in the first place.

But the strongest reason that import restrictions should not be introduced is because of the certain retaliatory actions that will be taken by other countries against the initiating country's own exports. If the home country shuts out imports from others, the certainty is that others will shut out imports from them.

In dealing with recession, maintaining the most efficient least cost forms of production should be a principle that should not be breached.

3. Attempts to direct economies from the centre are the worst of all possible solutions to recession. The belief that an answer to our economic problems may be found in handing over the management of our economic affairs to politicians and public servants is to lose all understanding of what is required to turn resources into value adding output.

    A politician will, perhaps, allocate money for schools, roads, hospitals or whatever because it makes good politics. But in so doing, nothing is known of what needs to be done next by those who allocate the funds.

    The various projects each require inputs of all kinds numbering in the thousands. Each of those inputs requires a hinterland of endless other firms supplying inputs. It is beyond the competence of governments to organize in any detail the entire network of production that would be required. The only way to create the required inputs in the required amounts to be available when required is to rely on markets and the price mechanism.

    Governments can perhaps fund a handful of projects. They cannot hope to direct the economy overall. Nor, in most instances do they believe they can. A government can provide funds to build schools, and can even build schools using their own employees. But they cannot provide the lumber, hammers or nails, the bricks and mortar.

    Government direction of industry – the centralized control and management of an entire economy – has been attempted at one time or another in the past and has in every case been a tremendous failure. The information requirements for centrally managing an economy are beyond all possibility of collection. No one can ever know everything that needs to be known if decisions are to be made in response to unforeseen events. The very concept of a centrally directed economy is a dystopian nightmare that can never be made to work.

16. The financial system

The financial system at its most basic is a system that allows goods and services to be produced, their sale converted into a medium of exchange of some sort, and that money then used to buy the goods and services produced by others. But it is more than this. The financial system is also an institutional mechanism designed to provide a haven for those who wish to save while transferring those savings to investors. It therefore offers, or at least attempts to offer, a safe harbour for that part of each person's income whose expenditure is to be postponed. Postponed present consumption of income already earned constitutes saving and it is that saving that is converted into investment.

Notice that saving occurs out of incomes already earned. Therefore, something has already been produced so that this income could have been received. Saving is thus not an absence of production, some kind of void. Saving is a transfer of production to someone else.

Irrespective of how it appears to the person who saves, postponement of present consumption by those who save allows part of the productive apparatus of an economy to be used to produce capital goods. If all incomes were immediately spent on buying goods and services for immediate consumption, no part of the productive structure of an economy would be available to produce investment goods.

All funds saved are intended to be used to buy goods and services at some stage in the future. The aim of saving is to postpone till a later date the decision to purchase. During each period, there are therefore individuals adding to the savings pool by not buying as much as their incomes would have allowed them to, while there are others who are removing productive value from the pool of saving by the purchase of capital goods.

In miniature, the process is shown in Figure 16.1. Incomes are earned, some of which are channelled into various forms of saving. Savings are incomes earned but not spent by those who have earned those incomes. The funds are instead placed into a savings institution (bank, pension fund, and so on) who then lend those funds to others.

Very importantly, it should be seen that what are saved are real goods and services. Those who are doing the saving only see the money side of

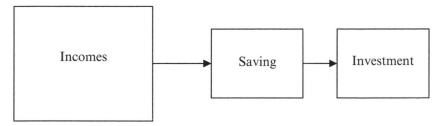

Figure 16.1   Basic framework of saving and investment

it, just as those who produce anything are seldom, if ever, paid with the products they have produced.

TO SAVE IS TO SPEND

Everyone receives money for their productions, but the money represents a share of the goods and services that had been produced. In exactly the same way, while the act of saving by an individual appears to be nothing other than placing money into a financial institution of some sort, from the global economic point of view, saving means putting to use whatever has been purchased by those who borrowed the funds. To save is to spend, but on a different set of goods and services chosen by someone other than the person who had originally earned the income.

Where savings are borrowed by business, then it should be understood that those savings are actually made up of the capital goods, the machinery, the factories and buildings that the existence of savings has allowed business firms to create.

It is, of course, true that savings can also be borrowed by others besides business firms, and these others include those who wish to borrow to buy consumer goods and governments who may wish to use available savings for their own purposes. A more complete picture is thus shown in Figure 16.2.

The money borrowed by consumers, to buy a car for example, or to finance the purchase of an overseas trip, does not add to the productive potential of the economy. It is a drawing down of productivity rather than an increment.

This is not a criticism, only a statement of fact. Borrowing to finance personal consumption, so long as the money can be repaid through other sources of income, is how economies typically operate. It brings forward in time the ability to purchase. Rather than having to accumulate the full purchase price of products, they can be bought at an earlier date with

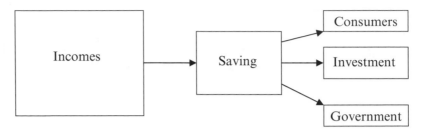

Figure 16.2   Flow of saving to all potential users

income earned at a later date used to repay the debt incurred plus the interest.

Government use of funds is, in theory, potentially as productive as the monies spent by private sector investors. The major difference, however, is that funds borrowed by governments are seldom repaid out of the revenues earned on the projects themselves (think of roads and schools), but from general government revenue.

The general expansion of the economy, towards which such infrastructure investments, if used sensibly, do contribute, is the form in which governments justify their borrowing of the nation's savings. In a well-ordered economy, this is what happens.

There is, nevertheless, no market testing of the value or productiveness of such projects. In the private sector, firms that cannot repay their debts disappear. In the public sector, the consequence is higher taxation, higher inflation, slower growth, and living standards below the level that might otherwise have been achieved.

Since in any economy the near certainty is that a government will repay the amounts it has borrowed, even if in a devalued currency or because it has raised its tax rates, there is typically less risk. But for an economy, the savings put to use by governments should be recognized as representing a portion of the output of the entire economy.

The more that government has use of a nation's savings, the less is available for use by the private sector. This is equivalent to saying that the more that the government has use of the nation's *resources*, the less there is for use by private sector firms. This is a *ceteris paribus* statement, of course. It is always possible that income earners will increase their level of saving. But if they do not, the more national savings are used by governments, the less there is for productive investment by firms.

THE NATURAL RATE AND THE MONEY RATE

In following the waves of recession, unemployment and inflation, it is helpful to recognize the existence of two parallel sets of market determinations for the price of borrowed savings.

There is first the *natural rate of interest*. It is a rate that is, in fact, invisible, almost undiscoverable within the flow of economic events. It is price of real savings as determined by the forces of supply and demand. The natural rate of interest is thus the price of that part of an economy's productive output that is available for others to make use of.

How much there is or how much would become available at different price levels is unknown. A reasonable proxy is available through the flow of funds into savings institutions, but it is only a rough guide. What is not, however, the equivalent to the flow of real savings is the flow of money and credit made available through the financial system.

The interest rates we do see, the *market* or *nominal* rate of interest, often called the *money* rate of interest, are the interest rates charged by financial institutions or other providers of credit. Credit may come in the form of money, bank accounts or other formats using domestic currency. Or it may simply be a form of permission to take goods or services upon a promise to pay a specific amount of money at a later date. It is therefore a known rate, almost always expressed in so many percentage points per year.

Such interest rates are often described as the price of money, but that is not quite right. What they are, more generally, is the price of market credit. They are the sums paid to gain access to available savings, but they are not the same.

It is a rate that is directly and often deliberately manipulated by the monetary authorities of every economy. It is the manipulation of this rate that causes a divergence between market interest rates and the natural rate.

Such manipulation, as can be imagined, has major effects on the state of an economy for good and very often for bad. The role of governments in the market for credit may be the single, most difficult area of economic policy. It is also the area that creates more havoc within market economies, even when the aim is to leave markets to sort themselves out on their own.

We will therefore look first at the natural rate, and then at the money rate before finally bringing the two together.

NATURAL RATE OF INTEREST

What must first be understood is this: interest rates are a natural form of payment. Since there are differences between individuals in when they would like to spend, a market for savings will always exist.

Savings will not be made available to anyone else unless those who borrow pay for the privilege of having use of some portion of a community's available resources. When interest is paid to the lender, it comes as a payment for the use of someone else's purchasing power and deserves a price just as if it were any other item of property being used by someone other than its owner.

There was for almost two thousand years a prohibition on the charging of interest that did not largely disappear within the advanced economies of the West until the middle of the nineteenth century, and even now such sentiments have by no means completely gone. Yet without a market for savings and the charging of interest that must come with it, an economy cannot grow and prosper.

The following discussion looks at the various elements that go into the pricing of savings, that is, that go into the determination of rates of interest.

Interest Rates as a Form of Rental

Interest rates are similar to rental payments, except the particular items that the borrower has chosen to use the funds to purchase were not items owned by the lender. Lending money at interest is a more abstract means of giving others access to the goods and services they would not otherwise be able to make use of themselves.

Part of the value given up in lending money out is the loss of immediate use of the funds. There is a need to pay for the postponement. The undeniable fact is that a dollar today is worth more to its owner than even the certainty of a dollar in twelve months' time even where the purchasing power has not changed. Interest rates are the payments that must be made to compensate for whatever reasons borrowers have to prefer spending in the present rather than at some moment in the future.

Interest as a Means to Identify More Productive Investments

But even beyond the requirement to pay interest, there is the need for the economy to ensure that those who use borrowed funds are the optimal users of those funds from an economy-wide perspective. The willingness to pay higher interest in a business context, if it is matched against a proper assessment of the uses for which the funds will be put (which is what lenders typically do), will tend to allow money and capital to flow to those who will make the greatest economic return.

Since savings are scarce, there is a return to the owners of available capital just as there is on the renting to others of any scarce resource.

If one bought a house and rented it out to others, the rental payments would be the return on the ownership of the house. Lending money is the same process without having first sunk one's savings into a particular form of capital. It is in many ways actually better, since borrowing the savings of others allows lenders to shape the realized form of those savings in any way they please.

Adjustment for Risk

But those who lend money out have as their first criterion a desire to have the money repaid. There is an enormous variety of risks associated with different lending possibilities. Lending money to governments will have a lower risk than lending money to a business which must deal with the endless uncertainties before it. Lending money for a short period will tend to be less risky than lending money for longer stretches of time.

There is therefore embedded into each interest rate charged a risk premium. This risk premium takes into account the likelihood that the money will be repaid, which builds into such considerations the length of time over which the money is to be borrowed.

The less risky the lender or the shorter the period of time, the lower the interest rate will tend to be, all other things being equal.

Moreover, there is not just one interest rate in an economy but a great many. There is, in fact, a different process of interest rate setting for just about every form of borrowing that takes place.

There is therefore within the money market the usual jostling that goes on in any market as those who buy, in this case the borrowers, look for the cheapest price (that is the lowest interest rates) while those who sell, the lenders, look for the highest price (that is the highest interest rate). But each, and particularly the lenders, look to balance the risk against the interest charged.

Many will choose a lower rate of return for the comfort of greater security. And in the money market, there is no perfect certainty anywhere. Even governments have been known to default on their loans.

The existence of a risk premium is therefore intrinsic to the market for available savings. The greater the risk, *ceteris paribus*, the higher the rate of interest will be.

Inflation and the Willingness to Lend

But finally, there is the relation between interest rates and the inflation rate. Since savings are transferred by lending money, the aim is to receive in return at least as much in purchasing power as was lent out plus the interest earned, which itself will contain a risk premium.

Inflation reduces the purchasing power of money. If inflation is running at 5 per cent per year, the value of a unit of currency one year later will buy only 95 per cent of what it originally would. Therefore, when inflation is running at 5 per cent, for those lending their money to others, if they are to receive in return at least as much in value as was lent out, the interest rate must include that 5 per cent inflation premium.

Moreover, it is the *expected* rate of inflation that matters. If inflation turns out to be higher than expected, borrowers come out ahead, since they pay their debts in a devalued currency because the inflation premium will have been less than necessary to compensate for the actual growth in prices.

It is a similar story when inflation is falling. If a fall in inflation is not expected, borrowers will be willing to pay a premium consistent with the prevailing expectation, while lenders will not accept anything less. The outcome works to the advantage of lenders, but who was to know?

It is for this reason that in attempting to contain inflation, part of the process is to lower inflationary expectations. If a lower inflation rate is expected, interest rates will be lower than they otherwise would have been.

Summary

In summary, the factors that go into the determination of interest rates would be dependent on a variety of factors which would include, but by no means be restricted to:

- the scarcity of available savings;
- the intensity of competing demands for those savings;
- the time period during which the funds are to be borrowed;
- the risks involved and the probability of being repaid in full;
- the expected rate of inflation.

Again, there is no such thing as *the* rate of interest. But every rate actually charged will be determined by these factors.

However, for convenience sake, the assumption of there being a single rate of interest is made to simplify the explanation. The rate can be seen as the representative rate, but it always needs to be borne in mind that any particular rate will be shaped by risk, the time period involved and the expected rate of inflation as well as a host of other factors that influence the willingness either to borrow or to lend.

SUPPLY AND DEMAND FOR SAVINGS

There is thus some unknown rate of interest embedded within every economy at which the level of savings is equal to the demand for those savings. Again, it is important to emphasize that saving here does not mean money and credit but refers to actual productive goods or labour time. It is these that are, for example, used in producing capital goods and other forms of investment. This is what the natural rate of interest allocates (and is represented in Figure 16.3 by the letter r).

Here we find the supply curve of savings. Each point on the curve is the answer to an **if–then** statement which begins from the vertical axis. If the rate of interest was at this particular rate, **then** the level of savings would be at the volume shown on the horizontal axis.

The demand curve for savings is also an **if–then** statement. **If** interest rates are at this particular rate **then** we know from the horizontal axis this

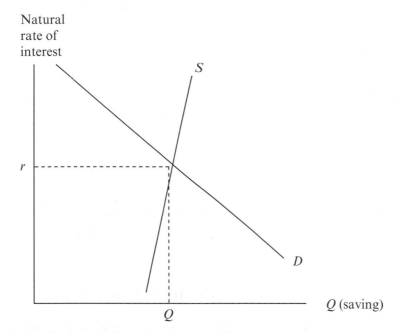

Figure 16.3   Determination of the natural rate of interest

will be the demand for available savings. And as already discussed, each of the curves has its underlying *ceteris paribus* conditions.

Where the two curves meet is the natural rate of interest, *r*, which is intrinsically undiscoverable. But the horizontal axis presents a reality of major importance. This is the volume of domestically generated output available for use in productive purposes.

The greater the volume of such savings, the more investment is possible. But whatever the volume of savings might be, that is all there is. How much savings there are limits how much investment there can be. The availability of capital is a major limiting factor in every economy.

MARKET RATE OF INTEREST

The market rate of interest, the money or nominal rate, is determined by the financial system. No one trying to borrow is unaware of what this rate is. Every lender makes a point of informing borrowers how much they will have to repay in return for any of the funds they receive.

But what is directly received is not the actual physical savings of the community but sums of money which can be used to buy the capital available.

Banks create money. They do not have an ability to limitlessly increase the availability of money but they do have an ability to increase the supply of money and credit at a rate well beyond the rate of increase in the actual level of savings. Banks have the ability to create an account where none had existed before or add a sum of money into an existing account.

And what is in that account is not an actual 'physical' sum of money, as there would have been in the days of the gold standard. The sum of money entered to someone's credit is no more than a data entry in the records held by the bank.

The determination of interest rates in the market for credit and money (designated by the letter *i* rather than by *r*) is shown in Figure 16.4.

The demand curve may not be much different either in shape or concept from the demand for savings generally. But the supply curve is different, and more importantly, the *ceteris paribus* conditions of supply are potentially very different.

DETERMINATION OF THE MONEY SUPPLY

The supply of money and credit is determined jointly by an economy's central bank in collaboration with the economy's banking system. There

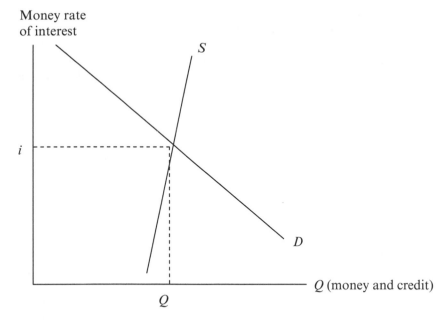

Money rate
of interest

Figure 16.4   Determination of the market rate of interest

are two elements that determine the full extent that an economy's money
supply may grow:

- the amount of *base money* in an economy;
- the *reserve ratio* imposed on the banks by either law or central bank
  regulation.

Banks are almost always compelled by law to maintain a particular proportion of their funds in liquid form; that is, in a form that is either easily convertible into the medium of exchange or that is in fact the medium of exchange
itself. These extremely liquid forms are the base money of an economy.

The most important parts of the base money are notes and coins in the
local currency or deposits by the banks with the central bank. Both can be
used at a moment's notice to meet the demands of depositors should they
wish to withdraw their money.

Banks, however, are in the business of lending money. And while it has
been a practice that has taken centuries to develop, it is now the case universally within banks across the world that they hold only a small fraction
of the value of their deposits in highly liquid form. Most of the assets of a
bank are in the form of loans.

Suppose banks are required to hold only 10 per cent of their total bank deposits as liquid assets. That would mean that for every $100 of deposits, they would be compelled to hold only $10 in cash or other reserve assets. If every depositor showed up on the doorstep of a bank, no bank in the world could, without assistance from its central bank, meet the demand from depositors for their money.

The total supply of money then consists of base money plus components of the bank deposits of the financial system. Since the interest is seldom in the volume of money per se, but is instead in the rate of growth of the amount of money, the particular list of deposits included in definitions of the supply of money is largely dependent on which aspects of the liquidity of an economic system there is interest in. But what gives money its 'moneyness' is its ability to act as a medium of exchange.

VARYING THE MONEY SUPPLY

Given the relationship between base money, the reserve ratio, the level of deposits and the willingness of others to borrow, it can be seen that raising the supply of money can occur in any of the following situations:

- an increase in base money;
- an increase in deposits;
- a fall in the reserve ratio;
- an increase in the amount of money borrowed;
- an increase in the willingness to lend.

These are the *ceteris paribus* conditions for the money supply. They are the underlying factors that cause the supply of money to shift. And while these are loosely related to the level of production and saving, they are also in important ways independent of anything going on in the real economy.

Much of this is determined by the central bank itself. Central banks can manipulate the flow of base money through what are called *open market operations*. These are efforts made to increase the level of base money by putting more cash into the hands of the public through buying bonds. Here the public has more money but fewer bonds.

Or on other occasions money is withdrawn from the hands of the public by selling bonds. The public has more bonds but less money. The aim in either case is to change the amount of base money in an economy.

The amount of base money is also affected by government spending and tax policy. High spending, low taxes and budget deficits increase the amount of base money. Less spending, high taxes and a budget surplus pull money out.

Once base money enters the economy it will find its way to the banking system where more money is deposited. More deposits leads to more loans and a further increase in the level of spending.

The central bank can influence the level of loans through variations in the deposit ratio. If it wishes to increase the money supply, the ratio can be lowered. If it wishes to diminish the money supply, the ratio can be raised.

But finally, there is the willingness of the banks to lend, which can be affected by the state of the economy and the relative optimism or pessimism of those who might be inclined to borrow. As an economy slows and pessimism spreads, there is less interest in borrowing, but the banks become more reluctant to lend.

Times improve and there is an increase in the demand for loans just as banks become more willing to lend their funds out.

To sum up, the notion that there is some amount of money that is 'the' money supply is untenable although sometimes argued. The level continues to change all the time, either through design or just by the ebb and flow of economic activity.

But it is the manipulation of the amount of money to vary interest rates which is amongst the most important causes of recession and economic instability, and has been since the early years of the nineteenth century.

How to bring stability into the financial system, and how to discipline the monetary authorities, are questions whose answers have thus far remained elusive. It is one of the reasons why the business cycle is certain to remain a feature of the economic system as far into the future as one might care to look.

THE MARKET RATE AND THE NATURAL RATE TOGETHER

Figure 16.5 shows the supply and demand curves for the market for money and credit side by side with the supply and demand curves in the market for savings. On the left is the determination of the market rate of interest, i. On the right is the determination of the natural rate of interest, r. Here $i = r$. That is, the market rate and the natural rate are the same. There is therefore balance in both the supply of credit and the supply of savings. What we have here is that the interest rate for credit matches the interest rate that allows the supply of savings to exactly match the demand for savings by investors.

We also see that, given the rate of interest, the level of investment is

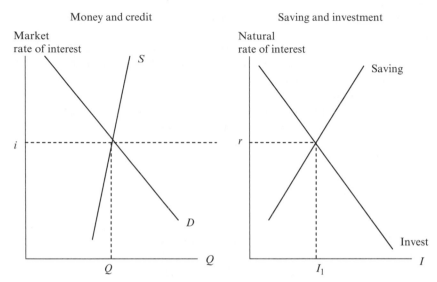

Figure 16.5   Market and natural rates of interest

determined by the point on the 'Invest' curve at that rate of interest. There is then a level of investment equal to I_1, which is just equal to the amount of savings available.

INCREASING THE SUPPLY OF MONEY

Into this situation we introduce an increase in the supply of money and credit (see Figure 16.6). Governments and central banks often take actions to lower interest rates, which means that they must increase the supply of money. Open market operations are the normal means in which this is done, and the effect is to move the supply curve of money to the right.

With this increase in the supply of money, changes take place in the financial structure of the economy that will have subsequent effects. Credit is cheaper and easier to get. Nominal interest rates are lower so the amount of credit sought has increased from Cr to Cr_2.

In following the dynamics of the changes, however, the limitations of the flat, timeless nature of supply and demand curves need to be recognized in thinking through all of the subsequent effects. So far as savers are concerned, nothing happens instantaneously. Therefore, in following the logic of the changes that take place, it is necessary to bear in mind that what will take place will take place through time. Nothing much happens immediately, but across the weeks and months, there are changes taking

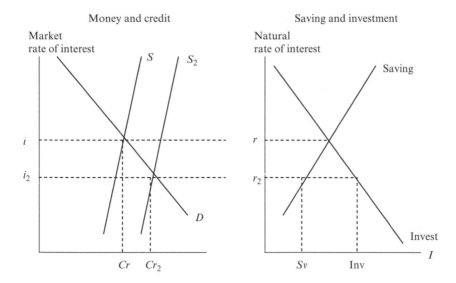

Figure 16.6   An increase in the supply of money

place as individuals across the economy react to the new circumstances they face.

With the fall in the market rate of interest, conditions have altered over on the real side of the economy. There we find a sudden excess demand for available savings. The level of real savings falls while the level of demand for such savings increases.

Note that in this simplified analysis neither curve shifts. Only the price – the rate of interest – has changed. In reality, with expectations of all sorts having shifted with the fall in rates of interest there are possibly no end of changes that might well take place. Here we assume no shift in the position of either curve.

With the lower rate of interest, looking first at the supply side, there is a lower return for the savings made available. The amount of available savings falls back from the former equilibrium level to a lower figure, shown in Figure 16.6 as *Sv*. There are fewer real resources being made available to investors.

Meanwhile on the demand side, lower interest rates have brought additional numbers into the market, looking for what savings there are. At the lower below-equilibrium interest rate, r_2, which is equal to i_2, there is a demand for investment goods at the level marked, Inv. There are more potential borrowers in the market looking for savings than there are savings available. The result, so far as the economy is concerned, is only harmful irrespective of how much apparent demand there is for the available savings (*Sv*).

CONSEQUENCES WHEN NATURAL RATE IS BELOW MARKET RATE

And what are these harmful consequences? Here is a list of some of them, after which they will be explained:

- slower economic growth;
- inefficient investments;
- higher inflation;
- inflation of asset prices (the 'bubble' economy).

Slower Growth

The belief that artificially low interest rates are good for an economy, that they will encourage higher rates of investment, is a notion that dies hard. It is a notion that is nevertheless deeply flawed.

Artificially low rates of interest will reduce the supply of savings. However much demand there might be – there would be even more 'demand' if we just gave as much credit as they wanted to anyone who asked – lower interest rates reduce the supply. There is just not as much capital for investment available than there had previously been.

Less investment means less growth. It is only the availability and utilization of additional supplies of capital that permit higher rates of investment to occur.

The actual level of investment in relation to the interest rate is shown in Figure 16.7. The downward-sloping section in the figure is the relevant section of the demand curve. The lower the interest rate, the more capital will be demanded until interest rates reach the equilibrium point. From then on, as interest rates fall it is only the supply curve which is relevant to the amount of investment.

Below the equilibrium point, whatever may happen to the level of demand, the amount of savings supplied falls away. The lower the level of interest, the less capital will be supplied and therefore the less investment there can be. *Imax* is the highest level of investment that will occur in this economy. Both higher and lower rates of interest will lower investment. Strange as it may seem, lowering interest rates beyond some point does not increase investment; it slows it down.

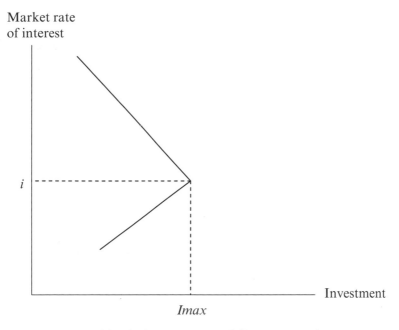

Figure 16.7   Actual level of investment at different rates of interest

Inefficient Investments

The excess demand for available savings means that lenders are able to choose, amongst the many additional demanders of funds, those with the lowest associated risks attached. There are more seeking the available savings than there are savings available.

The result is that many projects are undertaken that would not have been considered had rates been higher. The sorting mechanism of the price system is diluted. There are many less risky, less productive projects that will earn a positive return at the lower cost of funds. They get the funding while other, more difficult, less certain projects do not.

There are also many projects with a higher return to the investments that are not undertaken since the price mechanism does not ensure they are funded in preference to other projects with a lower real return. With interest rates no longer being used at the cutting edge to discriminate between projects, other criteria come into play, such as friendship with those in control of funds.

The consequence is that the actual investments that are undertaken are suboptimal. There is a lower real return with therefore a smaller contribution to growth.

Higher Inflation

If interest rates are below the equilibrium rate, there is more demand for resources to undertake investment projects than there is supply. Excess supply is the market condition out of which one can only expect prices to rise.

It goes further. The classic definition of inflation is too much money chasing too few goods. This is the precise condition put in place with the fall in interest rates below their equilibrium level. There is money and credit being created at a faster rate than the rate at which output is being produced.

For every dollar's worth of goods and services produced, there is more than a dollar's worth of purchasing power inside the economy. Loose credit markets make inflation inevitable, and in this case 'loose' refers to allowing interest rates to fall below the natural rate of interest.

Loose monetary policy is the most common cause of inflation. It is demand-driven due to the rapid growth in purchasing power allowed by credit conditions. Hyperinflations are most obviously driven by the rapid growth in money and credit, but even the slow, creeping inflations can be traced back to loosening credit conditions.

Whether due to budget deficits or open market operations by the central bank, the effect is similar. There is more money demand than there is supply. Prices inevitably rise.

Asset Price Inflation

There are in addition particular areas of the economy that can experience very rapid increases in prices through loosening credit conditions. These are in the market for various fixed assets.

House prices, share prices, the value of paintings and other works of art, tend to rise disproportionately to other goods and services in such an inflationary environment. These are typically the kinds of products with highly inelastic supply conditions over the medium term. Gold is often a refuge when inflationary pressures grow.

Money demand works its way through the economy, pushing up all prices generally, but some rise more rapidly than others. Where supply is inelastic, their prices will show rates of increase above the general average change in the price level.

Whether these assets hold their relative increase in value depends on supply conditions generally over the longer term. But the early stages of an increase in prices can cause a 'bubble' to emerge that is likely to be deflated to at least some extent as the economy moves through the various phases of the cycle.

GOVERNMENT DEMAND FOR SAVINGS

But it is not just business that seeks available savings. So too does government. And the more of a nation's savings that ends up in the hands of governments to be used for their purposes, the less is available to business.

A production possibility curve is shown in Figure 16.8 with consumption on the vertical axis and investment on the horizontal. It is also a straight line production possibility curve, indicating that resources are equally capable of producing consumption goods or investment goods.

In every economy some of its resources are used to provide goods and services for consumers while some are used to build the economy's productive capabilities. But also in every economy there is only so much that can be produced given the available technology, capital stock, labour, skill levels and general productivity.

In this economy, the level of production for consumption is equal to C while the level of investment is equal to I.

But note. The level of investment is dependent on there being saving. If everything produced were consumed, the level of consumption would occur where the production possibility curve reached the vertical axis. The

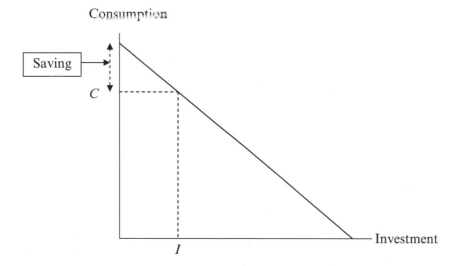

Figure 16.8   Production possibility curve with consumption and investment

actual level of consumption is less than the total level of consumption possible. The difference between the maximum possible level of consumption and the actual level of consumption is the amount of saving.

This saving allows investment to take place. The resources released from consuming are directed into the production of investment goods that improve the productive capabilities of the economy. Various entrepreneurs borrow funds and use those funds to purchase and produce capital assets. These are added to the productive base of the economy. The more such investments there are, the faster the economy will grow.

GOVERNMENT SPENDING AND NATIONAL SAVING

But it is not just businesses which use a nation's savings. Governments too take their share of available savings. Consumers save as before, but we will bring in government. Governments are already receiving part of their national income through taxation, but are also able to borrow should they wish for additional funds. This is shown on the horizontal axis of Figure 16.9.

Governments use part of the productive resources of the economy for their own purpose which, if used properly, will have a social communal purpose. But in whatever way the government uses these resources, if it uses them, the rest of the community cannot. There is only so much

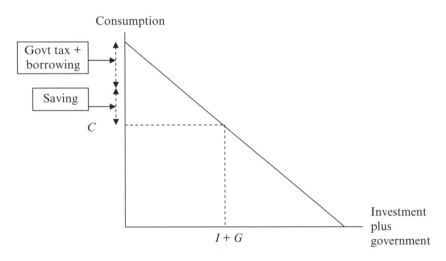

Figure 16.9   Production possibility curve with C, I, G *and* T

available, and the more the government has, the less there is for anyone else. When governments borrow, the effect is to limit the amount of savings available for business purposes.

CROWDING OUT

The production possibility curve in Figure 16.10 shows the trade-off between private investment and government expenditures. There are only so many resources, and the more available to one, the less available to the other.

This act of pushing business out of the way through increased government borrowing of available savings is referred to as *crowding out*. It is said that governments 'crowd out' business where their borrowings come at the expense of private sector borrowings. The private sector is said to have been crowded out by public spending.

In Figure 16.10, we begin with I_1 and G_1. If there is an increase in the level of government spending, it can only come at the expense of less private investment. But where governments are competing with business

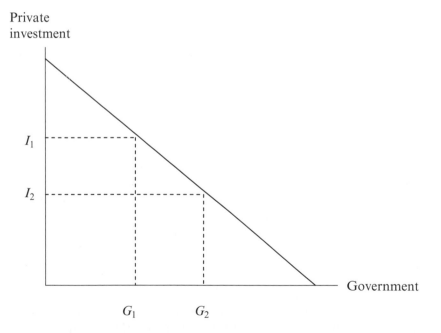

Figure 16.10   Private investment versus government spending

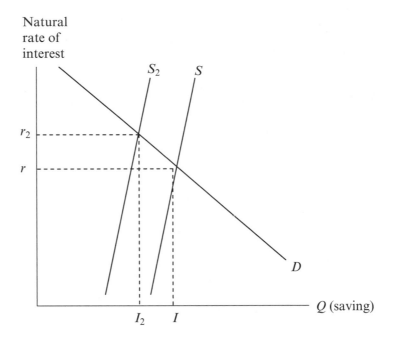

Figure 16.11   Crowding out

for resources to be used for investment purposes, the only way for governments to be able to spend more is for businesses to spend less.

This same effect can be shown more formally in the diagram showing
the supply and demand for savings in the determination of the natural rate
of interest (see Figure 16.11). The diagram shows the supply and demand
for savings as experienced by the private sector. The supply curve shows
how much saving will be provided at different rates of interest.

Here the interest rate is shown as *r* and the level of investment funds in
equilibrium is equal to *I*. With government entering the market for such
savings, the supply curve, as experienced by the private sector, has moved
to the left. There are fewer savings available at every rate of interest.

In a world of diminished availability of savings, interest rates rise to r_2,
while the level of investment falls from *I* to I_2. There is less private sector
investment, which has had to give way in the face of the government's
decision to compete for those funds.

Were the government's chosen investments as productive for the
economy as those of the private sector, it would make no difference
whether it was business or government undertaking the investment.

The reality is, however, that government spending is less productive than private sector investment. Government spending is, in fact, often unproductive, wasting the resources under its control and creating less value than it has used up in its productions.

It is a serious error to treat public spending as an equivalent to private spending. It is not. Not only is public spending less productive, but with its lack of productivity the increase in the number of jobs will be lower unless real wages are allowed to fall to accommodate the limited additions to value of public sector activity, assuming any value is created at all.

MONEY, DEBT AND RECESSION

There should, finally, be some appreciation of the dangers that are inherent in an economy that is dependent on credit and debt. Mistakes are regularly made by those who lend because they misjudge the risks. Economies will from time to time enter recession because of failings in the financial system that have led to savings being systematically placed with borrowers who cannot repay their debts.

Money and finance are odd products. Money values are an abstract measure of a quantum of goods and services. Money and credit in the modern world can, moreover, be created at the touch of a keyboard. Keeping the growth in the nominal amount of expenditure at or near the growth in the quantum of goods and services available for purchase is one of the most difficult, but crucially important issues for the management of an economy. If the amount of money and finance increases more rapidly than the quantum of goods and services, the effect is a rise in the price level. If, on the other hand, the amount of money increases more slowly than the flow of goods and services is increasing, there is a potential for prices to fall and for the economy to slow.

But in the situation of a typical financial crisis, there is an actual fall in the flow of credit in comparison with the past. And if the sense of danger increases, so that trust in the banking and financial system as a repository for their savings falls, or financial institutions lose trust in each other, a contraction in the system of credit creation can pull the entire economy down. Without credit to mediate transactions between buyers and sellers, the real economy will invariably go into reverse.

Savings and debt are the glue that holds the economy together. Finance was listed as the fifth factor of production. Without it virtually no enterprise can succeed. Businesses borrow and the financial system designs various forms of debt that are intended to mediate between those who save and those who seek to use productive resources that these savings have made available.

But the system of credit and debt depends on there being a strong level of trust between those who lend and those who borrow. Where such trust disappears for whatever reason, credit will be withdrawn and the economy will slow or even contract. Such financial crises are the most destabilizing form of economic dislocation and are the most difficult to prevent.

The financial system by its very nature will on occasion be driven towards major dislocation by an unexpected unfolding of events. The future is never perfectly foreseen and financial disasters must be an expectation. An economic system must therefore make contingent arrangements for such events which usually require the financial authorities taking action to stabilize the financial system by providing liquidity for markets in which credit has for some reason dried up. Liquidity is an essential component of the financial system and in an economy where liquidity is rapidly falling there is an imperative on the financial authorities to act.

A successful free market economy is not one in which the government disappears and does nothing in the face of major financial dislocation. It is one in which those in government understand how a market economy works and take appropriate steps when necessary to ensure that the financial system will continue to function when it is in danger of collapse. Governments are not in this way running the economy; they should be seen as managing it.

Yet even in saying this, the moral hazard in a system, where those who manage private sector financial institutions become convinced that the government will bail them out the greater are the financial problems they have created, can become a problem in itself. A properly regulated financial system where fraud and illegality are punished is of course a necessity. And financial institutions should themselves be designed in ways that ensure that those who make the wrong decisions are heavily penalized for their misjudgements. But at the end of the day, there will be honest mistakes in lending decisions and financial panics will occur. Institutional arrangements to deal with such problems as they arise is all that can ever be hoped for since there is no means to structure a financial system to ensure that only those who repay their debts on time will ever be allowed to borrow. Risk and uncertainty are in the nature of things, which is why recessions and financial panics are an inevitable part of economic life.

17. Controlling inflation

The explanation of inflation as too much money chasing too few goods, as clichéd as it might be, remains the most accurate short-form description we have, if what it says is properly understood. Since inflation is about the purchasing power of each unit of money in relation to the volume of goods and services sold, somewhere in all of that is what is required to understand the fall in the value of money relative to the prices charged for products bought and sold.

But where is that relationship, and even if it is understood, what tools does it give for creating conditions for rapid rates of long-term non-inflationary growth, the nirvana of economic policy? On this there are no settled conclusions.

QUANTITY THEORY OF MONEY

The oldest theory of inflation is still the best place to start and is still known by its original name as the *Quantity Theory of Money*. But as venerable as this theory is, it is deeply flawed. No sensible policy has ever been developed from it because of what it ignores and what cannot be known. It does contain an essential kernel of truth, but it leaves out too much of what needs to be understood to be of much direct use.

So what is this theory? Start with a unit of currency and a period of time, say a year. Each unit of currency will move from hand to hand as goods are bought and sold. The unit of currency received by one person is then used to buy something else. The number of times that a unit of currency changes hands during a period of time is known as its *Velocity of Circulation*.

Thus the total currency value of transactions during a period can be calculated as the number of currency units (M for money) times its velocity of circulation (V). Or as a calculation:

$$M \times V$$

It is also possible to see the entire turnover of the economy as the average price (P) of all of the transactions (T) that take place during that period of time. This is not the same as GDP since it includes all transactions and not just final sales. Money changes hands for all of the inputs as well.

The total money value of all transactions is therefore calculated as:

$$P \times T$$

The two expressions come to the same outcome, the nominal level of total economy wide transactions. The Quantity Theory of Money is therefore shown by this equality:

$$M \times V = P \times T$$

which is often shown simply as:

$$MV = PT$$

And because the number of transactions in an economy can never be known but is likely to be closely related to the level of nominal GDP, in the usual way this expression is now shown, transactions is replaced by real GDP (Y). Thus, in its simplest modern form, the Quantity Theory of Money is shown as:

$$MV = PY$$

That is, the number of units of currency in existence times the frequency with which each unit is used is equal to the number of units of output produced times the average price paid for each unit of output.

Much effort has gone into making this equation into a useful economic construct. It is an accurate equality since it is true by definition. The real question is whether it provides any useful policy advice.[1]

And the fact is that while economists have been manipulating this equation since at least the middle of the eighteenth century, there is so far precious little evidence that it actually provides any useful guidance for economic management.

There is, to begin with, no single definition of even something as simple as the stock of money. There are, in fact, many such definitions. Definitions of money have proliferated over the years, largely because of the attempts to find some definition of money that can be used to show a regular relationship between the growth in the stock of money and the growth in the price level. No such simple relationship has been found, irrespective of which definition of money one has chosen to use.

The velocity of circulation, the measure of the number of transactions within an economy during some period of time, has turned out to be anything but a constant. Not only does it vary, it varies in unpredictable ways. Partly it varies depending on the phase of the cycle. Partly it is the development of different forms of payment (for example credit cards) that causes the relationship to be unstable and partly it is the introduction of new forms of financial communication (for example the Internet). There are many other factors as well. Such changes are ongoing and constant.

It is in fact next to impossible to conceive of a definition of money that would provide a reliable base for all exchanges that take place within an economic system. Using the Quantity Theory of Money is useful as a rough explanatory guide to economic events but in spite of all the efforts made, has proven a poor guide to anti-inflationary policy. No policy that has focused on containing the growth of any particular definition of the stock of money has been successful in containing inflation. Economists have more or less given up trying to find one.

THE MODERN KEYNESIAN ROAD TO INFLATION CONTROL

Yet since there can be no denying that inflation is a loss of purchasing power per unit of currency, inflation must in some way be related to money.

Anti-inflation policy therefore remains focused on using the monetary system to maintain low rates of inflation. But the classical theory of inflation structured around the quantity theory has developed into an approach that now heavily relies on Keynesian aggregate demand. The approach to analysing output and employment is also used to analyse inflation and the inflationary process.

And while it will be noted only in passing, *monetary policy* should be clearly distinguished from *monetarism*. Monetarism is the theory that inflation can be controlled by controlling the growth in the money supply. It links two of the four elements in the quantity theory to achieve price stability. Control the growth in the money stock, and the rate of growth in prices is itself controlled.

Monetary policy is the use, not only of monetary aggregates, but also of interest rate and credit creation policies to effect chosen economic outcomes. And not just inflation but any aspect of the economy can be the target of such monetary policies. Monetary policy can be used and often has been used to affect employment, economic growth or movements in the exchange rate.

Moreover, monetary policy does not necessarily assume a close relationship between growth in monetary aggregates and the rate of inflation, nor does it necessarily assume that controlling inflation is the most important step in achieving economic stability. It is the use of money, interest rates and credit creation to improve economic conditions.

The following are the familiar ingredients around which modern monetary policy is conceived:

- estimates of the natural rate of unemployment;
- the upward-sloping short-run aggregate supply curve;
- the vertical long-run aggregate supply curve;
- the Phillips curve;
- interest rate adjustments.

There is probably more fashion in the area of monetary policy than any other area of economics but these are the basic ingredients that go into the framing of monetary policy at the present time. These were all discussed at greater length earlier on in the book. They are revisited here to see how they are combined in an anti-inflation policy.

The Natural Rate of Unemployment

The *natural rate of unemployment* is a particular rate of unemployment related to the rate of inflation. It is the unemployment rate which will leave the rate of inflation unchanged.

If the actual unemployment rate is below the natural rate, the inflation rate would be expected to accelerate. If on the other hand, the actual unemployment rate is above the natural rate, then the inflation rate would be expected to fall. If, finally, the actual unemployment rate is equal to natural rate, then the inflation rate would be expected to remain at whatever the inflation rate happened to be.

The natural rate is not constant but changes through time. It is estimated by those who are responsible for managing the economy, and in particular by the monetary authorities, and is derived from estimates related to the Phillips curve.

Why do they use this concept for monetary policy? Because since no one can know the future, by positing a relationship that states that an unemployment rate below the natural rate will lead to an acceleration of inflation, at least there is something one can know in the present that relates to that unknown future.

The fact that this relationship is almost completely specious – with almost no hard and firm relationship between today's unemployment rate and tomorrow's inflation – is, so far as policy makers are concerned, almost totally beside the point. It provides a framework for government action and is widely understood within markets.

Without this relationship, since we have given up using money supply growth as an indicator of future inflation, there would be almost nothing that could be used as a guide to policy. Better even a very shaky framework, it is thought, than having no framework at all.

Short-Run Aggregate Supply

Short-run aggregate supply (SRAS) is the relationship between the amount that will be produced at different price levels when all other factors in the economy are held constant. A higher price level means higher profitability since wages and other costs are frozen along the length of the curve, which is what is meant by holding all other things equal.

But as an economy tries to push beyond its natural limits it begins to strain against its various resource constraints, and at some stage costs begin to rise. And with rising costs the underlying conditions no longer remain equal and we move from the short run to the long run.

Long-Run Aggregate Supply

Long-run aggregate supply (LRAS) is the boundary between what is possible in an economy and what is not possible given its resource base, technical skills, labour force numbers and known technologies. It is the level of output towards which an economy gravitates when the unemployment rate is equal to the natural rate. It is an economy's potential GDP.

Trying to move beyond this level of production will in the long run only add to inflation, with no additional output possible. Only changes that make an economy more productive can allow economic growth to move beyond this level of output without creating inflationary pressures. All that expenditure beyond the capabilities of an economy can do is increase the rate of inflation.

The LRAS is shown in Figure 17.1. Increased aggregate demand only leads to an increase in the price level. *Yf* is the full employment level of output, which is the output at which the unemployment rate is equal to the natural rate. The only unemployment is frictional or structural.

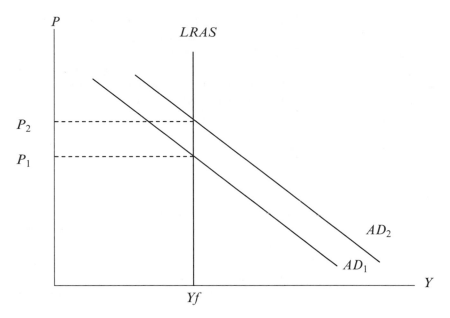

Figure 17.1   Inflation and long-run aggregate supply

Phillips Curve

The Phillips curve is derived from a study conducted during the 1960s of the relationship between movements in wages and movements in the unemployment rate in the UK between 1861 and 1957. The lower the level of unemployment, it was shown, the higher was the rate of growth in wage rates.

The relationship was then altered to make the comparison between movements in the price level (that is the rate of inflation) and the rate of unemployment. Low unemployment, it was concluded, led to high inflation. It is a relationship that has been calculated in every economy in which central banks have a role to play in framing policy.

The downward-sloping curve shown in Figure 17.2 is the traditional Phillips curve. The lower the unemployment rate, the higher the rate of inflation.

The vertical line is the long-run Phillips curve which is drawn at the natural rate of unemployment. Whatever trade-off there may be in the short run, in the long run, it is argued, there is no trade-off at all. It is similar to the LRAS curve. If the rate of unemployment falls *below* the natural rate of unemployment, *Un*, inflation will accelerate in the same way and for the same reason that inflation would accelerate if the level of GDP rose above its potential.

Inflation

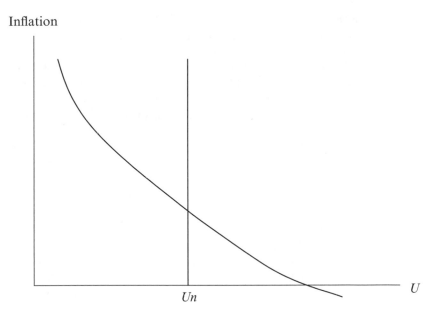

Figure 17.2   Short-run and long-run Phillips curve

To summarize: the rate of unemployment associated with an economy's potential GDP is its natural rate. There is therefore no point in trying to lower the unemployment rate below the natural rate, since all that will happen is higher inflation and no actual increases in the number of jobs. It is therefore the role of policy to keep the unemployment rate as close as possible to but not rise above the natural rate to prevent inflation from becoming entrenched. Keeping inflation down, it is said, is the most important role for governments in providing a platform for long-term sustainable non-inflationary growth.

Interest Rate Adjustments

Given the nature of long-run aggregate demand and the long-run Phillips curve as developed as part of the Keynesian macroeconomic framework, the aim of policy has been to estimate the natural rate of unemployment and thereafter ensure that the actual rate never falls lower than this estimated natural rate.

The basis for policy went even beyond that. The view was that if inflation were kept under control, recessions could be all but eliminated. Manipulation of interest rates became the instrument, with the aim being to keep the actual rate of unemployment above the natural. This was

argued to be the key to long-term and generally uninterrupted improvement in production combined with unemployment rates as low as could
possibly be achieved.

The variable used to control the unemployment rate was the rate of
interest. No longer was it thought that the aim was to keep unemployment
as low as possible as a prime aim of policy. Instead an inflation 'target'
was often chosen and interest rates were raised or lowered as needed to
ensure that the actual unemployment rate coincided with the natural rate,
which would ensure that the inflation rate was stable. Once stable inflation
was reached, the aim of policy was to keep the unemployment rate at its
natural rate.

If, however, inflation was too high, then policy would deliberately drive
the actual unemployment rate up above the natural rate until inflation was
again under control. Rates would then be brought down until the actual
rate was the same as the natural rate.

If, on the other hand, an economy was already at the desired inflation
rate but the unemployment rate went below the estimated natural rate,
then up rates would go again until unemployment went back to its natural
rate.

STABILITY

Here then was the answer to the problem of economic stability. Recessions
would be brief, assuming they occurred at all. But unlike with the original
Keynesian theory of aggregate demand, it was not fiscal policy that would
matter, but monetary policy. And while it was 'monetary' policy, the
instrument was not money itself, but the market rate of interest, the price
of money and credit creation within the financial system that mattered.

The basic aim of monetary policy was to get the inflation rate in an
economy to the desired rate and then use interest rate adjustments to keep
the unemployment rate at the rate consistent with that target rate.

Slowing aggregate demand to raise unemployment would require a fall
in one of the components of demand. Interest rate adjustments would be
aimed at lowering the level of private sector investment. The central bank
would raise interest rates arbitrarily, which then would lead to the situation shown in Figure 17.3.

Bad luck to the economy that the axe must fall on private investment,
the part of the economy producing long-term growth. Almost certainly
for political reasons, as little as possible of the reduction in demand and
employment would be allowed to fall on the public sector.

With the contraction in the stock of money from S_1 to S_2 in Figure 17.3,

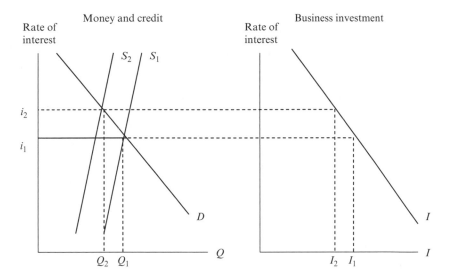

Figure 17.3   Increase in market rate of interest and its effect on investment

interest rates rise from i_1 to i_2. Some form of open market operation causes rates to rise. The effect on investment is shown on the right-hand side in the diagram, where the level of investment is seen to fall from I_1 to I_2 in response to the increase in rates of interest.

The effect transmits across to aggregate demand causing the aggregate demand curve in Figure 17.4 to move to the left from AD_1 to AD_2, lowering the price level. The effect of higher rates of interest has been to reduce the level of aggregate demand from the inflationary level beyond the economy's potential above the natural rate of unemployment to a lower more acceptable rate. Consumer demand would also be expected to fall with the increase in rates, which would move the AD curve even further to the left.

The equilibrium of the AD and $SRAS$ at a level beyond the capacity of the economy to sustain is the problem to be solved. The increase in interest rates therefore lowers aggregate demand until an equilibrium point is established where the $SRAS$, $LRAS$ and AD all meet at a level of production equal to the economy's potential. As shown in Figure 17.4, a stable equilibrium has been restored. Inflationary pressures have been reduced, the price level remains at P, while the level of production is exactly at the economy's potential at Yn.

The economy is at this point producing as well as could be expected; there is no cyclical unemployment and the price level is at the desired level. It is to achieve this outcome that inflation control through the judicious use of monetary policy was designed.

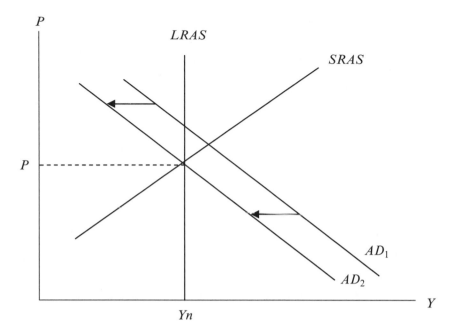

Figure 17.4   Stable equilibrium

WHAT'S WRONG WITH THE POLICY MODEL

In essence what we find is a model of inflation ultimately based on only a single factor, the rate of unemployment.

It is particularly notable that there is nothing explicit in this approach to inflation directly related to money itself, even though it is the value of money in relation to other goods and services that is the very meaning of an inflationary process. There is a price level in the form of an index, the index being comprised of untold millions of price movements. There are market interest rate adjustments which must presume some kind of subterranean adjustment of the amount of money which caused that rate to shift. But money itself is nowhere to be seen.

What we have is the movement of an aggregate demand curve relative to an aggregate supply curve where the entire world of buyers is buried in one curve while the whole world of entrepreneurial activity is buried in another.

To the aggregate demand and supply curves are then added the notion of a natural rate of unemployment and vertical long-run Phillips curve. Whatever Phillips may have found in the data on the UK between 1861 and 1957, no such smoothly continuous downward relationship is any longer visible in the data. The amount of work that has gone into finding some ongoing relationship between movement in prices and the rate of unemployment has been highly intensive. No such relationship can be found that reliably stands up across time.

The Phillips curve relationship has nevertheless found its way to the centre of economic theory because without it there is no Keynesian theory of inflation, there is no inflation forecasting model that can be constructed so that some event in the present can be said to affect price movements over the short to medium term, and there is no basis for an anti-inflation policy that can be implemented.

And finally, it is assumed that adjusting interest rates will merely lower the overall growth rate without consideration of the effects on the structure of production that rising rates must inevitably create.

CLASSICAL INFLATION POLICY

This last issue, the effect on the structure of production, may be of particular importance. The approach to inflation control ignores the fact that when interest rates are used to control inflation, the effect is to depress private investment. The space vacated by business can then be filled by increased activity in the public sector. Rising interest rates facilitate crowding out as governments inflate the money supply.

Indeed, the very meaning of 'inflation' originally meant an excess creation of the medium of exchange beyond the growth in productive output. Inflation meant an inflation of the money supply, one of whose consequences was rapid increases in the price level. Henry Clay, writing in 1916, made this point using gold as the stand-in for base money, the reserves of the banking system:

> Temporary changes in the demand for money can be met by banks increasing or diminishing their credits; ultimately, however, these credits depend on and are limited by the gold reserves of the banks. In the long run, therefore, the chief influence on the level of prices, which is the same thing as the value of money, is the relation between the rate at which the supply of gold increases and the rate at which the supply of other kinds of wealth increases. (Clay, [1916] 1924)

This was written when currencies were directly convertible into a certain weight in gold. The gold standard, as the system was called, ensured that a country could not just issue as much currency as it pleased, but was always disciplined by the need to be able to sell gold at the official price. It is a system now long gone and it is inconceivable that it should ever return.

But the problems of currencies whose gold price a government would not stand behind, that is, the problems of non-convertible currencies, were well known, an absolute commonplace amongst economists and even the general public in those days.

William Stanley Jevons, the originator of the marginal revolution in England, writing on these matters in his 1875 text, *Money and the Mechanism of Exchange*, made the point with great clarity:

> It is hardly requisite to tell again the well-worn tale of the over issue of paper money which has almost always followed the removal of the legal necessity of convertibility. Hardly any civilized nation exists . . . which has not suffered from the scourge of paper money at one time or another. . . . Italy, Austria, and the United States, countries where the highest economical intelligence might be expected to guide the governments, endure evils of an inconvertible paper currency. Time after time in the earlier history of New England and some of the other states now forming parts of the American Union, paper money had been issued and had wrought ruin. (Jevons, 1875)

Inconvertible paper currency allows the government to spend money by issuing new currency, in this way diverting the resources of the nation to its own purposes. It is a form of taxation by stealth. Jevons discusses this approach to government finance:

> The issue of an inconvertible money has often been recommended as a convenient means of making a forced loan from the people, when the finances of the government are in a desperate condition. It is true that money may be thus easily abstracted from the people, and the government debts are effectually lessened. At the same time, however, every private debtor is enabled to take a forced contribution from his creditor. A government should, indeed, be in a desperate position, which ventures thus to break all social contracts and relations which it was created to preserve.

And one last reminder of the depth of understanding that was once common but is now almost entirely forgotten. This is from an American text published in 1940 by Lewis Froman ('with the editorial assistance of Harlan McCracken'). There can be found the following:

> The difficulty with using a practically valueless commodity as the principal money of the country is that there is always the temptation to issue more and more of it. The substance of which it is made is easily accessible, and the government can raise money easily by this method. To be sure, it would be a form of taxation, but an indirect one, and indirect taxes are always more popular than direct taxes. Irresponsible governments, therefore, cannot be empowered with the issuance of un-backed paper money. With the pressure which is put upon most modern governments for the raising of revenue, it might be fair to say that most governments would be 'irresponsible' once they began to issue fiat

money. For this reason, therefore, it is desirable that money have an intrinsic value or at least a conversion privilege. (Froman, 1940)

Governments just keep pouring more money into their economies as a way of financing their own activities. The answer is to chain the domestic currency to some form of conversion, which no government will ever do. The consequence is that governments will continue to add to inflationary pressures without abatement.

Here all that can be done is explain. But the attempt to saddle the problems of inflation onto the market economy and the system of exchange will also be an ever-present temptation for governments. To try to stop inflation by pretending that the fault lies with entrepreneurial activity so that the solution is to get businesses to stop raising prices is an enormous folly that only adds to unemployment and does nothing about inflation.

The fact remains that with the government in charge of the issuance of money, no other entity in an economy can cause inflation other than the government and no other entity but government can ever bring an inflation to an end.

SOME FINAL CONSIDERATIONS ON INFLATION

Inflation is the result of too much money chasing too few goods. If money is recognized as what it is, purchasing power in the hands of buyers with governments included amongst those buyers, and if those with money to spend are attempting to buy more than 100 per cent of all available goods and services, then these circumstances properly represent the nature of inflation.

The question then relates to how this purchasing power gets into the hands of buyers. There are three main ways, often closely related.

Liquidity

There is first an excess supply of liquidity, that is, of spendable money. Although nominal interest rates are determined by the supply and demand for money and credit, there is also an inflationary component that can be embedded in lending rates.

The financial system, and in particular banks, creates money. Money is often no more than a line entry in the balance sheet of a bank.

Since banks hold only a small proportion of the total value of their loans in the form of cash and other reserves, banks can increase the total volume of money on loan by simply increasing the amount of money they create within bank deposits.

The *money multiplier* is an estimate of the total amount of money in circulation in relation to the amount of reserves held by financial institutions. An increase in liquidity beyond the actual available savings of the economy in general will put upward pressures on the price level.

Government Spending and Deficit Finance

The great inflations of the past have been due to large increases in liquidity caused by increases in public spending unfunded either by taxation or borrowing from the public.

The financial system generally and the banking system in particular are typically prudential lenders who aim to lend only to those who are seen as likely to repay their debts. To the extent that financial institutions behave prudently, there is little likelihood that a serious inflation can arise from a rapid increase in lending to those unable to repay. Where this occurs, bank failure is a brutal cure that nevertheless brings this excess into line.

Governments, however, can spend monies they do not have, since a cheque written by the government will be accepted at face value. Other than in very unstable regimes, it is certain to cash for the amount stated.

Governments can therefore create inflation first through their own spending and then, secondly, through their ability to create the liquidity that such inflations are dependent on. It is very difficult to sustain an inflation without deficit finance as the prime instigator and driving force behind the process.

Wages Growth

A crucially important element in the process of inflation is the certain demands that will come from wage earners for compensation for the loss of purchasing power that rising prices are certain to bring. Wage increases do not normally initiate the processes of inflation, but once an inflation begins, the role of wage earners becomes increasingly important.

The processes involved are a sequence.

- There are, first, higher prices caused by increased liquidity and deficit finance.
- There is then a growing resentment amongst wage earners at the loss of real incomes, which is translated into industrial militancy to restore lost purchasing power.
- Higher wage increases then fuel increases in business costs, which push prices upwards and add to the demands for higher wages by workers.

- The wage–price spiral becomes embedded with both wage earners and business attempting to maintain their own relative economic positions.
- Where business fails to keep prices high enough to cover costs, business activity contracts and unemployment goes up.
- The higher unemployment eventually puts a break on worker militancy and the demand for higher wages. But higher unemployment is almost certainly a necessary part in the process of eventually bringing inflation to an end, possibly not until many years have passed. The entire process is extraordinarily costly in wealth and personal welfare, which is why inflations should be avoided at all costs.

It is a very intense struggle all round. But the central problem remains with public sector deficits and the growth in liquidity. Only a restoration of some kind of balance between the growth in the amount of purchasing power and a growth in the level of production can allow for the simultaneous occurrence of low unemployment, rapid growth and stable prices.

CAUSES OF INFLATION AND ITS CONTROL

Let us once again return to the more complete model of the inflationary process presented in the previous chapter. What was shown was a process in which the growth in the amount of money and credit exceeded the growth in the underlying level of savings relative to the demand for such savings. This is shown once again in Figure 17.5.

The crucial element is where the growth in the supply of money and credit exceed the growth in the supply of physical capital and other resources needed for investment.

The increase in the supply of credit will either have been a deliberate act by government to lower interest rates to encourage investment, or more likely, a consequence of deficit financing where the amount of base money and bank reserves rise because public spending exceeds the level of taxation.

The result: less investment, investment on less productive assets, less value-adding production overall but more money and credit available. This is the classic situation of too much money chasing too few goods.

What to do is basically to reverse the process:

- end deficit financing;
- reduce the level of unproductive public expenditure;
- contain the growth in money and credit;

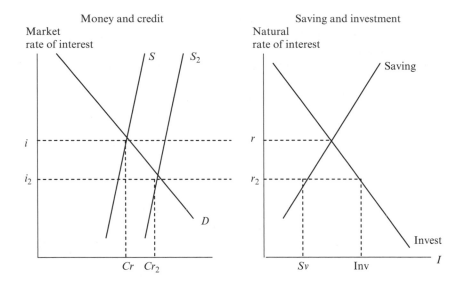

Figure 17.5   The inflationary process

- encourage higher levels of national saving;
- encourage higher rates of private investment;
- encourage higher levels of entrepreneurial activity.

And at the end of the day, it may be of the highest social value to let financial institutions fail where they have lent to borrowers who cannot repay their debts. Depositors should be protected, but the banks themselves should be treated as any other business that cannot meet its obligations, allowed to fail if those to whom they lend cannot repay their debts. It may be the only way in the modern world to ensure that money lent out is a proper reflection of the amount of savings that actually exist.

In essence, use the market. Prosperity can only come from market activity. Unless policy makers understand that, nothing they do will create economic growth for a nation or prosperity for those who live within its bounds.

NOTE

1. The way in which the equation has been used is to try to construct a relationship in form of:

$$\Delta P = k\,\Delta M$$

Delta (Δ) is the sign that means 'the change in'. The change in the price level is equal to some constant proportion (*k*) of the growth in the stock of money. This was the central equation in an economic set of theories that sought to control inflation by controlling the growth in the stock of money. This attempt is referred to amongst economists as *monetarism*.

Afterword

There are a number of people I owe a great deal to in getting this book into print. I began it at the height of the Global Financial Crisis at the end of 2008, at a moment when I could no longer bear teaching Keynesian economics. I had put up with it when things were going reasonably well, but the descent into recession, followed by the worldwide adoption of Keynesian stimulus policies, meant I could no longer in good conscience continue teaching in the way I had.

I am therefore endlessly grateful to my colleague, Bronwyn Coate, who allowed me to write the book as the basis for the course we taught together. Her support, encouragement and sensible advice meant a good deal to me as the book was being carved out of nothing more than my own ideas which had been developing in my mind over a goodly number of years. Neither she nor I knew what would come out during any given week. Her willingness to allow me to put onto paper my views on economics, and to use these as the basis for our classroom instruction, was essential for this project even to have commenced.

I am also grateful to my students in Economic Analysis for Business, especially the first tranche back at the start of 2009 who had no set text but had to wait each week for me to finish the chapter in time for distribution in class. Each group of students since then – and there have been four – has also had to put up with further iterations as I moved towards the completed work, and I am grateful for their indulgence and frequent commentary.

I would also like to thank Edward Elgar at Edward Elgar Publishing and Phillip Booth at the Institute of Economic Affairs in London. Both have seen the potential merit in this book and I appreciate their indispensable support. I must also mention the work team at Edward Elgar who are unfailingly skilled and helpful, and for whose professionalism I am deeply indebted.

Let me also mention the early twentieth-century economist, Henry Clay, from whom I have learned a great deal. In my view, his *Economics: An Introduction for the General Reader* is the best introductory book on economics written during the whole of the twentieth century. Clay had the advantage of having written before economic theory was affected by

Keynes and thus could write a compact and coherent text which perfectly summed up classical thought. It is as readable today as it was when first published in 1916 and it lasted long enough through many reprints for a second edition to be published in 1942. What of course spelled its demise was the advent of Keynesian economics, which rendered the classical view obsolete inside the classroom although it remained entirely relevant for understanding the economics of the real world.

Lastly in order of mention but first in my feeling of gratitude is my family, without whom nothing would ever get done. They make all the difference in my life. The book is therefore dedicated to my wife, Zuzanna, who has made the greatest difference of all.

References

Bagehot, Walter ([1873] 1919), *Lombard Street: A Description of the Money Market*, London: John Murray.

Becker, Gary and William J. Baumol (1952), 'The classical economic theory: the outcome of the discussion', *Economica*, **19**, 355–76.

Clay, Henry ([1916] 1924), *Economics: An Introduction for the General Reader*, 1st edn, London: Macmillan and Co.

Froman, Lewis A. (1940), *Principles of Economics*, with the editorial assistance of Harlan L. McCracken, Chicago: Richard D. Irwin.

Gellner, E. (1994), *Conditions of Liberty: Civil Society and its Rivals*, New York: Viking

Haberler, Gottfried (1937), *Prosperity and Depression: A Theoretical Analysis of Cyclical Movements*, 1st edn, Geneva: League of Nations.

Hayek, Friedrich A. (1931), 'The "paradox" of saving', *Economica*, **11** (old series), 125–69.

Jevons, W. Stanley ([1871] 1970), *The Theory of Political Economy*, Harmondsworth, Middlesex: Penguin.

Jevons, W. Stanley (1875), *Money and the Mechanism of Exchange*, New York: D. Appleton and Co.

Kates, Steven (1998), *Say's Law and the Keynesian Revolution: How Macroeconomic Theory Lost its Way*, Cheltenham, UK and Northampton, MA, USA: Edward Elgar.

Keynes, John Maynard (1920), *The Economic Consequences of the Peace*, London: Macmillan.

Keynes, John Maynard ([1936] 1987), *The General Theory of Employment, Interest and Money*, vol. VII of *The Collected Writings of John Maynard Keynes*, London and Basingstoke: Macmillan.

Knight, Frank ([1921] 1933), *Risk, Uncertainty and Profit*, London: The London School of Economics and Political Science.

Malthus, Thomas Robert (1986), *The Works of Thomas Robert Malthus*, edited by E.A. Wrigley and David Souden, London: William Pickering. Vol. 1: *An Essay on the Principles of Population* (1798); Vols 2 and 3: *An Essay on the Principles of Population*, sixth edition (1826), with variorum readings from the second edition (1803), Part 1, Part 2; Vol. 5: *Principles of Political Economy*, second edition (1836) with variant readings from the first edition (1820), Part I; Vol. 6: *Principles of Political Economy*, second edition (1836) with variant readings from the first edition (1820), Part II.

Marshall, Alfred ([1920] 1947), *Principles of Economics: An Introductory Volume*, 8th edn, London: Macmillan and Co.

Marshall, Alfred and Mary Paley Marshall ([1879] 1881), *The Economics of Industry*, 2nd edn, London: Macmillan and Co.

Marx, Karl ([1867] 1918), *Capital: A Critique of Political Economy*, translated from the German by Samuel Moore and Edward Aveling and edited by Fredrich Engels. Revised and amplified according to the fourth German edition by Ernest Untermann, Chicago: Charles H. Kerr.

Marx, Karl and Friedrich Engels ([1848] 1977), *Manifesto of the Communist Party*, Moscow: Progress Publishers.

Menger, Karl (1950), *Principles of Economics*, first published in German in 1871, translated and edited by James Dingwall and Bert F. Hoselitz, with an introduction by Frank H. Knight, Glencoe, IL: Free Press.

Mill, James ([1808] 1966), *Commerce Defended*, 2nd edn, in Donald Winch (ed.), *James Mill: Selected Economic Writings*, Edinburgh: Oliver and Boyd Ltd, pp. 85–159.

Mill, John Stuart ([1874] 1974), 'Of the influence of consumption on production', in *Essays on Some Unsettled Questions of Political Economy*, 2nd edn, Clifton, New Jersey: Augustus M. Kelley, pp. 47–74. Originally published in 1844.

Mill, John Stuart ([1878] 1921), *Principles of Political Economy*, edited with an introduction by Sir W.J. Ashley, London: Longman, Green and Co. First edition published in 1848.

Mises, Ludwig von ([1950] 1980), 'Lord Keynes and Say's Law', in *Planning for Freedom and Sixteen Other Essays and Addresses*, 4th edn, South Holland, IL: Libertarian Press, pp. 64–71.

Ricardo, David ([1817] 1951–73), *Principles of Political Economy and Taxation*, vol. I of *The Works and Correspondence of David Ricardo*, edited by P. Sraffa with the collaboration of M.H. Dobb, Cambridge: Cambridge University Press.

Ricardo, David (1951–73), *Correspondence 1819–1821*, vol. VIII of *The Works and Correspondence of David Ricardo*, edited by P. Sraffa with the collaboration of M.H. Dobb, Cambridge: Cambridge University Press.

Robbins, Lionel ([1935] 1945), *An Essay on the Nature and Significance of Economic Science*, 2nd edn, London: Macmillan.

Say, Jean-Baptiste ([1803] 1821), *A Treatise on Political Economy; Or the Production, Distribution, and Consumption of Wealth*, translated from the fourth edition of the French by C.R. Prinsep, MA with notes by the translator, 2 volumes, London: Longman, Hurst, Rees, Orme, and Brown. First edition published in 1803.

Sloman, John and Keith Norris (2002), *Macroeconomics*, 2nd edn, Frenchs Forest, NSW: Pearson.

Smart, William (1906), *The Return to Protection: Being a Re-Statement of the Case for Free Trade*, London: Macmillan.

Smith, Adam ([1776] 1976), *An Inquiry into the Nature and Causes of the Wealth of Nations*, Chicago: The University of Chicago Press.

Taylor, F.M. (1925), *Principles of Economics*, 9th edn, New York: The Ronald Press.

Torrens, Robert ([1821] 1965), *An Essay on the Production of Wealth*, New York: Augustus M. Kelley.

Walras, Léon (1954), *Elements of Pure Economics, or the Theory of Social Wealth*, translated by William Jaffé, London: George Allen and Unwin.

Index

Titles of publications are in *italics*.

acceleration principle 275
administrative role of governments 59
aggregate demand 206, 211, 220–21, 244–6
  failure 41–2
  and inflation 252–6
aggregate supply 244–7
  and inflation 252–6
  and technological improvement 258–9
  and unemployment 251–2
asset price inflation 312–13
axioms of a free market economy 8–14

Bagehot, Walter 215–16
balance of payments 176–8
bank credit 271–3
base money 305
basic rules of a market economy 13–19
basket of goods and services 168–9
Baumol, William J. 216
Becker, Gary 216
borrowing 84–6
  businesses 85–6
  government 86, 298, 313–14
  personal 86
business cycle theory 42–3, 200–201, 217–18, 260–81
  in economics teaching 286–7
  and entrepreneurial error 275
  and governments 282–4
  and macroeconomics 269–70, 286–7
  and political decisions 290–91
business loans 85–6
businesses 15–16

Capital (Marx) 195
capital 73–4
  Mill's fundamental propositions 74–80
  as the result of saving 75–6
capital accounts 177
capital flows, international 43–4
capital goods and GDP measurement 159
CBA (cost–benefit analysis) 137
centrally planned economies 53–4, 57, 295
ceteris paribus 54–5
change 10, 55
character of population and economic success 26
circular flow 222–7
  and government sector 224–5
  and international sector 225–6
classical economics 182–96
classical model, saving and investment 224
classical theory of recession 261–2
Clay, Henry 211, 329, 336–7
command economies, *see* centrally planned economies
comparative advantage 44–5, 188–9
competition 96–7, 285
  and the entrepreneur 82–3
consumer price index (CPI) 168–72
co-ordination 262–3
cost–benefit analysis (CBA) 137
counter-cyclical policy 292
CPI (consumer price index) 168–72
creative destruction 277
crowding out 315–17
current account 177
cyclical unemployment 249

debt 317–18
decision making 127–32
　by individuals 15
　marginal 33–4, 127–8, 136–8
deficit finance 332
demand 102–5
　aggregate, *see* aggregate demand
　for commodities is not demand for
　　labour 78–80
　created by supply 210–11
　different meanings 104
　elasticity 122–5
　failure as cause of recession 205–6
　financed by supply 17
　inelasticity 124
　for savings 303–4
　structure of 39–40
demand curves 88–9, 102–5
depreciation and GDP measurement
　159
diagrams 69–70
diamond–water paradox 198
discouraged workers 176
double counting and GDP
　measurement 158
downward-sloping supply curves
　113–16

economic activity 3
Economic Consequences of the Peace,
　The (Keynes) 202
economic growth
　and production possibility curve
　　66–7
　and value added 49–50
economic indicators, real movements
　171–2
economics
　definition 23–4
　history 181–203
　as political economy 4–5
　teaching approach 284–7
Economics: An Introduction for the
　General Reader (Clay) 336–7
education
　government involvement 61
　teaching of economics 284–7
elasticity of demand 122–5
employment 172–6; *see also*
　unemployment

entrepreneurial error and the business
　cycle 275–7
entrepreneurs 34–5, 80–83
　and competition 82–3
　and marginal analysis 137
　and J.-B. Say 190
equilibrium 54, 105–6, 107, 234, 247–8
ethics of population and economic
　success 26
exchange rates 44, 177–8
expenditure, circular flow 222–3
expenditure method, GDP calculation
　162–4
exports 226, 236–7
　and GDP measurement 162
externalities 197–8, 286

factors of production 71–87
finance 83–4
financial system 296–318
foreign sector and circular flow
　225–6
free markets, *see* market economy
free trade 44
　Smith's attitude to 187
freedom and free markets 4
frictional unemployment 248–9
Froman, Lewis 330–31
full employment 249
fundamental propositions on capital
　(Mill) 74–80

GDP (gross domestic product)
　154–67
　calculation 162–6
Gellner, E. 196–7
General Glut 207
General Theory of Employment,
　Interest and Money (Keynes) 6,
　204–6, 219–20
geographical differences and GDP
　measurement 158
government production and GDP
　measurement 157
government spending
　and deficit finance 332
　Keynesian model 235–6, 238–42
　and national saving 314–15
　in recession 62–3, 217, 240–41, 292,
　　293–4

governments
  borrowing 86, 298, 313–14
  and circular flow 224–5
  and cyclical activity 282–95
  economic role 16–17, 20–21,
    56–64
  and price regulation 119–22
  and recessions 62–3, 240–41, 288–90,
    292–5
  regulatory role 16–17, 59–60
  running businesses 15–16, 61–2
  Smith's attitude to 184–5
  see also government spending
Great Depression, US 283
Gross Domestic Product (GDP)
    154–67
growth rates
  average 180
  calculation 167
  effect of interest rates 310–13

Haberler, Gottfried 213, 215, 271–9,
    283
Hayek, Friedrich 210
health care as government business
    61–2
highly competitive industry 139
history of economics 181–203
home production and GDP
    measurement 156–7
honesty of population and economic
    success 26
horizontal supply curves 113–16
human capital 74

imports 225–6, 236–7
  and GDP measurement 162
income, circular flow 222–3
income method of GDP calculation
    165–6
inconvertible currencies 330
industry
  limited by capital 74–5
  structure 138–40
  supply and demand curves
    113–16
inefficiency 68–9
inelastic demand 124
inflation 117–18, 249–51, 319–34
  causes and control 333–4

and interest rates 302, 312–13
  problems 250–51
inflationary policy and short-run
    aggregate supply 252–6
infrastructure, role of government 60
injections 225, 237
*Inquiry into the Nature and Causes of
    the Wealth of Nations* (Smith) 23,
    182–7, 194, 198
interest 84–5
interest rates
  as a form of rental 300
  and growth 310–13
  and inflation 302, 312–13
  and investment 311, 326–7
  market rate 304, 307–8
  natural rate 299, 300–304, 307–8
  in recession 293
  and risk 271
  and unemployment rate 325–6
international economic relations
    43–4
international sector and circular flow
    225
inventory adjustments 226–7
investment
  as business decision 19
  intended and unintended 227
  and interest rates 311, 326–7
  and saving 185–6
invisible hand 182–3

Jevons, William Stanley 198, 199,
    330

Keynes, John Maynard 6, 202–3,
    204–6, 207, 212, 219–20
Keynesian macroeconomic model
    219–42
Keynesian policy 238–40
  and inflation control 321–6
Knight, Frank 36
knowledge 11

labour 72
labour force surveys 173
labour theory of value 194
  and Marx 195–6
land 71–2
law of markets, *see* Say's Law

leakages 224–5, 237–8
leakages–injections framework
    (Keynesian equation) 228–9
legal system and economic success
    24–5
    role of governments 16–17, 59–60
liquidity 331–2
loans, *see* borrowing
*Lombard Street: A Description of the
    Money Market* (Bagehot) 216
long-run aggregate supply (LRAS)
    254, 323

macroeconomics 27–9
    contrast with business cycle theory
        269–70
    in economics teaching 286–7
    Keynesian model 219–42
macroeconomy 40–41
Malthus, Thomas 191–2, 207
    influence on Keynes 204–5
marginal analysis 127–52, 198–200
    and decision making 136–8
    graphical presentation 148–52
    problems 134–5
    and theory of the firm 135–6
marginal cost 132, 133–4, 144
marginal decision-making 33–4,
    136–8
marginal product 132–3
marginal productivity of labour 133
marginal revenue 133–4, 141–2
marginal utility 132, 199
market activity 2–3
market coordination 30–31
market demand, *see* demand
market economy
    axioms 8–14
    basic rules 14–20
    definition 1
    and government 20–21, 58–64
    omitted from economics teaching
        287–8
    and political freedom 4
market failure 285–6
market mechanism 30–31
market prices 11–13
market rate of interest 299, 304–8
market supply, *see* supply
markets 89–90

Marshall, Alfred 2–3, 209–10
Marshall, Mary Paley 209
Marx, Karl 195–6
maximizing profits 131–2
McCracken, Harlen 330
measures of economic activity 153–78
    balance of payments 176–8
    consumer price index 168–72
    GDP 154–67
    unemployment rate 172–6
Menger, Carl 198
merchants, Smith's attitude to 184
microeconomics 27, 28–9
    teaching 284–6
Mill, James 210–11
Mill, John Stuart 74–80, 192–4, 217
    fundamental propositions on capital
        74–80
Mises, Ludwig von 212
mixed economies 57
monetarism 321
monetary factors and recession
    216–17
monetary policy 321–6
monetary theories of the cycle 271–3
money 18, 317–18
    determining supply of 304–6
    increasing supply of 308–10
    quantity theory 319–21
    and the structure of production
        274
    value of 211–12
    varying supply of 306–7
Money and the Mechanism of Exchange
    (Jevons) 330
money multiplier 332
money rate of interest 299, 304–8
monopolies 139, 285
    natural, and government businesses
        61–2
monopolistically competitive industry
    139
multiplier theory, Keynesian model
    241

National Accounts 154
national saving and government
    spending 314–15
natural monopolies and government
    businesses 61–2

natural rate of interest 299, 300–304, 307–8
natural rate of unemployment 249, 251–2, 322–3
nominal rate of interest 299, 304–8
non-monetary over-investment theories 274–5

oligopoly 139
On Population (Malthus) 191–2
open market operations 306
opportunity costs 129
over-investment theories 273–5
overproduction 215–16

'"Paradox" of Saving, The' (Hayek) 210
'paradox of thrift' (Keynes) 224
personal loans 86
Phillips curve 256–8, 324–5, 328–9
political decisions
  and recessions 289–90, 292–5
  and theory of the cycle 290–91
political freedom and free markets 4
politics and economics 4
population theory, Malthus 191–2
potential GDP 249
price ceilings 119–21
price floors 121–2
price movements
  and GDP calculation 166–7
  reasons for 117
price system 30, 31–2
prices 11–13
  effect of increases 93–5, 110–11
  and inflation 117–18
  should be set by businesses 19–20
  and volume of production 92–3
Principles of Political Economy (Malthus) 192
Principles of Political Economy (Mill) 192–3
Principles of Political Economy and Taxation (Ricardo) 188, 194
private sector
  and GDP 161–2
  role in government activity 58
product range and GDP measurement 157–8

production
  in anticipation of demand 37–8, 264
  decisions should be made by businesses 19
  destroying and creating value 48–9
  factors of 71–87
  structure of 51–3
    and recessions 41–2
  time and sequence 38–9
profit maximization 131–2, 141–8
property rights 27
Prosperity and Depression (Haberler) 213, 215, 270–79
psychological theories of the business cycle 279
public goods 62
public sector activity and GDP 161–2
public spending, *see* government spending
purely monetary theories of the cycle 271–3

quantity theory of money 319–21

rationality 128
real movements in economic indicators 171–2
recessions
  classical theory 261–2
  and debt 317–18
  and economic growth 266–7
  effects 265–6
  and government policy 288–90, 292–5
  and government spending 62–3, 217, 240–41, 292, 293–4
  Keynesian theory 205–6, 219–20, 240–41
  and political decisions 289–90, 292–5
  and Say's Law 208–10, 212–17, 261–2
  and structure of production 41–2
  unexpected 264–5
regulatory role of governments 16–17, 59–60
reserve ratio 305–6
resources
  inefficient use of 68–9
  natural 71–2

returns over time 129–31
Ricardo, David 188–9, 192, 194, 195, 217–18
risk and uncertainty 35, 82
risk premium, interest rates 301
Risk, Uncertainty and Profit (Knight) 36
Robbins, Lionel 24
rule of law 24–5

saving 296–7
    and capital creation 75–6
    classical model 224
    and government spending 313–15
    Keynesian model 223–4, 234–5
    Smith's attitude to 185–6
    as spending 76–8, 297–8
    see also interest rates; investment
Say, Jean-Baptiste 189–90, 212
Say's Law 6, 190–91, 201–2, 205–17
    and classical business cycle theory 260–61
schools as government businesses 61
seasonality and GDP measurement 159–60
seasonally adjusted employment data 175
self-interest 13–14, 183–4
short-run aggregate supply (SRAS) 246–7, 323
    and inflationary policy 252–6
Smart, William 200
Smith, Adam 23, 182–7, 194, 198, 200, 209
social conditions, effect on economies 24–7
specialization and the division of labour 186–7
stability 326–7
structural problems and recessions 213–15
structural unemployment 249
structure of production 51–3
    and recessions 41–2
supply 90–92, 95–101
    different meanings 100–101
    structure of 39–40
supply and demand 30, 32, 88–106, 107–26
    for savings 303–4

supply curves 88–9, 95–6, 99–101
    for savings 303–4

taxation 61
    in recession 293
Taylor, Fred 201–2
technological improvements and LRAS 258–9
Theory of Political Economy (Jevons) 198
theory of the cycle, *see* business cycle theory
theory of the firm and marginal analysis 135–6
time
    and economic return 129–31
    and sequence 38–9
Torrens, Robert 214–15
trade protection and recessions 294
Treatise on Political Economy (Say) 189–90
trend and GDP measurement 160

uncertainty 5–6, 9, 35–7, 82, 262, 279
under-consumption theories 277–8
underemployment 176
unemployment 68
    definition 174
    and inflation 256–8, 324–5, 328–9
    and interest rate 325–6
    natural rate 322–3
    in recessions 266
    types of 248–9
unemployment rate 172, 175–6
utilities, public 61
utility 50
    as determinant of value 199
    and value added 50–51

value 198–9
    destroyed and created in production process 48–9
    of money, Say's Law 211–12
    subjectivity of 50
value added 46–55
    and economic growth 49–50
    in production 47–8
    and utility 50–51
value added method of GDP calculation 165

values of population and economic
  success 26
variety of goods and services and GDP
  measurement 156
velocity of circulation 319, 320–21
volume of production and price 92–5

wages
  and inflation 332–3

in recessions 292
and unemployment 324
Walras, Léon 198
Wealth of Nations (Smith) 23, 182–7,
  194, 198
welfare 2, 60–61
what is saved is spent 76–8, 297–8
willingness to supply 111–13
withdrawals 224–5, 237–8